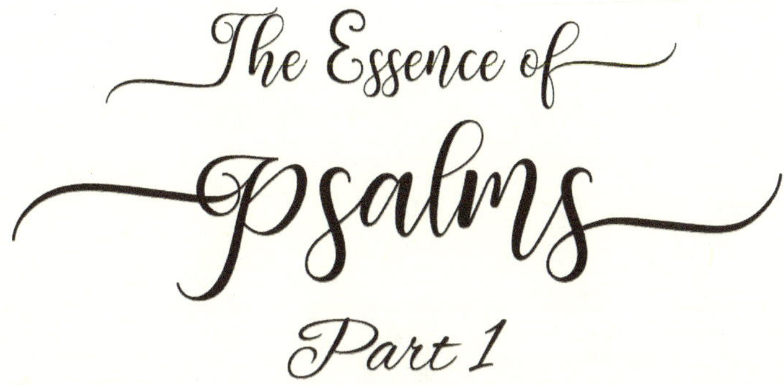

Dr. Shilpa Germaine Alfred

ISBN 979-8-89186-521-1

May the God of our Lord Jesus Christ, the Father of glory, give to you the spirit of wisdom and revelation in the knowledge of Him, the eyes of your understanding being enlightened; that you may know what is the hope of His calling, what are the riches of the glory of His inheritance in the saints, and what is the exceeding greatness of His power toward us who believe, according to the working of His mighty power which He worked in Christ when He raised Him from the dead and seated Him at His right hand in the heavenly places, far above all principality and power and might and dominion and every name that is named, not only in this age but also in that which is to come. (Eph 1:17-21)

In Lord Jesus Name,

Amen!!

Contents

Preface

The book of Psalms is an ocean. A careful, consistent, and inter-correlating study of this book reveals the magnificent attributes of our Almighty God, the glorious inheritance of His children, and the actual stance of the enemy. Most of the Psalms were written by King David, the legendary king of Israel. But it also includes Psalms written by Moses, the Kohathite priests, and King Solomon.

David was the "man after God's own heart". Do you know when this was declared? It was declared by the Prophet Samuel to King Saul in the second year of his reign, much before David was even born (1 Samuel 13:14). David hadn't heard this declaration with his own ears when Samuel spoke it. But he took his anointing seriously and steadily grew in it till the end of his life. We find that this book is written from the heart of the man who daringly trusted God and accomplished great victories, **but** who also failed repeatedly, yet was lifted up time and again by the grace and mercy of the Most High God. David's constant weakness was overwhelmed by the goodness and grace of God, which He revealed to him throughout his life every time he turned to Him. The Psalms store sound wisdom gained from a lifelong walk with God.

David's youth was characterised by a constant fellowship with God. He was a shepherd by occupation, and God had shown him the patterns of life while tending his father's 'few sheep'; even more so, after the Prophet Samuel anointed him for greatness. His Psalms vividly describe the lessons he learned that established a strong relationship with God. Because of this reason, despite the horrific mistakes he committed, he was able to receive the forgiveness of God provided by the Spirit of Grace (though he was under the old covenant). He believed the prophecies given about the coming Saviour and also himself prophesied about the Messiah.

David understood the importance of God's grace and mercy, knowing that deliverance belonged only to God. He had a wonderful understanding of God's creation and declared astounding facts that are proven today by science. Be it mankind, the plant or animal kingdom, or the magnificent water bodies, David saw God's hand and glory in everything.

David learned about and understood the facts that characterised a fallen world. There was an enemy out there who was deceivingly powerful. He knew he was weak in himself. And he very well knew for sure that God (The Almighty One) was his only hope of deliverance, and this deliverance was assured at all times since he trusted in Him. David longed for the days of grace as much as his forefathers and spoke concerning his heart's desire to be one among those who are saved by grace through faith, which he describes as being the "blessed man" to whom the Lord does not impute any sin.

Though much material is available to assist anyone who wants to know the treasure in Psalms, I would suggest that a good personal study, with a handy concordance and, of course, the perfect guidance of the Holy Spirit, would edify and enrich our relationship with God. The purpose of my book is to kindle a desire in the hearts of all the readers to study the word of God more deeply and draw on the inexhaustible revelation available to live a God-centred, fruitful Christian life.

This book is part 1 of the series that I will be writing as the Lord guides me. It contains a study of a total of 12 Psalms. I have begun the study with Psalm 23 (because I believe that it is epic in every sense), followed by Psalm 22 (an astoundingly accurate Messianic Psalm), and then continued chronologically from Psalm 1 to 10. I have quoted most of the biblical references from the New King James Version (NKJV). I request that the readers look up the references if I have not elaborated on them.

Giving all the glory to God, I prayerfully hope that this book gives you a good insight into the priceless treasure in the Psalms.

Psalm23

INTRODUCTION:

This epic Psalm, written by David, is probably one of the very few Psalms that is a vital part of every Christian household, irrespective of the hundreds of denominations that exist. Some have been reciting and teaching this in their households very religiously, thinking that this gets them a gate pass into heaven; some encourage their kids to learn this Psalm in order to show off their religious pride in society; few others do it for the most important reason of teaching the true love and character of God to their children. At the outset, I wonder how many of us would even bother to study and meditate on this Psalm to thoroughly absorb the nutrition that it offers. Let me assure you that a personal detailed study is indeed beneficial to any Christian who yearns to progress in his/her relationship with our ABBA Father.

At a time when everybody is gloating about their love and sacrifice for God, this Psalm will further root us in the foundation of the "**Father's love for us**", which is indeed the required fuel to propel us in the Christian life and walk of faith. This irrefutable revelation of "God's love for us" is what kept the Apostle John going even beyond the age of 90, having been exiled to the Island of Patmos.

This Psalm was written by David based on his understanding of life in relation to his primary occupation as a shepherd. It was based on 'knowing' and 'understanding' God in his '**daily routine**.' How often does the word bring out this perspective in the life of the saints, and we neglect it? **'Whatever you do, work at it wholeheartedly as though you were doing it for the Lord and not merely for people' (Colossians 3:23)** is the primary principle that every saint in the Bible followed, and it catapulted them into greatness. David worked with the Spirit of excellence, a virtue to be possessed by every child of God, and he perfectly understood how much more excellent the God he served is! His encounter with the wild beasts in the wilderness while shepherding his little flock gave him the confidence to face Goliath.

This Psalm clearly sets the theme of human life. It's a combination of 2 valleys. One valley is very welcoming with green pastures and still waters, beautiful beyond measure and a paradise for many. The other is the one with the shadow of death looming all over it, having death traps like thieves, steep ledges, landslides, loose rocks falling, threat from wild animals, extremes of weather conditions, sudden eruption of hidden volcanoes, overgrowth of toxic plants, damp air, and sudden floods due to storms on mountain tops. This valley has death written all over it!

Primarily, God did not create life to be this way. 'The fall' impacted the perfect course of life and made it crooked. Added to this was our wilful disobedience, our ignorance of the truth, and our stubbornness in holding onto the traditions and doctrines of men. As a result, mankind had to walk this trail. But the believer has an advantage because the Lord has already prophesied through Isaiah the prophet (Isaiah 40:1-5) that the Messiah would bring forth salvation, as a result of which this rugged terrain of life would be rectified and made straight for those who would receive it. This is the difference for the believer! God's presence, guidance, strength, and grace in our lives exalts the valleys, brings the mountains low, makes the crooked places straight, and rough places smooth! However, this cannot be claimed by unbelievers or experienced by ignorant believers (who don't study the word of God and renew their minds to His truth) either.

David sees God in both these places. In the first, He is the source of all the "good." In the other, He is the defender of His children, chastening us in love (with His staff) and avenging us against our enemies (with His rod).

All along, He has authorised us to use the weapons of spiritual warfare - The Holy Communion and His Anointing on our lives. Finally, we have the assurance of His goodness and mercy being our portion forever, chasing after us, all the days of our lives!

Many times, we are tempted to pride ourselves based on a few good traits we possess. Most of us would go one step ahead and even rejoice in our self-righteousness. But we can see David make a difference here in his approach to such a thought process. He knew he was good at his job. He understood the fact that if he could be so good at what he did, how much more would God excel in His care and concern for His children? When we apply this same principle in things that we pride ourselves in, it will wreck pride in our lives and we can appreciate the love of God for us much better. This would rid us of a great deal of fear, anxiety, pride, and self-righteousness. None of us can outdo God in any of His virtues.

David was the 8th son of Jesse, the Bethlehemite. According to the culture of those days, the youngest among many kids was usually not given any inheritance in the father's property and was rather put in charge of the household herd or flock. Hiring a shepherd was usually expensive, and they could rarely be trusted with good quality shepherding. Hence, one among the children, usually the youngest (or the weakest), would be chosen for the job. This was probably the case with David as well. But I cannot really buy the story that Jesse did not get him to the sacrifice because he did not think he was worth it. It is an assumption. I will explain this in detail further on.

David's father, Jesse, was a good man. Much can be said about his character from the information given in the Bible. He was a generous giver, had great respect for other people, was hospitable, caring and loved his children. He feared God enough to honour the Prophet Samuel's invitation to come to the sacrifice, which he was performing in Bethlehem in the presence of the elders. What caught my attention is the fact that Jesse named his sons very meaningfully. He named his final son as 'DAVID,' meaning "BELOVED." That speaks aloud of Jesse's love for his son David. What more? David's name is unique in the Bible! Which father would repeatedly call his son 'beloved' and then neglect him?

When I named my 2 children, I called them by names that would usher the blessing of God on them every time they were called by it. Very few people understand the paramount significance of naming their children meaningfully. Jesse knew the importance and significance of names and I believe that David was indeed loved by him. When children understand that they are loved, they go all out to please and satisfy their parents as much as possible. David was one such teenager who did his best to take good care of his father's few sheep; so much so that he was willing to put his life on the line to protect the flock from predators. That shows responsibility taken well at an age that very few others show it!

The Apostle Paul warned Timothy to keep away from old wives' fables and endless genealogies (1 Timothy 1:4). The assumption of David's rejection by his father, Jesse, stems from one such fable in the Talmud, which runs rampant in the Jewish community. It concerns the story regarding David's mother, Nitzevet, and Jesse's rejection of both David and Nitzevet. If you have sound Biblical knowledge, it doesn't take long to realise how flawed this story is. I sincerely request every one of you to look it up before you believe the rejection theory.

1 Samuel 16 begins with the Lord commanding the prophet Samuel to forsake his mourning over Saul, take up the horn of anointing oil, go to Bethlehem, and anoint one of Jesse's sons as the next king of Israel. The very next verse says that Samuel shared his concern with God, fearing a death threat from Saul if he did that. Hence the Lord advised him to accomplish this task under the banner of performing a heifer sacrifice there. This was supposed to be a "**cover-up**" for the anointing. After the death of Eli, Samuel went back to his parents' place in Ramah and settled there. He would regularly go around the nation and perform sacrifices at the high places. A few important people in that city would be invited to take part in those sacrifices (1 Samuel 9:13). Saul was also anointed as king privately at one such sacrifice (1 Samuel 9:27, 10:1).

When Samuel arrived at Bethlehem, the people trembled upon his arrival. When they questioned him, he answered, saying he had come to sacrifice to the Lord. It is important to note that he asked them to sanctify themselves and come for the "sacrifice" and not for the "ordination ceremony of the next king." Jesse and his sons were among the invited. The heifer sacrifice was the only information provided by Samuel to the elders of the city and also to those invited. Jesse honoured the prophet's invitation. **The "Anointing for kingship" was a secret only between the Lord and Samuel.** If Samuel had openly said it and the rest of the crowd knew it, the word would have gone to Saul in no time, and both Samuel and David would have been targeted by him right away, isn't it? David's brothers were more than enough to betray him to Saul. The whole 'heifer sacrifice cover-up' would have been meaningless if Samuel had announced the future kingship of David at this event. Not even Jesse or his sons (including David) knew the purpose of the anointing other than the basic meaning it conveyed: "**set apart as holy.**" This was more than enough for young David to take his anointing very seriously, practice it on a regular basis, and explore it. It was also the reason for him to suffer his brothers' envy. No wonder God called him 'a man after His heart'!

Prior to the anointing of David, only Saul was anointed as king (again privately) at one similar sacrifice by the prophet Samuel. Saul was actually looking for his father's lost donkeys when his servant suggested that they meet with Samuel (the Seer) and ask him for help. When they searched for and found Samuel (by divine providence), Saul was invited to the sacrifice and anointed as king privately. The Lord had already instructed Samuel of these happenings the day before. Hence, the practice of 'anointing for kingship' was literally unknown in those days. It was routine among the Levitical priesthood to anoint the Levites who entered into the service of the Lord in the Tabernacle. This signified being set apart as holy/ consecrated to the Lord.

Many people gladly blame Jesse for neglecting his youngest son by not bringing him for the sacrifice. But they do not consider that David was a responsible shepherd, attending to his shepherding work seriously. Shepherding was a task involving staying away from home for regular long intervals to find pasture to feed the sheep. It seems very absurd to me that Jesse would have strictly told his 'beloved' son to mind the sheep and taken the rest 7 for the sacrifice. If we study Jesse's character from the information given about him in the Bible, this does not fit in. It would be absolutely rude! Moreover, when Jesse was questioned about any other remaining children, he replied immediately saying the youngest one was out in the field, shepherding the flock. If David was indeed rejected by his father, I doubt if Jesse would have even brought his name before Samuel. In fact, I believe that David chose to stay in the field so that his work wouldn't be neglected! This goes very well with David's character; after all, he fought lions and bears to save his sheep!

Most of us love to show off our sincerity before the eyes of men. But the Lord honoured David's attitude towards his little flock and knew that great things would be accomplished through him because of his submissive spirit. God knew that all along! Moreover, this was a major event through which God taught an important lesson to Samuel and to all of us: **"But the LORD said to Samuel, 'Do not look at his appearance or at his physical stature, because I have refused him. For the LORD does not see as man sees; for man looks at the outward appearance, but the LORD looks at the heart' (1 Sam 16:7)."** The Lord guided Samuel to send for David, and they all waited until he arrived. Then he anointed him in the presence of all people, including his father and older brothers. This meant that David was "set apart for something great." That was indeed an honour from the Lord. Now the onus was on David to find out and pursue the purpose of his anointing.

David's 3 older brothers were recruited into Saul's army. Being soldiers, they must have been well-built and would have prided themselves in their stature and status. The fact that Samuel had to look past all the 7 sons and make everyone wait until David arrived from the field was not taken well by his brothers. God very well established His character when He revealed to Samuel (and in turn to the rest of the world) that He never looks at the outward appearance of man but only looks at his heart.

Jesse had only a few sheep (1 Samuel 17:28), and David was put in charge of them. Much can be inferred from the Bible about the way David took care of his father's sheep. His flock would have been very blessed because he was a very responsible shepherd. His brothers chose to elevate themselves by following Saul in the army (or rather, being recruited by him into the army because of their physique). But David was submissive to his father in the responsibility given to him and was faithful in it. God always sees how faithful we are in the least, in whatever we have or is given to us. He sees whether we are responsible with what belongs to another man, when it is committed to us. Until we prove ourselves faithful in that which is least **and** that which is another's, we cannot expect to have more **or** that which is our own. This is a simple test of character. This is common in parenting also. Until we are convinced that our children are responsible for the little things we give them, we will not give them anything big like a cell phone or the house keys. It would be foolish if we did otherwise.

God had been observing this young man who was out in the wilderness, shepherding the flock. The manner in which he took care of the sheep was honoured by God; he was anointed by Samuel in the sight of all his brothers. The Spirit of the Lord came upon David from that day onward, and we can witness the wide array of talents he received after that. David immediately returned to continue his job as a shepherd. But he saw the supernatural power of God enabling him to protect his sheep better from wild beasts, acquiring the talent to play musical instruments skillfully, to be prudent in speech, and in the eyes of others, he appeared to be a mighty man of valour, a man of war and handsome (1 Samuel 16:18). Finally, he was called in to serve Saul by playing music for him when the distressing spirit was upon him and was recruited as Saul's "armour bearer." Yet, occasionally, he went back to feed his father's sheep in Bethlehem.

During one such vacation, Israel was at war with the Philistines in the valley of Elah, and the big-mouthed giant, Goliath, came up with a daring challenge. At the same time, Jesse loaded some food for his older 3 sons who were in the army, along with a gift for the captain of their thousand, and asked David to deliver it and inquire how they had been faring. Hence, David responsibly handed over his little flock to another person and rose up early the next day to run the errand. Upon reaching there, he heard the giant's blasphemy. David displayed righteous indignation towards the giant's challenge since he was empowered by the covenant that he had with God. This fuelled him to fight and kill the giant with a single smooth stone, shot from a sling. Further on, he was recruited into Saul's army and was set over the men of war. He no longer returned to shepherd the sheep but stepped into the next phase of his life. But all this while, David had a good experience being a shepherd to his father's few sheep, and he relates this relationship to that between God and himself.

It is anything but easy to be a shepherd, especially in those days. I seriously believe that if a person did not have a passion for this job, there is no way he could succeed at this. There is much difference between shepherding done in those days compared to now. Most modern shepherds have their farms and ranches, ready feed and stay put there all through the year. Most sheep are domesticated and reared for specific purposes like for wool, meat, and milk. A few modern shepherds may even treat their sheep as pets if they are few in number. But now, this occupation has been totally commercialised, and there hardly remains any bond of love between the sheep and their shepherd. I would like to familiarise you with the shepherding practices of those days and certain well-established facts about sheep, so that the revelation that this Psalm provides is more effective.

Sometimes, we are unable to appreciate and acknowledge the goodness of God in our lives because we happen to fail in our duties and responsibilities and tend to put God at our level. This is an indication for us to work hand in hand with God's grace so that we will understand His love for us better. The perks of being obedient to God's leading and His faithful deliverance, even when we disobey but repent and turn to Him, are brought out beautifully in this Psalm. This Psalm reiterates God's provision, guidance, restoration, deliverance, correction, comfort, covenant, anointing, victory, faithfulness, support, goodness, love, and an eternal relationship.

One more important point to be noticed in this Psalm is that whenever David mentions God first (He/ the Lord/ His/ You/ Your), it is always connected with positivity. When he refers to himself first (I), there is some negativity involved (for example, even though I walk through the valley of the shadow of death). God will persistently lead us into good things. But when we decide to dictate our lives, eventually we end up in dangerous places. But God is faithful to deliver us from it if we turn to Him for help.

1. THE LORD IS MY SHEPHERD; I SHALL NOT WANT.

David had a good understanding of his profession as a shepherd and also about the nature of sheep. David willingly identified himself with his forefathers who also were shepherds. During those days, this profession wasn't respected much by the non-Jews. Almost every heathen tribe (non-Jews) in those days would employ or hire people outside their caste and tribe to take care of their sheep because this profession and the caretakers were considered an abomination. Despite these racial differences, the children of God soared to heights in the midst of these heathen tribes, for example, Joseph and David. David wrote this Psalm out of the revelation and assurance of the goodness of God.

For most of us, the concept of shepherd and sheep may not be clear; most of us relate to it in the modern-day sense. We tend to overlook their immense significance in interpreting this Psalm. Hence, before we go any further, I would like to present some basic facts about shepherds and sheep from my research.

Shepherding/ shepherd:

- ✡ It is a ubiquitous profession and is one of the oldest professions (5,000 years old), originating in Asia Minor.
- ✡ A shepherd has to tend (care), herd (lead), feed, and guard (protect) the flock.
- ✡ Large flocks had to be moved from pasture to pasture and required a great deal of maintenance.
- ✡ The duty of the shepherd was to keep the flock intact, protect them from predators, guide it to the marketplace for shearing, milk the sheep to make cheese, help in birthing the lambs, groom the sheep, etc.

- ✡ They constituted an important part of the economy and would usually be wage earners.
- ✡ They usually lived apart from society, being largely nomadic. This was usually a job of solitary males without children or, most often, the job given to younger sons who did not inherit any land. In other societies, each family would have a family member (a child/youth/elder) who couldn't help much with hard work, and hence they would be put in charge of the flock.
- ✡ They would normally work in groups, looking after one big flock or each bringing their own and merging their responsibilities. This way, it would be easier for them to effectively protect their flock from predators and thieves.
- ✡ While moving from place to place, if they passed through inhabited places, they would refill their food and water bags to sustain them for the days ahead in the lonely places.
- ✡ Most of the olden day shepherds would have to graze their flock in rugged and mountainous areas rather than low lands and river valleys because the latter would be preferred for agricultural purposes.

Being a shepherd was no easy task. It still isn't. Even though most of my research on this topic was online, I had the privilege of observing a shepherdess with her flock of goats in the pastures around my home, and her routine was enlightening. I live in a sparsely populated area, with a good stretch of pastureland, shrubs, and thorny trees all around. A certain old shepherdess was (and still is) a frequent visitor to this place along with her flock of goats. Even though she stays close by and returns home every evening, all through the day, her routine gave me a good view into the life of a shepherd. I strongly believe that this was divinely ordained by God to help me understand things better.

Almost every day she would come in shortly after breakfast time, a basket with some food and a long thick stick in hand, calling out with a peculiar tone which, I guess, her flock of goats definitely understood. She would look for shade under one of the thorny trees and sit for hours on end, moving her resting place as the shadow of the thorny tree moved. Occasionally, she would call out to her flock, which was happily grazing or resting. She would take a walk around the place to make sure that there was no unwanted herb that her flock would feed on and fall sick. She took short naps in between. Most of the time, she would just observe her flock that was spread all over the place, occasionally turning her gaze to the sky or people or vehicles moving around. She would be very alert to the presence of stray dogs and wouldn't hesitate to shoo them off instantly. At times, when she came close to my house, our eyes would happen to meet, and she would say a friendly hello, initiate a small random conversation, and then move on. She has never asked me for money, food or anything else. She always sounded self-sufficient and would talk fondly about her flock. She carried a very basic cell phone, and I have never seen her whiling away on it while her flock grazed the pastures. But she gladly gave me her number and asked me to contact her if I ever wanted to buy a goat for a feast!

The pasture land around my home is also home to snakes of all sizes (venomous and non-venomous), rats, chameleons, a small black tortoise, and a mongoose! Apart from these creatures, there are a group of wild pigs and packs of stray dogs that are always on the hunt to kill and eat these pigs. That is a ghastly sight to see. My city is mostly hot and humid, and during the monsoon, it generally floods because it was a lake bed previously.

Most of us would overlook the labour of this shepherdess. If we just go with a glance, we would miss out on a lot of things that she was doing, which we fail to understand. Not only does she have to protect her flock from these city predators, but she has to protect herself too. Her little occasional walks around the place are not just to stretch her legs, but to make sure there are no poisonous herbs, shrubs, berries, or flowers around that could harm her ignorant flock that is just about happy to graze on anything. Sometimes I can see kid goats in her lap while under the shade, and she would be comforting them fondly. A little before sunset, she would call out to them in a particular tone, and her flock would start exiting the field at a particular point. She would wait until the last one was out of there and then would follow her flock back home. Her flock knew the way back home very well, and they marched ahead with confidence, with their mistress at the tail end.

I hope I have shared quite a bit for you to ponder on and understand the job profile of a nomadic shepherd. I personally believe that any moral profession is respectable, whether it be cobblers, shepherds, or doctors. Though there are some nobler than others, at the end of the day, Proverbs 16:26 is established - "the person who labours, labours for himself, for his hungry mouth drives him on." Respect for every moral profession should be first practiced by us and also taught to our children early at home. This can avoid a lot of problems going forward. The world tends to exalt certain professions beyond their true worth or value, and the little ones get programmed to enter the rat race and waste their lives. The danger of being biased by such exaltations should be avoided at any cost. **Rather, we need to teach our children to tune their hearing to God's voice and His leading in order to prosper in their vocation. Their part in decision-making is of paramount importance, and hence godly parenting/guidance is absolutely essential.**

As I already mentioned, the life of a shepherd is anything but easy. Only if this is combined with a passion for the same, a good job can be accomplished. If this is forced on anyone, it can turn out to be a real drag since this profession requires '24 hours a day, 7 days a week, 365 days a year' care for the flock. In case the shepherd needs a break, he has to make sure that his substitute will do justice to his flock too.

Today, this profession has taken a major turn into being primarily commercial. There is not much bonding between a shepherd and his flock. Ready feed is available, and the flock is fed from troughs instead of lush pastures. If we go by the way shepherding is done today, we would miss out on the real-life experience of a shepherd that David shares in this Psalm. The present-day nomadic shepherds of the Middle East are similar to the shepherds of the olden days, and they are off for a couple of months, taking care of the needs of their flock. They lead their flock through wildernesses, mountains, valleys, and forests, and encounter threats and danger from wild beasts, serpents, scorpions, thieves, harsh weather conditions, etc. These nomads share a good relationship with their flock as compared to the modern-day shepherds.

David often risked his life when it came to protecting his little flock. The anointing definitely catapulted David into a much higher place. The desire in his heart to be a good shepherd certainly mattered to God, who sent Samuel to anoint him and let him know that he was set apart for something special. Along with the anointing came great power so that people saw a mighty man of valour in him, who could subdue lions and bears on one hand, and on the other, he could play the most melodious music on the harp! The best part is that David himself knew this truth and extrapolated it to the challenge he faced against Goliath. He never credited himself for any of his victories in his lifetime; he knew that his absolute source of victory was God. He knew that if God's anointing on his life could bring him so much higher, how much more powerful and loving would the One who gave the anointing be? This perspective is most needed and has to be possessed by every child of God. God's anointing made David flourish in his profession as a shepherd and also was introduced to new ones along the way, as God was preparing him to be the next king.

David developed great compassion and responsibility for his sheep and a sense of accountability to his father for the job given to him. This can be inferred from the fact that he fought the lion and the bear to just rescue one sheep! Who among us would even risk putting our lives on the line in order to save an animal? David did! He saw how the Lord's anointing brought him victory against these wild beasts with just a sling. All these virtues - loving care, responsibility, accountability, compassion, etc. matter even today and are absolutely applicable to every aspect of our lives. This understanding of the much greater love of God for mankind kept David dependent on God all through his life, and we can see this in other Psalms written by him as well.

After being appointed as Saul's musician and armour bearer, David was allowed to take short breaks and go home to be with his family in

Bethlehem. During these breaks, most of us would just lie around lazily and have nothing to do with work. Not so with David. He would go back and tend his father's sheep. Again, when it was time for him to return to Saul, he would responsibly hand over his flock to another person. David never wasted a moment during these years but learned about life as much as he could because he knew that this knowledge and experience would be handy going forward. He was faithful in the little things. I am sure that no matter where he was, his flock was always on his mind. Lord Jesus honoured this perspective when he expounded later on Him being the Good Shepherd in John 10:11-18. So it is very beneficial for us to have a good understanding of this Psalm in order to grow in our relationship with God.

Sheep:

I have heard people say, all my life, that sheep are dumb or stupid animals and that is the reason this comparison is being made to show that even humans are stupid. I almost believed it! But thank God for the revelation he gave me while I was researching this topic, and I believe that it will amaze you too. I am assured that nothing that God created is stupid, dumb, or irrelevant. Every work of God's hand created in the 6 days of creation is the work of His wisdom. His wisdom does not bring forth meaningless stuff. Yes, there was 'The Fall', corruption crept in and it affected all creation equally. But the mind of mankind has been steadily upgraded by God to such an extent that now even the vast space is being explored! There have been innumerable great inventions and discoveries. The fall separated our spirit from God, and even babies born today are born with a spirit that is separated from God (dead/sinful spirit). But God has continued His loving kindness and mercy towards mankind and has allowed them to function in a glorious way. Unfortunately, man has shut out God in the very place where He has to be magnified and has taken all credit for himself. Even in their fallen state, sheep possess the following features:

- ✡ Sheep are herbivores and exhibit a variety of unique characteristics.
- ✡ They are one of the most easily domesticated animals and are a part of the cattle family.

- ✡ They have excellent peripheral vision, a keen sense of smell and taste, good depth perception, and are good communicators (among themselves).
- ✡ Mature sheep have 32 teeth, with 20 deciduous teeth- which is very similar to humans!
- ✡ The sheep's main asset is its wool. This has been and still is the main reason for rearing sheep, apart from being a source of meat and milk.
- ✡ Sheepskin is unlike leather. It is tanned along with the fleece intact (called pelt). It is resistant to flame and static electricity, has excellent insulating properties, is hypoallergenic, and serves as a natural insulator.
- ✡ The quality of wool matters and sheep are classified based on that. White wool is always preferred over other colours, and the texture determines what can be made from it. For example, dense and highly crimped wool is used for textiles, while the long, hair-like wool is used for making carpets.
- ✡ They have been domesticated and used as sacrificial animals by the Jewish community because they are kosher. Even today, many other religions continue the practice of sacrificing sheep.
- ✡ The life expectancy of sheep is 10-12 years, with a maximum of 20 years.
- ✡ Their peripheral vision is so good that they can see up to 270-320 degrees without even turning their heads unless hindered by facial hair (wool blindness).
- ✡ Sheep tend to move out of the dark into well-lit areas and prefer to move uphill when disturbed.
- ✡ They have been reared for various purposes throughout history: for wool (clothes, carpets, and jackets), for milk and dairy products, and for meat.
- ✡ **Feeding habits:** They are grazers, meaning they put their heads down and feed on ground-level vegetation like grass and herbs.

Their feeding is limited, and the shepherd has to carefully inspect the pastures for unwanted plants (e.g. tomato plants) that may be toxic to the sheep before the flock spreads out to graze. Sheep generally crop plants very close to the ground and can overgraze a pasture much faster than other cattle. Therefore, intentional rotational grazing is required to give plants time to recover. They can also act as herbicides by grazing on invasive plants!

- **Behaviour**: Sheep are well known for flocking with 4 or more sheep at a time and they are strongly and naturally inclined to follow a leader to new pastures. They don't defend their territory but form home ranges. A sheep can get stressed when separated from the flock. Some flocks exhibit hefting, meaning they keep to a small local area for life.
- Their primary defence mechanism is to flee. However, cornered sheep may charge, butt, or threaten by hoof stamping and adopting an aggressive posture, even lambs. However, in areas without natural predators, sheep do not exhibit strong flocking behaviour.
- They are food-oriented and can be led away by buckets of feed.
- They practice dominance hierarchy through fighting, threats, and competitiveness. Sometimes, they become bullies. Horn size plays a role. Usually, sheep with the same horn size enter into a duel to determine dominance.
- **Intelligence and learning ability:** Sheep can recognise individual human and ovine faces and remember them for years. Their neural systems in the temporal and frontal lobes are very similar to humans, with a greater involvement of the right brain hemisphere. They can differentiate emotional states through facial characteristics. They can be trained to respond to names given to them and also respond to clicker training.
- **Vocalisations:** Bleats, grunts, rumbles, and snorts are the usual methods of vocalisations. For contact communication, they usually bleat. Certain vocalisations are specific in signalling distress, frustration, or impatience. They are silent when in pain, isolation,

or labour. For courting, they usually rumble, and they snort to show aggression.

- They prefer sweet and sour tastes and reject bitter-tasting food. There are a variety of plants that are good for us but toxic to sheep. Hence, the shepherd has to keep a keen eye on the pastures to which he leads his flock.

- If a sheep falls ill, its system is adapted to hide the obvious signs of illness to prevent being targeted by predators.

- **Reproduction:** Usually, a group of ewes are mated by a single ram (dominant or chosen by the breeder). The ewes mature at 6-8 months, and the males from 4-6 months. About 8% of sheep show homosexuality. The gestation period is 5 months, and labour lasts 1-3 hours. Usually, single or twin lambs are birthed. The shepherd has to assist in the extraction or repositioning of the lambs. The lambs stand within an hour and start feeding. If not accepted by their mother, they have to be bottle-fed or fostered by another ewe. The ewe has only 2 teats.

- When it comes to treating diseases in sheep, prevention is always better than cure. Hence, many vaccines are available, and preventive methods for parasitic infestations have to be undertaken. But in olden days, these were not available. Hence, their own remedial measures were used for the prevention of diseases. Certain diseases like orf, anthrax, etc., are transmissible to humans.

- The group of predators preying on sheep includes canids, felines, bears, birds of prey, and feral hogs. In pre-modern times, shepherds used their presence as the best way to prevent predation.

- By-products of slaughtered sheep include meat, fat used to make candles and soap, bone, and cartilage used to furnish carved items, and to make glue and gelatine. The intestines are used to make strings for musical instruments, surgical sutures, and tennis rackets. The waterproof substance lanolin in wool is used for cosmetics. The ram's horn, shofar, was very significant in the olden days. It was used as a musical instrument and also as a container for the anointing oil.

✡ Due to the constant comparison of sheep with goats in the word, I would like to provide some contrasting information regarding this as well. Sheep and goats are separate species. Hybrids rarely occur and are always infertile. The table below shows the basic differences between sheep and goats and will help us understand better why this difference is being used to explain certain characteristics between the real children of God and the pretenders.

Sheep	Goat
They are grazers (explained above).	They are browsing animals i.e. they tend to feed on taller vegetation by reaching up.
Prefer to eat soft items like grass and other tender plants.	They prefer the woody parts of shrubs and trees. But they also feed on grass.
The tail hangs down.	The tail is held upwards.
They don't have a beard.	They have a beard.
The upper lip is divided.	The upper lip is not divided.
Naturally polled (no horns)	It is very rare for them to be naturally polled.
No unique or strong odour during rut for rams.	They have a unique and strong odour during rut.
Feed well on monoculture pasture.	They fare poorly on monoculture pasture.

After being enlightened with all this information about sheep, I believe that you would gladly agree that sheep are unique in certain aspects and also similar to humans in many ways. When I read about the similarity in dentition between humans and sheep, it surprised me! God's wisdom is beyond words! While reading through the points mentioned above, we would have identified ourselves with the sheep in certain aspects, especially regarding their behaviour. A sheep is anything but dumb. But it does have a few timid characteristics, like fleeing on account of any danger. Very rarely does it stand up for a fight with its predators; this characteristic is similar to most humans.

This animal, being Kosher, was in almost every Jewish household in those days. God made it easy for the people to offer sacrifices from something they already had. They didn't have to go looking for a rare animal somewhere in the forest. They could just give from what they had. Similarly, the other kosher animals were also easily available in their own houses or in the common marketplaces.

The prophet Nathan used the loving relationship between a master and his only pet sheep to convict David when he committed adultery with Bathsheba. David understood this love and got very angry with the guilty person in the story (which was actually himself in real life). Today we have plenty of people showing this type of love to dogs and cats, etc. There is a possibility of great bonding between a man and his pet, and sometimes it is beyond our understanding. I guess it needs to be experienced to be understood. But David knew his relationship with his sheep and that he would cross any limit to protect them and provide for them. Along with this, he had a revelation of the New Covenant salvation by faith. Hence, he went on to write this epic Psalm that would benefit us today if we really understood what it reveals.

Our heavenly Father always outdoes the best love mankind can show to anyone. He created us. We defected and continue to do so on a daily basis. It may be subtle or frank. But God is well aware of our weaknesses. He always encourages us to come up higher and look at all things through His perspective. He is not obligated to us just because He created us. An obligatory lifestyle is not the norm for the children of God either. We need to do things with the right attitude or not do them at all. Out of pure love for His creation, He sacrificed His only Beloved Son for mankind and made "The Way" for us to reach Him. This relationship begins here on earth, and knowing Him and His Son is what commences eternal life here on earth itself (John 17:3) and continues beyond physical death into eternity.

Very similar to the concept of a shepherd and his sheep, Almighty God loves and cares for His children infinitely more and deals with us with great compassion. Not only does He provide us with the very best, but He also watches over everything that is dangerous for us. But still, we dare to venture into trouble, willingly at times! In these moments, He is always there to help us, as He clearly told in the parable of the lost sheep. He will go behind and rescue that one lost sheep gladly. He faithfully takes care of the babes as well as the juveniles, adults, and the older ones. His love extends to all races, tribes, and nations. Every child of God is bestowed with 100% of His love and goodness. But the extent to which it manifests in them is related to the extent they are willing to receive it for themselves. On God's part, He is absolutely impartial. The hesitancy in receiving is always from our end.

The shepherd never abandons sick and old sheep. From the day they are born until they die, they stay with the shepherd. The sick ones are cared for, and the old ones are accommodated with love. No matter our physical or mental state, our ABBA Father is much more loving and caring towards us and has promised to never leave us, nor forsake us. He is the One who keeps His word always!

When we live life with this revelation of God being our All in all, we will never lack any good thing from the Father. I have previously spoken of the way the Father provided for Lord Jesus when He walked the earth. We should not go by our negative circumstances. Rather, we will definitely overcome them if we choose to believe this truth and allow His goodness to flow in our lives.

2. *HE MAKES ME TO LIE DOWN IN GREEN PASTURES; HE LEADS ME BESIDE THE STILL WATERS.*

Honestly speaking, every time I read this verse in the past (i.e. before I actually sat and meditated on it), I always thought of it as a shepherd leading his sheep to green pastures and beside still waters. But as I meditated on it, God revealed a different perspective of this verse, and this revelation is just so beautiful! So far, I haven't come across this revelation in all the teachings I have heard, so I am very excited to share this.

It is true that every shepherd's aim is to find the best and safest pasture for his flock and also to provide clean drinking water from freshwater pools/streams. Knowing that God similarly deals with much more care and love towards His children, there is also something more to be understood here. **When David was tending his flock with utmost care and wanted them to have the best, it was the grace of God that enabled him to do his work in a "RESTFUL manner."** This needs to be explained further.

When flocks of sheep are led to pastures, they don't immediately hit the ground and lie down. They are led by their hunger to feed joyfully in these pastures. A variety of grass, legumes, and herbs constitute green pastures. It is the perfect diet for the sheep, consisting of all essential nutrients and minerals. This serves the purpose for which they are reared. Adequately fed sheep give a good quality and quantity of wool, have good immunity against diseases, and provide good quality milk and meat. Hence, on being brought to such nutritious pastures, they feed to their satisfaction and then basically sit with their forelimbs folded, hind limbs stretched, slanting on one side, and ruminate to their hearts' content. They actually don't lie down on their sides because it does not suit the digestive system of any ruminant. From my childhood, till today, I have observed many cows in my area. I have never actually seen any cow lying on its side. If it was, either it was very sick, injured, or probably dead.

When David said 'He makes me to lie down in green pastures,' he meant that God not only satisfied him with the best needed for his flock but also that God helped him to do his shepherding job **"stress-free."** I hope you get the point.

Let me explain it this way. There are 2 individuals, A and B, doing their job. While Mr. A depends on his strength, intellect, and charisma to come up in life, Mr. B is totally dependent on God and does his work free of stress. Mr. B knows that God has already made the way and provided everything needed for him to have an abundant life. He approaches life from the perspective of a victor rather than working towards victory. Hence, at the end of the day, Mr. A is filled with pride, self-exaltation, and, of course, a great deal of stress because there is a lot of weight on his shoulders to stay successful. He has sleepless nights added to restricted time with people who really matter. But Mr. B is calm, restful, and still very successful in his work because he is drawing on God's grace and favour on the work of his hands. While resting in the Lord's finished work, he has superb health, is stress-free, and enjoys life with his loved ones. He is content with all that God has blessed him with and, in turn, he is a blessing to others.

This is possible! The only way to go about life is to do it resting in the finished work of our Saviour and knowing that God:

- Opens the right doors,
- Closes the wrong ones,
- Holds the perfect time for everything in His hands,
- Is always gloriously rich in His love for us,
- Sends forth adequate supply of provision into our lives,
- Bestows favour on us as dew upon the grass,
- Knows the dangers that lurk around us and protects us even when we fail to recognise it,
- Brings in the right connections and relationships into our lives,
- Removes people and things that don't edify us,
- And knowing for sure that His will for us is to have hope and a future!

This list can go on as we keep adding all His promises given to us in the Word. All His promises are 'Yes' and 'Amen' in Christ Jesus our Lord! If we continue in faith and patience, all His promises will be fulfilled in our lives. It is possible to go about our work restfully/stress-free. I have seen the effects of parenting using my own strength, and it has frustrated me. But then I pray to God to help me receive His grace for godly parenting, and that is enjoyable and a much better place to be in. When we receive God's strength to do the things we need to do, it makes a huge difference. It is something to be 'experienced' rather than just theory. For that reason, it is worth casting away our pride, humbly receiving His grace to accomplish the task set before us and give Him all the glory!

The picture of a sheep resting in the green pastures says a lot about its confidence in the shepherd. A sheep is sensitive to danger because of its good peripheral vision, sense of smell, and hearing. But because of the relationship the shepherd and his flock share, the sheep have a greater sense of security with him around. On the other hand, if David is referring to himself when he says that the Lord makes him lie down in green pastures, he intends to say that God is helping him also to rest while his flock is happily feeding and resting. He is not fretting and stressing while shepherding his flock. This is important because a shepherd has to always look out for any danger to his flock. But the green pastures have short grass, and he doesn't have to worry about camouflaging predators. It is not easy for predators to hide or even camouflage in such pastures. Hence, much of the danger is ruled out. Rough and dry terrain harbour more predators because it is easy to camouflage/hide by the rocks and attack the flock. To be led to green pastures is a blessing in many ways. They also have the advantage of having a healthy source of water nearby.

A shepherd cannot dream of or crave any comfort while grazing his flock. He has to be content with what he gets. Shepherds in the Middle East would be glad to find a small tree so that they could sit in its shade while doing their job. David says that God's care for him was so excellent that even his resting place in the wilderness was taken care of! Similarly, God is with us every step of the way to help us do our work with excellence. He provides us with the resources to do our job efficiently for His glory.

The striking fact about green pastures is that they are natural and not artificial. The vegetation is not planted by anyone. It is God who covers the terrain with pastures to feed these animals. However, these days there are people who own farms and cultivate such pastures for their flocks. But it was not so in the olden days. These pastures were planted by God and are usually perennial (growing all year round). It is fresh, nutritious, and like daily bread for the sheep, unlike stocked hay fed to cattle. Sheep prefer tender grass to hay. David intends to say that God faithfully gave him the provision for each day, and it was always the best. God was his source! Green pastures also denoted that the area was well watered by dew, rain, and a good water source. The land was fertile. Dew denotes divine favour (Proverbs 19:12) according to the word, and every child of God is blessed with favour whether they recognise it or not. If we are aware that we carry God's favour, life would be a lot different for most of us. Rather than longing and striving for the approval and applause of mankind, we would dare to carry out great godly exploits. Green pastures are favoured ground! They are a call to rest! The very sight is welcoming and inculcates a feeling of great joy!

The still waters are mentioned after the green pastures. Other translations also call it quiet waters, peaceful streams, restful waters, waters of refreshment, and quiet pools of fresh water. The very sound of it is so soothing! How many of us would feel safe walking next to or even standing beside roaring and violent water bodies? The very sound of it would make us shudder and be nowhere near it. But the very thought of still, quiet, peaceful streams of water gives us a welcoming feeling and a sense of calm. There are people who crave the adrenaline rush of river rafting, but not me! I believe most people would love, enjoy, and prefer the serenity of peaceful waters any day.

These restful waters would welcome both man and beast. For the shepherd and his flock, the combination of green pastures and still waters would be paradise on earth! Multiple purposes would be served by these waters - for drinking, refilling his water skin, cleaning his sheep, as well as himself, etc. The pastures around these waters would always be green, providing continued sustenance to both for many days. It is akin to every need of theirs being met!

Water is very significant in the Word. Its use is multipurpose. Lord Jesus said that He is the source of Living Water, which, if a person drinks, he would never thirst again. All of us who are thirsty to have a fulfilling life are asked to come to Him, and He will satisfy us with living waters so that we won't despair of life anymore. This Living Water is the Holy Spirit, whom Lord Jesus promised to all those who believe in Him (John 7:38, 39). The guidance of the Holy Spirit is such that there is a continuous supply of grace and empowerment all the time. More than being conscious of what we cannot do, He reminds us constantly that Lord Christ is All-sufficient for us and that we can accomplish His perfect will through Him who strengthens us. I hope every one of us realises the true potential of the Holy Spirit working in and through us! It is certainly much greater than the power possessed by the most powerful human on earth! We can do ANYTHING the Lord wants us to do. The Holy Spirit is the ultimate source of inexhaustible power and energy with which the Lord's goodwill can be accomplished in and through our lives. He is the first instalment that God has given to each of us who are saved, of all that the Lord has promised is ours (Ephesians 1:14). Hence, the starting point for us to believe in God's goodness and receiving from Him is to be aware of the gift of the Holy Spirit and being baptised into Him. There is a big difference in having a sip of water from a glass every once in a while and diving into the Rivers of fresh water and it satisfies us in every way. Lord Jesus Himself began His earthly ministry after the Father bestowed on Him the fellowship of the Holy Spirit following the water baptism by John. Thereby He set the precedent for every believer. None of us can accomplish God's purpose for our lives effectively without the empowerment of the Holy Spirit. He never leaves us once He comes to live in us. That is the major difference between the Old and the New Covenant. These rivers of Living Water flow from within us to feed many lives around us (Proverbs 21:1) and this causes a ripple effect.

The word of God is the water that continuously cleanses the believer. The word has that power. As the word goes into our hearts, it drives out all the unnecessary stuff. Similar to the manner in which we take a bath to clean our body from filth, the word cleanses our hearts from all filth. Hence, a believer is encouraged to renew his mind daily by meditating on the word of God (Romans 12:2). His word refreshes and rejuvenates us just like how water quenches our thirst and refreshes us in a physical sense. All these need to be experienced firsthand in order to understand it better. That is why David says in Psalm 34:8, "Oh, taste and see that the Lord is good!"

Once I saw an experiment done to explain this, and it was awesome. The person demonstrating this concept had black-coloured water kept in a transparent jug. Then he poured clean water from another jug into the jug of coloured water. The outcome was very predictable. The clear water quickly displaced all the coloured water, and very soon, the entire glass had crystal clear beautiful water! I hope you get the picture. It can't be explained better than this! If only a jug of ordinary tap water can do that, how exceedingly much more can the **WORD OF GOD?!**

When we submit completely and surrender control to God, this is the perfect standard He conforms our life to - "Green Pastures and Still Waters." The problem often arises when we, every once in a while, try to take back what we have submitted to God and aim for greener pastures (for so it seems) and adventurous roaring waters devoid of God. It is then that we foolishly invite trouble (paraphrase of Proverbs 27:8). When Lot was given the privilege to choose a land and separate from Abraham, he chose the lush green plains of Jordan near Sodom and Gomorrah, in spite of knowing the city was wicked. Moving forward, his life never lacked distress!

Proverbs 19:3 says, "the foolishness of a man twists his way, and his heart frets against the Lord." We tend to ignore and shut Him out when He convicts us, and only when we reap the consequences of our actions, do we let Him in, expecting Him to sort out everything overnight! Yet the Lord is faithful and delivers us when we call upon His Name in truth! We make our own ambitious plans and never seek to know what His will for our life is. Almost all the time, our bright ideas get us into deep trouble, and we ask Him to bless such plans. Even we wouldn't bless such self-destructive ideas if our children request us to, knowing that it will certainly harm them. Then why should we be so adamant for God to bless such self-centred ambitions? We have the audacity to go one step ahead and say that God doesn't answer prayers, making us a saint and Him a villain. Shame on us!

We need to understand that it is for our own good that such selfish and self-destructive prayers go unanswered. God knows what is best for us. When we delight in having a close relationship with Him (by studying the Word, meditating on it, and living life with Him), He puts His desires into our hearts and steers our thoughts in that direction. He blesses prayers prayed along those lines, and we get to enjoy the benefits of His good plans as He brings them to pass. This far outweighs anything we can come up with our intellect or smartness.

3. *HE RESTORES MY SOUL; HE LEADS ME IN THE PATHS OF RIGHTEOUSNESS FOR HIS NAME'S SAKE.*

a. He restores my soul:

God's concept of restoration is one of the most beautiful revelations I have received and experienced personally. It goes beyond anything any man can offer. Though I have been a Christian all my life, due to my own foolishness, I fell into a lot of trouble in my mid-twenties and desperately needed both deliverance and restoration. The way this came to pass in my life was when God opened my eyes, ears, and heart to His Word. As I delved deeper into His Word, I was assured of His willingness to forgive, deliver, and restore me. Then He gave me the grace to believe it, confess it by faith, and very soon, it became my reality. I still practice this principle even today and reap its benefits. It is undoubtedly possible for us to live the good life that God has ordained for each of His children, provided we first believe that!

God's concept of restoration is at a much higher level than the world's standards of restoration. The world can only compensate meagrely compared to the loss suffered; it cannot restore. I firmly believe that restoration belongs only to God; He owns the copyright! If someone loses something, the world would probably search and return it, either in the same or worse condition; never greater. Very rarely does monetary compensation satisfy.

However, the biblical concept of restoration is astounding. If every broken person gets a hold of the truth of God's love and His willingness to restore, the world would be a much better place today. God's restoration does not stop at replacing that which is lost. It goes much beyond that to added benefits, provided we are willing to receive it, overlooking the magnitude of the loss.

God's restoration is manifold. When Adam and Eve attempted to cover their nakedness using fig leaves, God performed the first sacrifice in the Garden for the remission of their sins and used the skin of the animal to provide a sturdier, effectual, and lasting covering for their nakedness. It is equivalent to taking down 2 birds with one stone. He not only dealt with sin but also dealt with the consequence of sin (nakedness). Adam and Eve could have refused the tunic of skin and persisted in using fig leaves to cover themselves. The loss would have been theirs. This holds true for us even today. God has offered much more to mankind than it can receive naturally (due to ignorance or frank pride). The one who will benefit is the one who humbles himself and receives His gift of restoration, which is a part of salvation.

When God created the universe, His standard for every aspect of life was unique. This standard is perfect and cannot be challenged by anyone, anytime. He instituted these standards as statutes and commandments in the Bible. For example, marriage had to be between a male and a female and had to last a lifetime. Anything that deviates from this set standard is a perversion, and the world passionately pursues this perversion under the influence of satan. He gave us the blueprint of marriage through the first couple He created and went on to state the clauses for a godly marriage, which were further emphasised by Lord Jesus in person. Similarly, God ordained His standards, qualifications, and requirements for restoration in His Word through statutes. Let's take a look at it from the Old Testament and follow it up with an example in the New Testament.

The Lord's heart is always for His people, and He goes all out for them. In Leviticus 6:1-7, God instituted the 'law of restoration.' The victim here is the one who has been wronged by another on any account given in verses 2-3: stolen, extorted from, negligence in safekeeping, or lost and found. The standard of restoration that God set was the full value of the item with an additional one-fifth of its value added to it. So, in total, it amounts to 120%. In other words, the victim became a gainer! This additional 20% compensation was under the law and known by almost all the Jews, but I am not sure how many of them seriously followed this standard practically.

When we study the concept of restoration in the New Testament, we see our Saviour demonstrating this clearly in all His miracles. He healed a man with a withered right hand in Luke 6:6-11. The very setting of this miracle was one where man tested God's goodness because of their useless traditions and misunderstanding of the meaning of the Sabbath. Lord Jesus did not back off but went ahead and healed the man. Verse 10 explicitly states: "And looking round about upon them all, he said unto the man, 'stretch forth thy hand'. And he did so: and his hand was restored whole as the other." Not only did our Lord heal him, but He restored his livelihood and gave him the ability to feed himself and his family. That is the nature of our God! When He healed the lepers, they were made whole (Luke 17:19); I believe their fingers which were eaten away by the microbe grew back to normal healthy fingers. In other words, He gave them back their health and livelihood.

This gift of restoration had a significant impact on the people He restored. The best example is Zacchaeus, the short-statured chief tax collector from Jericho. In Luke 19, Zacchaeus, most likely a Jew, sought to see the Lord as He passed by. There was something about Jesus that drew people of ill repute and encouraged them to live a pure life. Tax collectors in those days had a very bad reputation and were considered on par with drunkards and prostitutes. They were hated by their own people (Jews) because of their job profile, which made them loyalists to the Roman government and because they extorted much more than what was right. Lord Jesus attracted the hearts of guilt-ridden people like a magnet because He taught kingdom principles in which these people, who were condemned by the masses and religious leaders of those days, had a chance at living a life connected to God through repentance.

Zacchaeus "ran ahead of Him" and climbed a "sycamore tree" to see Him as He passed by! Have you ever seen government officials climbing trees? I bet not. Dignified people rarely climb trees. The most common tree climbers are kids because they don't care 2 cents about what others would think of them. But Zacchaeus displayed this innate childlike nature just to get a view of the Lord! So what if he was short? **There is always a way to overcome, and the answer is usually standing tall right**

before our eyes. Desperate people do desperate things. It can either be good, like what Zacchaeus did, or bad like what Judas Iscariot did; we need to choose wisely. This man is a good example of the positive use of our desperation - **look to the Lord**! He will never disappoint us. When Lord Jesus came to 'the place,' He 'looked' up, saw him, and called him by 'name'! I don't think Zacchaeus expected this. What more? The Lord invited Himself to stay at Zacchaeus' house that day! I'm sure Zacchaeus was so blown away by the reward he received for the right use of his desperation! Over all the people in the crowd who thronged Him, the Lord gave this honour to Zacchaeus just because he strived for clarity, sacrificing his ego and dignity. By his unique act of worship (persevering to see the Lord), Zacchaeus stood out and became more pronounced as he sat on the tree compared to the crowd that hovered around the Lord. I hope with all my heart that this speaks to you.

Now, let us understand how this gracious move of the Lord caused a ripple effect in the life of Zacchaeus. The Lord told him to make haste and come down. He immediately obeyed, came down, and received the Lord joyfully. Every part of this event is special, but one stands out and must have had a deep impact on Zacchaeus. The very name Zacchaeus means "pure/clean." By occupation, he was just the opposite. But this did not make the Lord call him anything different. He still called him by his name! The Lord called him and reminded him to come up higher because he was a son of Abraham too. With all the hatred and disgust the Jews had for the tax collectors, I wonder if anyone would have called him by his name in a long time, especially if his name meant exactly the opposite of what he was indulging in. I am sure all these happenings would have elated him. Zacchaeus opened up the door of his house and heart to receive Grace - the Person of our Lord Jesus Christ. When grace came in, it turned his world the right side up, and he became a 'giver'! He stood up before the Lord and declared that he would give half of all that he had to the poor and restore 'Four-fold' to anyone from whom he had taken anything by false accusation. This takes us back to the law of restoration in the book of Leviticus. This is where we see Grace Supercede The Law. The law commanded restoration of the loss with 20% of its value added to it, thereby making it 120%. But Zacchaeus raised the standard to 400%! Zacchaeus' victims were now super-gainers! His victims would have fallen on their faces, thanking God for being victimised by Zacchaeus instead of any other tax collector because they stood to gain four-fold. The restoration under grace is much greater than the restoration under the law. Lord Jesus raised the standard of restoration to a higher level because He made grace priceless! Grace elevated the standard of compensation and restoration.

Now, having learned about the restoration under grace, may we never make the mistake of looking to man for the same. Man can never match up to God's standards. Go to Him! Let Him restore you! His restoration is beyond anyone's comprehension. Don't miss out on it!

Now that we are convinced that God's will is to restore us, it is important for us to know the starting point of restoration. Regardless of the loss (whether physical, spiritual, mental, emotional, financial, etc.), restoration always begins in one's understanding. It begins with the knowledge of John 10:10, which explicitly says that every loss is from the enemy, satan. When we stop blaming God for all the wrong things happening in our lives and know in our hearts that His thoughts towards us are always to give us hope and a future (Jeremiah 29:11), we can receive grace from God and work hand in hand with Him and allow Him to restore our loss. Sometimes the loss may be the life of a person. In this case, we might think that it is impossible to be compensated. But even in such cases, Lord Jesus set the example more than once when He raised Jairus' daughter, the widow's son in Nain, and Lazarus from the dead. His Apostles followed suit. He showed us that it is not impossible. Even today, I have heard many powerful testimonies of people raised from the dead!

In the Book of Daniel, chapter 4, Nebuchadnezzar, the king of Babylon who ruled the kingdom in the east, gives us a wonderful revelation on restoration. This concept of restoration has practically paralleled in my life too, and hence I stand witness to this. On account of his insolent pride in thinking that he was the source of all his splendour, glory, and wealth, the Lord warned him through a dream. This dream was interpreted by Daniel, and the warning was made more clear. Yet, he ignored it for almost a year and continued to be swelled up with pride.

One fine day, he opened his mouth to glorify himself, and immediately the word which God spoke came to pass. He was turned into a beast, driven from men, stayed along with the beasts of the field, ate grass like oxen, his body was wet with the dew of heaven until his hair had grown like an eagle's feathers and his nails like bird's claws. He was trapped in an animal's body for 7 years until all his pride drained out.

After 7 years, **"he lifted up his eyes to heaven."** That speaks volumes! As a person who ruled the earth, his gaze would have been horizontal if not downward, looking down on others, but never up. But now he realised his sin of self-exaltation (similar to the sin of Lucifer) and looked up to the God of heaven and earth. The first thing that was restored to him was his **understanding** (Daniel 4:34), not his kingship or kingdom. **Understanding means to know God (Proverbs 9:10).** It is to acknowledge that He is the Supreme Potentate of the universe, and there is none beside Him. Nebuchadnezzar's pride made him discredit God for his success. He finally realised that it was God who had kept the breath in his nostrils and who was the source of all his glory and splendour. When he realised this, the next thing he did was to abound in praise and thanksgiving to God. Once his relationship with God was restored, everything else - reasoning, glory, his kingdom, honour, and splendour, etc. - was restored. His counsellors and nobles who had driven him out 7 years ago came back to him. The kingdom and more excellent majesty were further added. I believe that he was one saved heathen king who finally believed in God!

When we understand this passage, we should also have the same attitude. Just acknowledging His goodness will make us abound with thanksgiving in the middle of our loss. This leads us to seek Him, His kingdom, and His righteousness. Then the promise in Matthew 6:33 goes into action, and God's restoration takes effect in our lives. We need to cast away all pride. Every saint in the word of God held onto these godly principles, even through tough times and was a recipient of God's manifold blessings.

This has very well been my experience too. I had gotten into a big mess due to my own foolishness. **BUT THE LORD's LOVE AND FAITHFULNESS** drew me near. He first restored my relationship with Him and brought it to a whole new level. As I started spending more time with Him, in prayer and studying His word, His word taught me first to be established in His righteousness and then to receive His promises by faith. This restoration was beautiful and continues to this day! I would encourage everyone who has been victimised by satan to go to God and allow Him to restore you.

b. He leads me in the paths of righteousness for His name's sake.

Righteousness is the established character of God. It goes hand in hand with all His virtues - His holiness, His kindness, His love, and His justice. This banishes every trace of negativity that ignorant people attribute to God. He is the pinnacle of perfection! Nobody in all eternity can point a finger at God and accuse Him of anything bad.

'The fall' caused man to lose his position before God. God was and is still enthroned as before, while man was pushed away from Him by a huge barrier called sin. Always remember that God never backed off. It was us who backslid while He faithfully stays where He is, waiting for us to return (Luke 15:11-32). Hence He made a way for man to come back to Him through the offering of innocent, unblemished animal sacrifices (which depicted the death of our Saviour). Through these sacrifices, sin was only covered by the blood but not removed (under the old covenant). The removal of sins forever would be accomplished when the Messiah died on the cross. But the Lord graciously made a way for man to come before Him. When Lord Jesus died on the cross, all our sins were abolished (totally removed), and the barrier of sin was broken down for good! **Our Saviour became 'THE WAY'** for us to return to God and stand before Him blameless.

Before the fall, Adam and Eve lived in the perfect environment. They were always in the company of God, hearing directly from Him, living in perfect health, and with every provision met. They lacked nothing. Life was full of joy, peace, love, and every good thing one could imagine. The path of righteousness is characterised by all these features. Adam and Eve did not know their 'need' because they didn't have any. The Father had faithfully supplied them with everything. They had the righteousness which God had given them, but forfeited it by their disobedience. Now they had 2 problems: the barrier called sin and the loss of righteousness.

In order to solve both these problems, the Omniscient God of the universe provided the solution even before He established the earth: The Lamb of God, The Beloved Son, would come in the flesh and deal with both and rectify it forever. He would not only abolish the power of sin but also restore the righteousness that man had lost. Both these were accomplished at the cross by Him.

The Lord lived a perfect life on earth. The sin of Adam could not penetrate His flesh at conception or birth because it was 'The Word' that impregnated Mary. Neither man's sperm nor the woman's ova had anything to do with His conception. **It was purely The Word only.** When Mary wholeheartedly accepted the Angel's proposal to bring the Messiah into the world, **'The Word' became flesh in her womb**, similar to the way the whole creation came into existence—by the Word that proceeded from the mouth of God! It is as simple as that! God said, "Let there be light," and there was light! Just as simple as that! But for God to be born into this world as a human, a virgin was necessary. The Lord waited until that 'one woman' came along who would wholeheartedly accept His proposal beyond all odds—Mary. God took the onus to convince her husband, and she brought forth the sinless Messiah into this world. Even after being born, He lived a perfect and sinless life until the end and fulfilled every jot and tittle of the Law, thereby becoming the only Human fulfilling the righteous requirements of the Law and 'earning' righteousness. He legally owns righteousness.

Shortly before His betrayal and crucifixion, He enforced the New Covenant at the Last Supper and established the Holy Communion as a sign of the New Covenant. Then He went ahead with the will of the Father and submitted to the death on the cross. Now here was the place of divine exchange. As Judas was bringing the soldiers to arrest Him, the Saviour began to take on the 'sin of the whole world,' from the first man Adam to the last human born before the world ends. The judgement, scourging, mocking, more scourging, crown of thorns, the walk to Calvary, and finally crucifixion happened. He was nailed to the cross for 6 agonising hours, which is beyond the reach of any human understanding. **An eternity of punishment that was rightfully ours was completely fulfilled in about 18-20 hours in the flesh (body and**

soul) of our Lord. This was the place where He traded with us and gave us His righteousness in exchange for our sins in addition to bearing our punishment! I bet there is no other noble trading in the history of the world that can even come close to this! Who would trade gold for rotten eggs? Yet our Lord, because of the love He had for us, gave us the best gift ever! He died because of our sins and rose again because of our justification.

For those who still don't understand why only the forgiveness of sins wasn't sufficient, I would like to explain it in a simple manner. Just imagine a well-dressed person stumbling and falling into slush. In order to get clean, he has to go home, take away the dirty clothes, and bathe. After this, how many of us would loiter around naked instead of putting on clothes? None of us would do that, right? Just cleaning ourselves from the dirt will not do. We need to put on fresh clothes so that we can get on with the rest of the day. Similarly, at the cross, our Lord dealt once and for all with sin. Sin's power over us was totally destroyed, and the huge man-made barrier was broken down. Still, man stood 10 steps behind because he lacked the proper attire to appear before God. This gap was closed when the Saviour clothed us with His righteousness, and we can approach the Father now with the righteousness of our Lord Jesus Christ.

The Righteousness of our Lord becomes our identity on the day we are born again. No longer is our identity in our carnal self. This gifted identity is superior to any other that exists because even the heavens and the angels recognise this identity, and the demons tremble because of it. By profession, I am a medical doctor. But this title is applicable only to this earth; to be more specific, my degree is recognised and accepted only in India. I cannot practice abroad with this degree. I still have to write and clear many qualifying exams and do additional courses as specified by that country in order to practice my profession there. Even on this earth, there is so much variation in recognising a degree and job profile. As far as the heavens and the angels are concerned, my degree does not increase my status before them as compared to my fellow brothers and sisters from a different profession. They seriously don't care whether I am a doctor or a cobbler. They are more concerned if I am a child of God and possessing His righteousness. Then they will act on my behalf. Though the importance of this identity is not appreciated or understood well by the world, the saints in the Bible repeatedly demonstrated the power of this identity. It is undeniable! When we are clothed with the righteousness of our Lord, as Hebrew 4:16 says, 'we can come boldly to the throne of grace that we may obtain mercy and find grace to help in time of need.'

This righteousness is a gift. The only way to have it is to receive it. Since Lord Jesus is the Beloved and Favoured One, we also become the beloved and favoured of the Lord. This righteousness is everlasting, beginning at salvation and stretching into eternity. However, forgiveness of sins is the primary requisite and is followed by the impartation of His righteousness to us. Both entities go hand in hand and cannot be separated from each other.

Now that we have been made righteous, i.e., right before God, the Lord faithfully leads us in the "Path of Righteousness" for "His Name's sake." We are commanded not to seek vengeance or walk the perverse road even though there may be a good reason for doing so. God is called "The Righteous God" in many places in the word. That is one of His Names. Since His Name is Righteous, we, His children, should also live righteously. We cannot take the liberty of living otherwise no matter how well we can justify it. The Path of Righteousness can be understood very well if we take the time to study the lives of the saints in the word. Now let us try to visualise this path as I put it forward one by one:

- ✡ In spite of the unfair and harsh treatment meted out to **Joseph** by his brothers at the age of 17 and all that followed after he was sold in Egypt, including the false accusation by Potiphar's wife and being forgotten by the butler for almost 2 years after his reinstatement, he never avenged himself on any of these people who did him wrong when God exalted him to the second-highest position in Egypt. He extended kindness and mercy towards his brothers even after the death of his father Jacob. He could have taken matters into his own hands and justified his actions. But no! He preferred to walk the path of righteousness (not avenging himself) because he served the God of Righteousness and allowed Him to defend and avenge him.

- ✡ Having lost their beloved homeland, their royal positions in the kingdom of Judah, and treated as refugees in the land of Babylon, **Daniel, Hananiah, Mishael, and Azariah** walked this path when they blatantly disobeyed the kings' orders to follow the world's system and got thrown into the fiery furnace that was heated sevenfold and also into the hungry lion's den. They preferred to walk the path of righteousness (not compromising, irrespective of the consequences) because they served the God of Righteousness and allowed Him to defend and avenge them.
- ✡ Having been anointed for greatness as a young lad, the shepherd boy **David** found his strength in the covenant he had with the Lord. He floored and beheaded the giant Goliath, **BUT** refused to harm Saul because he feared the Lord. Saul was also anointed by the Lord, but he recklessly persecuted hardworking David for almost 13 years out of sheer envy. David preferred to walk the path of righteousness because he served the God of Righteousness (confidence in the Lord and fear of the Lord) and allowed Him to defend and avenge him.
- ✡ Having nurtured self-confidence because of being brought up in Egypt and knowing that he was a Hebrew by birth, the foretold deliverer, **Moses**, fled after killing an Egyptian, fearing the wrath of the Pharaoh. Yet for 40 years, he walked in the wilderness, attending to his father-in-law's herd and flocks until the word of the Lord brought him back to Egypt to deliver God's people. He boldly stood before the Pharaoh and commanded him to release the Israelites so that they could worship the One True Living God, dwelling in the Promised Land. The hard-hearted Pharaoh was rewarded by God with devastating plagues brought forth by the word Moses spoke. He did not take matters into his own hands as he had done 40 years ago. He patiently waited until the Lord had His way and brought out the armies of Israel, led them to Sinai, and brought them to the Promised Land. Pharaoh kept changing his mind repeatedly, and the final time he did that again, the entire

Egyptian army was wiped out by the waters of the Red Sea. His own people turned against him many times in the wilderness. Yet he preferred to walk the path of righteousness, for he served the God of Righteousness (patience and boldness), and he allowed Him to defend and avenge him and the Israelites.

- Being barren for years, and ridiculed time and again by her counterpart Peninnah, even in the place of worship, yet being loved dearly by her husband Elkanah, **Hannah** preferred to pour out her hurting heart and soul before the Lord in the tabernacle at Shiloh. Even though all the ridicule was in the open, she did not seek sympathy from humans but preferred to harness her feelings and set her case before the Lord of Hosts! She asked Him for a son so that she could dedicate him back to His service in the Tabernacle and take away her reproach. The Lord answered her prayer by confirming it through the word of Eli, and she returned home confident in the promise that was given to her. She conceived and brought forth the child who became the final judge, a prophet, priest, seer, military leader, and the one who anointed the first 2 kings of Israel! So great was her reward! In addition to Samuel, God blessed Hannah with 5 more children (3 boys and 2 girls). Scholars say she was 130 years old when she birthed Samuel. She preferred to walk the path of righteousness (depending on God for consolation and honour), for she served the God of Righteousness, and she allowed Him to defend and reward her.

- Being an orphan who was brought up under the parental affection of her older cousin Mordecai, **Esther** learned obedience and submission. God granted her favour in the eyes of all the people, including the King of Persia. Her simplicity and humility propelled her to be chosen as the queen of Persia. As usual, satan had his agents upfront to totally wipe out the Jewish race. At this time, Esther was unaware of the plans hatched against her people. But being informed by Mordecai and being told that 'she was in that position of influence for such a time as this,' she found the grace and boldness to stand before the King of Persia and petition him for the lives of all the Jews, her people. Instead of being beheaded for appearing before the king without an invite, her request to **"defend themselves from their enemies"** was attested by the king and made official in all 127 provinces that he ruled over. She preferred to walk the path of righteousness (boldness and selflessness) for she served the God of Righteousness, and she allowed Him to defend and reward her as well as save the lives of thousands of Jews.

✡ Being a Moabite woman and the daughter-in-law of a Jewish couple, **Ruth** clung to her mother-in-law Naomi, who had literally lost everything in life and was far away from home. Her customs would have allowed her to remarry and have a great life if she had gone back to her parent's house. **But Ruth chose the God of Naomi over the abominations that her people worshipped, and God flooded her life with His favour and goodness.** The Lord arranged her second marriage with one of the most elite and wealthy bachelors of Israel, and she became the great-grandmother of King David! She preferred to walk the path of righteousness (sacrificial love) for she served the God of Righteousness, and she allowed Him to defend and reward her.

✡ Having indulged in a great deal of sexual immorality in the land which was the gateway to the Promised Land, **Rahab** (the mother-in-law of Ruth and the mother of Boaz, and the great-great-grandmother of King David) was taught as a little girl that the God of Israel, Who is God in heaven above and on earth beneath, had dried up the waters of the Red Sea for His people to cross over and how they had recently killed the 2 most powerful Amorite kings on the east side of River Jordan. She knew that all the hearts of her people had grown faint, discouraged, and melted, and the terror of the Israelites had fallen on them. She boldly confessed her heart before the 2 spies that the God of Israel was The True God. She requested that her kindness be repaid by sparing the life of her household with a "true token." I even wonder if her household appreciated her worth because she was a prostitute. Yet she pleaded with the spies for their lives also. The spies handed her a line of scarlet cord (a sign of redemption) as an apt token to be hung in the window through which she would let them down. This scarlet cord became a powerful sign for the saving of her entire household. Years later, King Lemuel's mother taught him that the virtuous woman wouldn't fear snow for her household, for all her household was covered/clothed with scarlet (Proverbs 31:21)! She preferred to walk the path of righteousness (declaring her faith in the Almighty God and obedience to the covenant given to her) because she believed in the God of Righteousness, and she allowed Him to defend and reward her.

- Being the most important patriarch of the Jews, **Abraham** followed his father Terah along with his wife Sarah and nephew Lot to Haran. For some reason, Terah wound up his journey in Haran and died there. But Abraham went forward, sought peaceful relationships always, and believed in the promise made to him, sojourning in the land of Canaan. Being barren, Abraham and Sarah grew in faith as the days went by and found that their dead reproductive systems were made alive by the power of God, bringing forth their promised son, Isaac. They considered Him faithful, Who had promised. Before they exited this earth, they were more than convinced that myriads of people would come from them, and a nation would be born through which the Messiah would come to save the world. Abraham "looked behind him" on Mount Moriah after the Lord stopped him from sacrificing Isaac and saw "The Ram" that God had prepared for sacrifice in the place of Isaac. He saw Lord Jesus there (John 8:56)! They preferred to walk the path of righteousness (rooted in faith and absolute trust in God) because they served the God of Righteousness, and they allowed Him to make them the patriarchs and the primary examples of faith.

- Being a Levite by birth and a scribe and priest by vocation, **Ezra** had little doubt about his calling. He honoured the desire God had put into his heart to live out his calling as a scribe and a priest. He boldly requested the king of Persia to allow him to take his fellow Levites and priests (about 1500-2000 men) along with their families and relocate to Judah in order to teach the people who had returned earlier with Zerubbabel about the commandments, laws, and ordinances of the Lord. He acknowledged the good hand of God and His favour upon him. He came to Judah and introduced godly discipline and worship there. There were many Israelites who had settled quite well in the land of captivity and were flourishing there. They did not desire to sacrifice all that by going back to Judah and starting all over again. But not so with Zerubbabel, Ezra, and Nehemiah. Ezra's heart burned with the desire to teach the word of God to his people. He preferred to walk the path of righteousness (knowing he was favoured and equipped for his primary calling) because he served the God of Righteousness, and he allowed Him to strengthen him and prosper his work.

✡ Being the trusted cupbearer in the court of the Persian king, **Nehemiah** had come a long way. Yet his heart longed for the good of his people who had returned and were in great distress in the land of Judah. The glorious city of God had the temple restored but no walls around it to protect them from scavengers like Sanballat and Tobiah, who constantly sought harm for Jerusalem and its inhabitants. He also was aware of the favour of God on his life, made audacious requests to the king of Persia, got his approval for every one of them, arrived in Jerusalem, and built the wall of Jerusalem in a record-breaking 52 days! This included clearing the debris that lay around and putting to good use the stones that were already there. Along with this, he had to shut his ears to the discouragement and threats of his enemies, stay focused on his purpose, sacrifice his rights to the governor's portion, and even design a battle array and enforced it to protect the work that was going on. He preferred to walk the path of righteousness (knowing he was favoured by God, bold, hardworking, sacrificial, and focused) because he served the God of Righteousness, and he allowed Him to defend and reward him.

✡ Being the Pharisee of the Pharisees and an influential, highly educated, blameless Jew according to the law, Apostle **Paul** forsook all his worldly glory for the knowledge of Christ. He was honoured to be the first Apostle to the gentile world, appointed by Almighty God, and he endured suffering at the hands of many. He was also greatly rewarded by the Lord with astounding revelations concerning the Gospel of Grace. Paul wrote more than half of the New Testament, and his letters and epistles are major pillars of Christendom today. He preferred to walk the path of righteousness (enduring persecution for the sake of the Lord, possessing boldness and a supernatural life) as he served the God of Righteousness, allowing Him to defend and reward him.

The path of righteousness is impossible to walk in our own strength, but the good news is that we are not required to do so. It is the Lord's grace that leads us on this path because He is the God of righteousness; that is His unique name. This "path" is characterised by open heavens above, the company of an innumerable number of angels ministering to everyone who walks in it, and the host of heaven supporting it. It is a path characterised by absolute power and godly peace. Along this path, we see memorials standing high, of all the saints who have walked in it, some of which I have highlighted above. Certainly, the first memorial would be of our Lord Jesus Christ, who set the standard for this path and walked in it Himself.

Many times, unfair things happen, and the Lord does not leave us alone to face them. He stands by us and prevents us from resorting to unfair means to justify ourselves. He is also the God of justice, and vindicating us is His job; He excels at it! This is the reason why we must refrain from avenging ourselves after we have been restored by God. Restoration is a part of salvation, and the path of righteousness is the path that a born-again believer must take after restoration. David has brought this understanding into this verse.

Our God is the great I AM. He is the giver of every blessing. The path of righteousness is studded with precious gems: wisdom, knowledge, understanding, health, healing, deliverance, joy, peace, a sound mind, boldness, sacrificial love, confidence, etc. He has equipped us with all these traits so that we can use them to build His kingdom here on earth. This path has the strongest security because God Himself guards it. The restoration of our souls and being led in the paths of righteousness for His Name's sake are the pillars of the New Covenant Salvation. David had a good understanding regarding this.

4(a) YEA THOUGH I WALK THROUGH THE VALLEY OF THE SHADOW OF DEATH:

After having clearly addressed the positive aspects of life, David turns his attention to the other side, starting with the word "yea." We often tend to overlook the importance of these small words if we merely skim through the word of God with a religious reading. Every word, every number, every tiny detail holds a revelation in the word of God. Don't overlook it. The undeniable truth that he was about to declare further in this verse was etched on his heart, and he was assured of this truth.

Here, he speaks about a valley that was not welcoming and, in fact, seemed to have death written all over it. Most of the time, we find ourselves in such valleys due to our pride, stupidity, self-righteousness, foolishness, or ego. David acknowledges this because he didn't say that "the Lord led me into the dark path." God has granted us the privilege to choose between life and death, and this key is in our tongue (Proverbs 18:21). The results we obtain have everything to do with the words that exit our mouth.

When the Lord leads, He does it perfectly—through green pastures and still waters. However, when "we" walk according to our own wisdom, we often end up in gloomy valleys because we choose to leave God out or willfully ignore Him. The remarkable part is that our loving heavenly Father is right there. He never moved from His position when we chose to move from ours. Portrayed as the father of the prodigal son by Lord Jesus, His gaze is fixed in the direction of our return, and when He sees us from afar, He rushes to welcome us home.

Shadows operate on natural principles. They are visible only when there is light; they can never be seen in darkness. Shadows form when an object blocks the path of light. Let's consider a few well-known characteristics of shadows:

- ✡ They rarely match the actual size of the obstructing object. The closer the object is to the source of light, the larger the shadow because it obstructs more light rays.
- ✡ A shadow has no mass or energy. It doesn't have any substance to it.

- ✡ A lion can kill, but its shadow cannot harm anyone.
- ✡ Some shadows can be welcoming, like that of a tree on a hot day, while others can warn us of an impending threat.
- ✡ When I was a child, I learned how to create shadows of animals and birds on the wall using candlelight and my hands and fingers. I could make them bigger or smaller depending on the relative position of my hand to the light source. This demonstrates that certain shadows can appear deceptive too.

When we are walking through valleys looming with deathly shadows, it is utmost important for us, as children of God, to discern these shadows. As said before, many shadows look bigger than the actual size of the object. Some are deceptive, having no semblance to the object. Knowing that shadows cannot harm us in any way is always very pacifying. Some shadows may warn us of danger ahead, and we can be more prudent in our choices and decisions.

Satan signifies death in every aspect, and his agenda is to always try and block the light of God. He targets us with greater vigour if we have the word implanted in us, intending to dislodge it. **It is the word in us that threatens him;** it's not our personality or any virtue. The shadow disappears when the object is directly perpendicular to the source of light. **Hence, if we need to discern these deathly shadows, we need to look at them from "God's/word's perspective".** The word has clearly declared that satan is a defeated foe, and his eternity is sealed in hell. If we are well placed near God and in close proximity to Him, there is no way that satan can deceive us. On the contrary, if our perspective shifts away from the source of light, satan's gimmicks appear larger to us. God stays on His ground always. We need to be in close proximity to Him. If we move away, we are making a place for satan to come in between and block God's light and form shadows. How do we get back? By realising our mistake, repenting of it, and returning to the Father. He will take care of the rest.

4(b) "I WILL FEAR NO EVIL":

Satan's work is always deceptive and fear-instilling. But we have to renew our minds to the fact that he is a defeated foe and is powerless unless we give him ours. There is no substance to his threat. But if we fear his deception and give in, we end up giving substance to it. That is exactly what he wants.

It is necessary to practice godliness every day. When we practice godliness, we automatically fight fear and dread. It is something we need to learn to do. As we keep at it, even the smallest ones, God perfects us. God's love plays a major role in fighting fear and dread. If we are totally assured in our hearts of God's love for us, it makes us overcome every fear. In fact, fear flees in the presence of God's love. When we master this, most of our problems are solved. Knowing that we have a loving heavenly Father and Saviour Who has given us everything pertaining to life and godliness supplies us with divine grace-filled courage that keeps our hearts steady when fear knocks. Added to this, if we are intimate with God's word, He gives us His Rhema word to assist and encourage us through the situation.

David makes a wilful choice to keep away from fear. How many of us can boldly say the same? It is a deliberate choice we have to make. The attack of fear is always initiated in our minds. That is where "what if" starts. If we can quench all these arrows in our minds with the shield of faith, the battle is already won. On the contrary, if we give into fear or deception, we empower the negative and allow satan to wreck us.

When does a shadow actually disappear? Only in 2 places: absolute darkness and when the light source is perpendicular to (right above) the object. People living in darkness (without the knowledge of God) primarily cannot see anything. So shadows actually don't matter to them. But if we want to totally negate the effect of a shadow, we need to have a heavenly perspective. When the light source is directly above the object, the shadow automatically disappears under it. Hence, we need to have God's perspective to look at things happening around us. Not only does the size of the object reduce, but its shadow also dissipates. A godly perspective will diminish and negate every threat.

Most of us know that the true value of something is often underestimated until it is lost. It takes darkness to appreciate the light. It takes a storm to appreciate sunny weather. It takes barrenness to appreciate abundance. It takes sickness to appreciate the value of health! In the absence/ lack of a blessing, the true value of it is understood. Lack brings out the value of the blessing. Fallen human nature is such that it absolutely ignores God in good seasons, but bad seasons automatically make a man go on his knees and pursue God for His intervention and deliverance. God can never be the source of evil. When we go through trials, it opens our eyes to the goodness of God, and we get to know Him more because we are pursuing Him. But this is not the way it's meant to be. It is even better to seek God in the good times. Our hearts will be able to understand Him better (without the distraction of bad happenings) if we seek Him when all is well.

The study of the sun is very challenging. Scientists are persisting in exploring more and more about it. One feature that has helped them study the sun better is an eclipse. When the moon comes in the way, it has helped the scientists appreciate the features of the sun's atmosphere better. For some people, objects blocking God's light and casting shadows have probably driven them to seek God and know His love for them better. This is the way I came to know God, too. But I am glad that God worked all that bad stuff out for my good, and here I am today!

Having spoken about valleys looming with shadows of death, I just want to put in a note here about 'welcoming shadows'. As mentioned earlier, the shadow of a tree is most sought-after on hot days. The Israelites were led through the wilderness under the shadow of a huge cloud. Think of it! For 40 years, they never had to suffer the heat of the scorching sun as they walked in the wilderness. Psalm 91 says that we who dwell in the secret place of the Most High God will dwell under the shadow of the Almighty. We, as a family, felt this so strongly during the COVID pandemic. It needs to be experienced firsthand in order to know its value. This is why David says, 'Oh! Taste and see that the Lord is good! Blessed is the man who trusts in Him' (Psalm 34:8). We need to discern the shadows in our lives.

David makes a clear distinction in this Psalm between the 'Lord leading us' and 'we walking in our strength'. Notice the difference between '**the Lord** leading us in green pastures and still waters' and '**I walk** through the valley of the shadow of death'. It is obvious that we fall into trouble when we try to take God's place in steering our lives. Most of us don't even think twice before we blame God for our problems. At times, we underestimate and degrade Him as being worse than the meanest human. Which one of us would harm any of our children if total control of their lives were in our hands? Would we allow them to suffer on any account? None of us, of course! But there are times that they behave stupidly and make wrong decisions that hurt them and us. This happens when they reach a certain age, and most of their activities become private and beyond our reach. Their actions are the source of sorrow. Then would it be right to blame the parent? Absolutely not! If we train them to walk in the fear of the Lord, we do well and prevent them from making bad decisions to some extent. But sometimes they go astray, and it is ugly. Then they hurt God, themselves, and us.

When we go through troubled waters, it is wisdom to go to the Lord first and ask Him to show us where we went wrong and what we need to do to rectify that. He is faithful to show us where we faltered and went astray into troubled valleys instead of valleys with green pastures and still waters. He will also point the way out of it and lead us out from there into the good part. All it needs is our submission and obedience to His word and promises.

The only persecution that the Lord has allowed for His children is **'the persecution for His Name's sake'.** Not sickness, poverty, etc. Satan has got the church to believe that sickness and poverty are from God and has succeeded in making many believe that doctrine and embrace it. We need to grow out of such a mindset by renewing our minds to the word of God despite all odds. Just see the Lord Jesus in the gospels and study the work of the disciples after they were empowered by the Holy Spirit.

Our Saviour healed every sickness and disease. There was not a single person who came to Him and went unhealed. That is proof enough of His stance on healing. Do not embrace ungodly ideologies while listening to the traditions and doctrines of men. Read the word for yourself and study it under the guidance of the Holy Spirit. God has promised in Hebrews 8:10 and 11 that He will put His laws in our minds, write them on our hearts, and all of us will know Him! This is the most beautiful truth of the New Covenant. The One and only Mediator between our Father God and us is our Lord Jesus. He is more than sufficient to reveal the Father to us through the Holy Spirit, and He will guide us into all truth. When we accept and embrace things that are not from God, due to our ignorance of His word, we give way to satan to wreck our lives. Think about this: if we are sick, poor, or decrepit, how efficiently can we serve the Lord as compared to being healthy and having enough and more to spare so that we can be a blessing to others? This is just common sense!

"The Lord gives and the Lord takes away" is the favourite verse for many people who want to portray themselves as self-righteous Job. They portray God as this mean person who delights Himself in giving and taking away. I challenge those people to study the entire book of Job before even agreeing with Job on this point. The absurd statements of some people are recorded in the Bible, and we need to discern their theory of God before we voice it out like a parrot. For example, in Genesis 30:18, Leah names her fifth child Issachar and says, "God has given me my wages because I have given my maid to my husband." That would sound funny to most of us, right? Just because Leah said something like that, it doesn't make it true of God. God never endorsed surrogacy through maids at any time. Giving her maid to her husband was definitely 'Sarah's style of getting bright ideas' and all of us know that it is wrong. Leah probably didn't know any better and made that statement. The problem happens when we foolishly proclaim the same thing just because Leah said so. This is the same problem with Job's statement, and for some reason, people take pleasure in quoting him just to pacify their understanding during a time of loss. But it is certainly a bad witness of a good God!

4(c) FOR YOU ARE WITH ME;

From the very beginning, God has been persistently and sincerely showing mankind that He is the One who is always with us and for us. While satan tries his level best to corrupt this truth and assure men that God is withholding something from us always, our Lord goes the extra mile to prove otherwise. "I will never leave you nor forsake you" is the word that He spoke and demonstrated under both the New and Old Covenants, again and again. The world saw the impossible being made possible because of the manifestation of His word. The saints who believed this truth stood out as beacons of God's light in a dark world.

In Deuteronomy 31, Moses voices this promise twice. In verse 6, he assures this promise from God to the Israelites, and in verse 8, he assures his successor Joshua personally of this promise. Knowing the anxiety that both the Israelites and Joshua would face (since Moses' time was up) and that they would be entering the Promised Land under the new leadership, Moses urges them to look up to God, their everlasting source and strength.

This virtue is the foundation of the character that is most important for every child of God: **to be fearless.** Fear is faith in evil happenings. It is having confidence in the negative. Fear has ruled in the hearts of mankind for ages, pushing man towards sin. The Bible also speaks of **"the fear of the Lord,"** which is a reverential fear of God that causes man to walk away from evil and sin. These 2 fears are not alike. One pushes us towards sin while the other causes us to do the right thing, walk away from it, and endows us with courage and confidence. It is necessary for us to have the fear of the Lord, which helps us to live for God and fulfil the excellent destiny He has planned out for our lives. In doing so, we find ourselves having a healthy mind, soul, and body. It edifies us and causes us to be a blessing to others too. The other fear is sickening, debilitating, and paralysing. There is confusion, strife, bitterness, and oppression when we give into this negativity. This difference helps us to discern which fear we need to resist (fear of evil) and which one we should embrace (fear of the Lord). When we are assured of God's perfect love for us, an assurance that when "He has given up His beloved Son for our sake, how will He not with Him freely give us all things?" (Romans 8:32), then fear of evil will certainly be cast away from us.

Praise and worship are effective weapons against this fear. A jar of coloured water can be effectively cleaned out in 2 ways. One way is to just pour it out and fill in clean water after a good rinse, **or** keep pouring clean water into the jar until the existing coloured water is diluted and displaced. Fear of evil in a man's heart cannot be emptied out just like that unless it is replaced with the love of God. One of the most effective ways to get rid of this fear is to study the word of God, praise, and worship Him until His oil of joy and peace empties out all the worthless virtues in our hearts. There is none who beats or equals God in ridding us of all fear. When we make it habitual to praise God day and night, even without being conscious of it, fear is totally cast out.

In the New Testament, the author of Hebrews reiterates this promise again in Hebrews 13:5. In this context, he assures us of another truth: God's everlasting providence. He says that since God is with us, we don't have to covet anything. God supplies us with what we need (to satisfy us) and even more in order to be a blessing to others. The "more than enough provision" is for us to serve mankind on His behalf. It is not for us to hoard up and build our lives on. No matter how the ways of mankind may impact our lives, God's providence always, always, always comes through for His children, unless we do something stupid in between. Proverbs 10:3 says "The Lord will never allow the righteous soul to famish". Inflation, economic depression, famine, pestilence, etc. have never been a challenge for God at any time. He has always gone ahead for His children and made His supply ready for them. If we pay attention to His leading, we can overcome any difficulty we may be facing.

The hallmark of every victorious saint in the Bible is the firm assurance in their hearts and verbal acknowledgment of the unfailing presence of God with them. This perception endowed them with abounding grace to accomplish their calling. It gave them supernatural strength and courage to face every challenge and overcome it. We need to follow their example, as they are our counsellors (Proverbs 24:6). These saints practiced the presence of God in their day-to-day lives. If we don't do so consistently, it is not possible to master it when the storm hits. Proverbs 24:10 says that 'if we faint in the day of adversity, our strength is very small'. This is like a self-assessment test. When the warning signs are glowing and the slightest disturbance causes an explosion of fear in our hearts, it is time for us to get serious with the word, seek God, and practice trusting Him consistently.

The Lord sent His Holy Spirit to be with us always after He ascended into heaven. This is how He never leaves us or forsakes us. In the Old Testament, His children saw Him lead them as a visible pillar of cloud by day and as a pillar of fire by night. They had soothing light and warmth 24x7. How much more soothing, calming, and assuring should His presence be to us now?

4(d) YOUR ROD AND YOUR STAFF, THEY COMFORT ME.

The rod and staff were the most important paraphernalia of a shepherd. David includes almost every aspect of the shepherd's character and possessions in this Psalm. Unless we go the extra mile and research these things, we will lose out on precious revelation that the word gives and fail to claim all that our God has faithfully provided for us.

Apart from carrying limited supplies of food and water, the nomadic shepherds carried objects like the rod and staff to guide, defend, and protect their flock and themselves. Along with these essentials, they would also carry a sling, and a small knife/dagger, and those who were passionate about music would also have a small musical instrument like a harp or a flute made from reed. David probably carried a small harp with him every time he was on the job and delighted himself in singing to God.

The purpose of using the rod and staff was different. The rod was short and thick, while the staff was slender, long, and curved at one end. While the rod served to defend the flock from enemies and as a weapon of offence and defence, the staff was used to correct and rescue the straying sheep or the one which had fallen into a pit. The staff also served as a resting aid for the shepherds while walking and standing.

The rod was mostly used as a weapon of defence. The shepherd would use the rod against predators and thieves, who threatened the flock or himself. He would not hesitate to grievously injure or even kill (if necessary) anyone who intended to harm him or his flock. Very rarely would he use it to warn a sheep that was straying from the flock by throwing the rod near it but never harm it. This would alert the sheep, and it would turn around to join the flock. But its main use was to fight, wound, and put the enemy to flight or death.

The staff, on the other hand, defined the shepherd to his sheep. It was a long slender branch, curved at one end. Sometimes there would be a second curve at the end of the first, like a hook, which would serve as a peg to hang a lantern (after dark) when the staff was fastened to the ground. A shepherd could use it to shift his body weight from his legs onto it when his legs felt tired. It was an excellent aid to balance oneself on rocky terrain too. Apart from all these advantages, the staff was mainly used to pull back or redirect a straying sheep. It was also used to lift a sheep from the pit by securing the curved end around its neck. It was mainly meant to correct his flock but never with the intent to harm. It was the least painful and most effective method.

When we see the purpose behind these 2 objects used by a shepherd, we can quite simply understand their purpose in God's hand for our lives: the rod to rout the enemy and the staff to correct us. The Lord already used His rod against satan when He went to the cross and condemned him to an eternity in hell along with his entire army of fallen angels. Unfortunately, men who reject salvation will join them. On the other hand, correction is an essential element of every godly relationship. It is evidence of true love that cares for our good. This is the purpose of His staff in our lives. For whom the Lord loves, He corrects, just as the father disciplines the son in whom he delights (Proverbs 3:12). This can probably be understood by most parents because they experience the same. But when it comes to the Lord disciplining us, some of us just can't wrap our brains around it. That is the sad reality. We need to be more aware of the ways of God. That being said, God never corrects us with sickness, disease, accidents, death, etc. Those are not His works, just like how we won't purposely make our children fall sick and endanger their lives in any way. We may end up with bad repercussions due to our stupidity. But the Lord stands ready to rescue us when we repent and allow Him to intervene.

Moses fled from Egypt after murdering an Egyptian at the age of 40. He was trying to fulfil God's calling on his life in his own strength and severely failed. For the next 40 years, he spent his life in the wilderness shepherding his father-in-law's flock. This was preparation to shepherd a stiff-necked multitude for the subsequent 40 years through the wilderness to the Promised Land. All through these 40 years of preparation, Moses had a staff in his hand. This staff rose to fame when the Lord called him to deliver the Israelites from Egypt. This staff was called the "Rod of God" in the hands of Moses. From being used to shepherd his flock to clobbering the Egyptians with terrifying plagues, this staff/Rod of God was feared by all. Not only did it herald the onset of plagues every time it was lifted up in the hands of Moses and Aaron, but it was also used to perform many great miracles like parting the Red Sea for the children of God to pass through, bringing forth water from 'The Rock' on Mount Horeb for the Israelites, and defeating Amalek in Israel's first battle at Rephidim.

David knew how gloriously effective God's rod was against His enemies. I suggest that we should study the Book of Exodus to understand the power of the 'Rod of God'. It will make our faith abound when we know that God does avenge His children, when we submit to Him and that there is none who can play the fool with us and get away with it.

The rod was the shepherd's "identity". By obeying the Lord's word to him, Moses submitted his rod, his identity, to Him. When his identity was submitted to God, the impossible and supernatural happened. Have you ever considered what your identity is? How do you identify yourself? What would be your immediate reply if I were to ask you who you are? Most often, I have introduced myself as a medical doctor. It meant that I expected recognition and respect from people for being an intellectual person who had won the rat race of this world and qualified as a member of the high-class society. Even though I may not have portrayed this obnoxious attitude outside, it was the truth in my heart. I can truly confess this because every time somebody disrespected me on this aspect, my ego was hurt, and my flesh went into a fit. The Lord showed me that this is where I had to make a change speedily. I had a huge identity problem. This became one of the first steps in renewing my mind. I had to first shift my identity from my profession to being 'the child of God,' deeply loved, graciously and completely forgiven, blessed beyond measure, and highly favoured! Do you know that this is the highest and most coveted identity a human being can possess today? There is nothing in the universe that can be set above this identity. This was signed off as our inheritance by our Saviour Lord Jesus Christ. All other identities are far, far, far inferior to this. This is what happened when Moses turned over his rod to God.

When we study Exodus, we can picture how the Rod of God shook Egypt when Moses and Aaron lifted it up. It struck fear in the heart of Pharaoh, all his nobles, and people. The moment Moses held it up, the destruction of Egypt was commanded and put into effect. We have just come through one plague, and it has taken almost a good three years for things to normalise. Imagine plagues happening one after another, in a short span of time, and most of them overlapping each other! I wouldn't dare to imagine living at a time like that! Most surely Moses' rod, which became the Rod of God, was the most feared object in all of Egypt.

The Lord used the rod to turn all the waters of Egypt (streams, rivers, ponds, pools of water, and the stored water) to blood, and this remained as such even till the Israelites were freed. Pharaoh was very selective in asking Moses to request God to withdraw the plagues. By the time the Angel of Death entered (plague number 10), Egypt's waters were still bleeding, the stench of dead frogs filled the air, man and beast were infested with lice, the livestock was dying due to pestilence, the Egyptians were covered with boils and sores, their crops were totally destroyed, and there was thick darkness all over Egypt except for the land of Goshen, which was set apart by God and was unaffected by the plagues. God visibly and tangibly showed that He stood for Israel. Egypt was totally destroyed, and this was verbally declared by Pharaoh's own servants (Exodus 10:7). There were some among them who feared Moses enough to heed his warning and protect their belongings from the fiery hail. The final blow destroyed the firstborn of both man and beast among the Egyptians and raised an outcry so loud that it could never be compared to anything before or after it.

While the Egyptians took some time to come to terms with their profound and unbearable loss, the Israelites had reached the Red Sea and had camped by it. Once they woke up from their distress, the Egyptians were more enraged and beyond any sign of repentance. Rather, they were overcome by bitterness, deciding to pursue and bring back Israel to serve them again. In their attempt to do so, they lost their lives! Here again, we see the Rod of God in action in Moses' hand. Following the outcry of unbelief from the Israelites, Moses cried out to God for deliverance. I bet that opening up the Red Sea was not a thought on anyone's mind, including Moses. The Lord commanded him to stretch out the rod over the sea and divide it. The moment he obeyed, a strong east wind kept the waters divided all night long, and the Israelites crossed over on dry ground. The raging, blinded Egyptians tried their best to harm the Israelites only to have the waters of the sea completely destroy Pharaoh, the Egyptian army, their chariots, and horses with another stretch of the Rod of God over the parted waters. Not so much as one of them remained (Exodus 14:28). This Rod of God was beyond awesome! The Israelites saw the Egyptians' bodies wash up on the shore the next morning.

When the Israelites began their journey through the wilderness, they constantly complained of the slightest discomfort. All they had to do was request God to provide for them. Somehow, this never struck their minds. They preferred to grumble and complain. When they grumbled at Marah (because of bitter waters), the Lord simply made it sweet just by instructing Moses to put the wood from the tree (which He showed him) into it. It was a piece of cake for God! The people just didn't get it. The Lord instructed Moses to go ahead of the people with the elders of Israel and strike the Rock at Horeb (on which He stood) with the Rod of God. When he obeyed, water gushed out from the split Rock and nourished the Israelites and their livestock.

When Israel reached Rephidim, Amalek came up against them for war. Being the descendants of Esau, they were constant troublemakers for the Israelites. Moses instructed Joshua to fight them while he stood on the mountain with the Rod of God in his hand. During the battle, the Israelites prevailed when Moses had his hands raised. But when he lowered them (due to tiredness), the Amalekites prevailed. Aaron and Hur, who were with Moses on the mountain, rolled a stone under Moses, seated him on it, and supported his hands to keep them raised. As a result, Israel won their first battle against Amalek.

In conclusion, I would like to reiterate that when our identity is in Almighty God, The Most High, Possessor of the heavens and the earth, the enemy will definitely be routed!

5(a) YOU PREPARE A TABLE BEFORE ME IN THE PRESENCE OF MY ENEMIES;

"The Table" was and is still an integral part of life for every child of God under the Old and New covenants. A feast has always excited the heart of mankind. In ages past, promises, covenants, and vows made to each other and to God were always sealed with the sacrifice of an animal (shedding of blood). This was a serious event, and every person involved in it (Jew or non-Jew) knew the consequences of breaking an oath sealed by the shedding of blood. The sacrificed animal was later cooked, and people would eat it together at "The Table" like a feast and go back home satisfied, knowing that each person would keep their part of the deal in "fear and reverence" to the spoken word. The point of all this was to "Keep the word" spoken by one person to another, an agreement, a covenant, or a vow made to another man or to God. The word, which was mostly verbal in those days, was respected and honoured. Objects like stones, staffs, signet cords, or rings were often used as witnesses while making these covenants. Written contracts came much later because man's word alone could not be trusted anymore.

God created this entire universe by His word. From the unseen came the seen. From the invisible came the tangible. This is His decree and the manner in which everything works in the Kingdom of God. He still places a very high value on spoken words because man was created in His image. God's intent is to keep it that way. In other words, every word that man spoke was supposed to be kept. Unfortunately, the fall corrupted this, and since then, most of us do not realise the magnitude of power in our words. Today, we really have to take a big risk in trusting someone only based on their word. We are careless with our words, and most of the time, we don't mean what we speak. Words have been used to propagate personal agendas, deception, lies, flattery, false witness, etc.

"The Table of God" however revolves around the spoken Word and has everything to do with keeping it at whatever may be the cost because the Word of God cannot be corrupted at any cost or by anyone. God means and does what He says. God is not obligated to prove anything to anyone; yet He humbled Himself to look upon us and give us such precious promises. He humbled Himself to make covenants with mankind for our benefit! I just can't wrap my brain around God's meekness. He humbled Himself because He knew our weakness. With His love, He draws us near. So we should be very sensitive to Him and keep our eyes and ears open to His word. When He 'Assuredly' says something to us, it is a doubly established promise!

Let's take a quick look at biblical covenant-making. The first covenant was made by God when He reprimanded satan, Adam, and Eve in the Garden of Eden when they disobeyed His word. Having tried and failed to cover their nakedness with fig leaves, God intervened and clothed them with skin. God performed the first sacrifice in the Garden of Eden (most probably) before their eyes, teaching and demonstrating to them first about redemption through the blood. Only after that did He send them out of the Garden. I believe that God taught Adam and Eve to repeat these sacrifices regularly and pass it on to the next generation because we see their son Abel doing the same (performing a blood sacrifice which was accepted by God). While this offering of blood through animal sacrifices continued, God gave significant 'signs of the covenant' like the rainbow to Noah, circumcision to Abraham, inspiring dreams to Jacob and Joseph.

These covenants were taken seriously by the people who received them, and I personally get excited when I see the goodness of God being displayed in the sky for all to see. While there is no record of Joseph performing sacrifices to remind himself of God's work in his life, I believe the dreams God gave him were more real to him and kept him going. When God led the armies of Israel out of Egypt, He sealed all His covenants with them with the blood of the sacrifice that He commanded them to perform.

On the other hand, men also made covenants with each other. Once a covenant was made, it was accompanied by signs and ceremonies. The rainbow and circumcision were both signs of the covenant made by God with men. However, the signs and ceremonies observed by people to make a covenant effective are too elaborate to be listed here. But today, these signs and ceremonies are least significant because they have been largely replaced by paperwork and legal agreements. That is how far it has all deteriorated. I have listed a few contextually important ones here.

- ✡ In Genesis 21:22-32, we see Abraham making a covenant with Abimelech, king of Gerar, and his commander Phicol, at the latter's request. Here, Abraham brought up the issue of certain wells he had dug, which Abimelech's servants had stopped. Abimelech swore ignorance in the matter. To clarify and wrap up this issue, Abraham gave Abimelech sheep and oxen, and the 2 made a covenant, with Abraham pledging not to harm or deal falsely with Abimelech and his descendants. Abraham specially set aside 7 ewe lambs and gave them to Abimelech as a sign that the disputed well indeed belonged to him (Abraham). The place where they made the oath was named Beersheba, signifying the well of the oath.
- ✡ In Genesis 26, a famine in Canaan made Isaac move to Gerar. Abimelech was a family friend by now. However, Isaac repeated the same mistake that his father had made and called his wife, Rebekah, his sister. They probably did it out of the fear of the immoral people who inhabited that place, who helped themselves to any beautiful woman they wanted by getting rid of their husbands. However, Abimelech had learned his lesson and stayed away from her. At one point in time, he saw them both being

intimate, questioned their motives for the lie, and decreed a death penalty on anyone who would dare touch them. I would call that divine protection in a heathen land! Isaac began to prosper and continued prospering until he became very prosperous and stifled Abimelech and his people to the point of envy, and he was asked to leave. Isaac moved to the valley of Gerar and reopened the wells his father had dug (which the Philistines had closed with earth). He even named all those wells! Which of us would do something like that? These patriarchs took every work seriously and connected it to God always. But his efforts in opening up these wells were faced twice with opposition from the herdsmen of Gerar. Isaac did not waste time quarrelling with them. He went on to dig a third well, and no one opposed that. He called the well 'Rehoboth' and later shifted to Beersheba. The favour of God on Isaac was so evident and threatening to the Philistines that Abimelech, Phicol, and his friend Ahuzzath came to Isaac to make an oath that Isaac wouldn't harm any of their men. It just took one man with the favour of God to threaten an entire nation! As an execution of this covenant, Isaac prepared them a nice feast! The next morning, they reaffirmed that oath and went on their way.

✡ In Genesis 31:43–48, Laban makes a covenant with Jacob for mutual safety after the latter leaves Haran to return to his home country (the Promised Land). Jacob selected a stone and set it up as a pillar. Then his brethren heaped up stones together, and they all ate on that heap. This pillar and heap of stones stood as a witness between Jacob and Laban; they agreed that none would cross the pillar and heap of stones to harm each other. Jacob swore by the fear of his father Isaac, offered a sacrifice on the mountain, and called his brethren to eat bread. Then the covenant was established, and each left to his place. Who would think that stones would stand as witnesses? Who would think that stones could talk or witness against people? All these things need to be pondered! When the Lord Jesus made His final entry into Jerusalem, riding on a colt as prophesied in Zechariah 9:9, the Pharisees told Him to rebuke the disciples who were shouting praises to Him. In response, He said in Luke 19:40, "I tell you, if these should keep silent, the stones would immediately cry out." What did He mean by this? Did our Lord utter something senseless? How can stones shout? Which stones was He referring to? Let's rewind a bit. Zechariah was one of 2 prophets (the other being Haggai) who prophesied and encouraged Zerubbabel to complete building the temple in Jerusalem after returning from the 70 years of Babylonian captivity. Initially, they had laid the foundations of the temple, but the work seized there because of great opposition from the people who had settled there. These prophetic words of encouragement propelled the temple work to completion, even as the prophets Zechariah and Haggai continued to prophesy and stood alongside Zerubbabel. We all know that by then, the lifespan of people had shortened to below a century. But there were objects there that would outlast the people who lived in those days. That's right! The stones! Zechariah prophesied in and around Jerusalem. The temple stones and the stones in the debris of the walls of Jerusalem had heard him prophesy about the entry of the Saviour King, who would come riding on a colt into Jerusalem one day, and on that day there would be a great shout of rejoicing. Every word of God surely comes to pass. This prophecy also came to pass, and the Pharisees just did not get it, in spite of their pride in 'knowing all the scriptures'. Sometimes they deliberately withstood understanding the scriptures because they were prejudiced against the Lord Jesus. In reference to this prophecy, which would definitely be fulfilled no matter what man would say or do, the Lord Jesus imperatively says that even if He forced the people to stop praising Him, the stones that heard Zechariah's prophecy would do all their work instead! That is awesome because it immediately shut the Pharisees mouth! I would love to meditate more on this.

For the Jew, "The Table" held a special, personal, and sacred significance. In Leviticus chapters 1 to 7, God instructed the children of Israel regarding 5 different sacrifices, each carrying a strong reminder of the Saviour's sacrifice, which they had to observe. These are The Burnt Offering, The Grain Offering, The Peace Offering, The Sin Offering, and The Trespass Offering. The person presenting the offering and the priest performing the sacrifice received ordained portions to partake of, from all the sacrifices (except for The Burnt Offering), after the first portion was offered to God. In the case of the Burnt Offering, the entire animal was burnt on the altar, except for the skin, which was given as a portion to the priest who conducted the sacrifice. The priests could tan the hides and use them to make tents, bags, belts, and more, or even sell them to tanners. In either case, it provided them with a source of income.

Among the other sacrifices, both the offerer and the priest received significant portions to share as a family. These gatherings often turned into literal feasts because these sacrifices made a person blameless before God. People eagerly anticipated these feasts and made it a tradition to partake in these sacrifices every year. Jewish families would journey to the place where the Tabernacle was located, almost like a pilgrimage. They would offer sacrifices to God, feast on their portions along with their entire families, and return home blessed. These feasts were unlike any other because they brought the satisfaction of knowing that their sins were covered by the blood of the Sacrifice, and that they were endowed with God's blessing.

Shortly after the Lord rejected Saul's kingship, He commanded Samuel to go to Bethlehem and to anoint Saul's successor, a man after God's heart—one of Jesse's sons. Samuel was guided by God to pick David, who did not arrive with his father for the sacrificial feast initially with the other sons. Though many say that Jesse was careless regarding David, I would rather say that David was quite a faithful son in attending to his father's little flock and taking his job seriously. Added to that, I believe he was little in his own eyes. Compared to David (who was just a shepherd), his brothers (the older 3) were employed in the Israeli army. They accompanied their father to the mouth-watering feast. However, none got to dine until David arrived there, and Samuel rose up and anointed him in the midst of his brothers. Every one of them knew that this anointing was very significant and even sparked envy among David's brothers. Following the anointing, the Spirit of the Lord came upon David from that day forward. This moment and the feast that followed were indeed very special to this young shepherd boy, who least expected such an honour. David would have understood the depth of God's love for him as the Spirit opened his eyes to see it. This table was definitely special for him because, after this, his character was established as that of a valiant man, a skilled musician, a man of war, prudent in speech, and a handsome person! David could clearly see the difference between what he was and what he became after the anointing. This formed the foundation of the courage with which he fought the lions, bears, Goliath, Philistines, Amalekites, etc. until finally he was crowned the king of Judah at the age of 30. The effect of this table continued till the very end of his earthly life.

Having understood the importance of "The Table", let us now study the characteristics of the enemies. The enemies of the children of God come in all shapes and sizes. Their characteristics included gigantism, state-of-the art weapons, chariots of iron, magnificent horses, spears, javelins, and a very mean spirit. They all had the same agenda: to usurp more land and power. They were cunning, brutal, and barbaric. During the deliverance from one such enemy (Egypt), the Lord instituted the Passover for His children. This was first observed the night before they were liberated from Egypt. By then, Egypt was reeling from the devastation caused by the arrogance of their hard-hearted pharaoh. The chosen Passover lamb (which signified the Messiah) was sacrificed at twilight on the 14th day of the first month, its blood applied to the doorposts and lintels with hyssop (to protect their firstborn specifically), and the lamb roasted wholly in fire was eaten with bitter herbs and unleavened bread (every part of this being significant). Anything remaining until morning was supposed to be burnt. They had to eat it with a belt on their waist, sandals on their feet, and a staff in their hand because their deliverance was that close! In haste, they would be sent out of the land of their bondage once they partook of the Passover meal. This became a perpetual covenant between God and them until the Saviour arrived in person and fulfilled it. This covenant initiated supernatural victories against their enemies from the time of their liberation from Egypt and even after entering and possessing the Promised Land. They were instructed to observe this Passover at the beginning of each year (the 14th day of the first month). The year started off with the remembrance of the Saviour's sacrifice. This observance was precious to God because it was a powerful declaration of deliverance for His children and because it was the ultimate solution to the fall that separated man from Him. This was the most important of all 'The Tables'.

At the final Passover that the Lord Jesus observed with His disciples, He materialised this symbolism into reality. He confessed that He longed to have this Passover with His disciples in the "Upper Room". After supper, He took the unleavened bread, thanked God for it, broke it, passed it to His disciples, and commanded them to partake of it, remembering Him. In a similar manner, He blessed the cup of wine (unfermented grape juice) and commanded them to partake of it in remembrance of Him. What does this "in remembrance of Him" mean? Let us aim to understand this first.

All through the ages, God had been prophesying through men and demonstrating the substitute death of the Saviour, His beloved Son, our Lord Jesus Christ, through sacrifices. But sadly, even until the Saviour died on the cross in person, not one man fully understood this truth. While Abraham, David, and a few others got very close to understanding this and foresaw it, they were long gone before the Saviour arrived. People gradually turned the Passover into a ritual, and the true meaning was fading away. If they had their facts and beliefs in line with each other, they would have all believed the Lord when He walked on the earth. Even at the time of the last supper, none of His disciples fully comprehended the meaning of what the Lord Jesus was doing. They were with Him for all 3 and a half years of His earthly ministry and were repeatedly told about the redemption He would accomplish, yet they did not comprehend this important truth. But the Holy Spirit revealed the true meaning of this to them once He descended on them on the Day of Pentecost. At this last supper, the Lord Jesus once again reiterated the significance of His sacrifice to them and shifted their focus from the symbolic Passover sacrifice to Himself—the real deal! Once this sacrifice was over, there was no need for any other sacrifices. His sacrifice was the perfect final fulfilment of all the sacrifices that God had commanded His children to observe until then.

The total penalty for the sin of mankind was taken by Him willingly, and 'mankind' was completely pardoned. This penalty was directed against His flesh (body and soul), as stated in Romans 8:3, while His Spirit remained pure and untouched by the sin of mankind. Therefore, every evil that is directed against our body (sickness, disease, etc.) and soul (depression, anxiety, mental issues, etc.) was already dealt with 2000 years ago by our Lord. These infirmities in our soul and body were a direct consequence of sin—a door that Adam and Eve opened to satan. This death affected most of creation as well. But God did not abandon us. The Saviour's ultimate sacrifice was more than a perfect answer to all this. God Almighty reconciled the whole world to Himself through His beloved Son (2 Corinthians 5:19). This reconciliation was executed at the cross of Calvary. This was powerfully symbolised and commanded to be observed by our Lord further on, by the present and future generations through the Holy Communion.

For the New Covenant believer, the Holy Communion is the "Ultimate Table". It is the exact same remembrance of the Last Supper instituted by our Lord Jesus Christ. It is a powerful remembrance of the finished work of our Saviour. Its meaning is profound! If we are ignorant of its meaning, we lose out on the most important need for redemption or salvation. By shifting the focus from the roasted Passover lamb to the unleavened bread and wine (literally nullifying the need to observe any future animal sacrifices), the Messiah would fulfil the prophecy spoken from the ages in just a few moments. Hebrews 10:10–12 explicitly states that His sacrifice was **only once** for all time and all people. Hence He put an end to the Passover sacrifice (an observance of that which had to be fulfilled) and instituted the Holy Communion (an observance of that which is already accomplished). The unleavened bread and wine signify His body and blood, respectively. His body was mutilated and massacred for our sake. He took it all! All this so that we can be made whole! Therefore, Isaiah prophesied "By His stripes we **are** healed" (Isaiah 53:5), and the Apostle Peter confirmed "By His stripes we **were** healed". Every evil attacking mankind this day in his body and mind was dealt with. **THIS IS THE TRUTH!** The more we renew our minds to this truth and stay consistent with our right beliefs, the faster we receive our deliverance. God is not withholding anything good from us. **Romans 8:32 is a golden verse, and it states, "He who did not spare His own Son but delivered Him up for us all, how shall He not with Him also freely give us all things?"** May this verse resound in our hearts continually so that we are fully assured of His good intentions for us. May it be the lightening that strikes satan dead in his tracks of deception in our lives. The full acceptance and acknowledgement of this truth makes us overcomers instead of victims. Ignorance of this truth makes us misunderstand God and certify false allegations against Him. Choose wisely!

Most of us know that blood is vital. No blood, no life. In the medical field, blood speaks volumes. We cannot belittle the magnificence of this tissue. Any abnormality in the body can almost always be detected by a blood test first. This is the reason a routine blood analysis is the standard investigation for diagnosing a disease. Based on this, a diagnosis is made, and treatment is initiated, or further specific investigations are conducted. But the scriptures written ages ago confirmed that blood spoke (Genesis 1:10); in fact, Abel's blood cried out to the Lord from the ground! What did it cry out? Hebrews 12:24 answers that; it cried out for justice. The blood of Lord Jesus speaks better things than that of Abel! His blood speaks justification on our behalf to the Father. The blood of our Lord was absolutely pure (sinless). His flesh was without blemish. He was the perfect sacrifice. While His flesh took the brunt of all our punishment, His blood was the cleansing flow. Every drop of it was shed to cleanse all creation from the death that had entered. The punishment part was taken care of by His flesh, while the cleansing part was done by His blood. Today, we are made perfect and whole because of the combination of these 2 elements. Perfect redemption was achieved by the mutilation of His flesh and shedding of His blood.

Do you now see the difference between the Old Covenant sacrifices and the Lord's sacrifice? Under the old covenant sacrifice, the animal was killed (no doubt) in the most painless manner. The entire volume of blood was drained (life is in the blood). Once it was absolutely dead, its body was divided into parts, and each served its purpose. Part of it was burnt on the altar, and the rest was cooked and eaten by the priests and the offerer of the sacrifice (except for the burnt offering). The blood was shed to **cover** man's sin. It never took it (sin) away. This is the reason that these sacrifices had an expiry date and had to be repeated every year. The blood of the sacrifice was used to cleanse the elements of the tabernacle, to anoint the High Priest, sprinkled on the lepers for cleansing when they were healed, etc. But the sacrifice of our Saviour abolished sin totally as well as cleansed our hearts and conscience from sin and its guilt. Lord Jesus' sacrifice was final and never to be or will be repeated. It's a one-time deal. **Today, sin is not the issue; our ignorance of the truth is!** If we acknowledge that we are indeed dead to sin and alive to God in Christ Jesus our Lord, we will not allow sin to reign in our mortal bodies so that we should obey it in its lusts (Romans 6:11, 12). **It is all a matter of renewing our minds to the truth of the perfect sacrifice of our Lord Jesus Christ and His finished work.**

Blood is not the only thing that speaks. In the word, we see trees, waves of the sea, the earth, celestial bodies, stones, rocks, etc., called to witness covenants since the days of old. When God promised Abraham that his descendants would be as numerous as the stars in the sky and as the sand on the seashore, the stars and the sand stood as witnesses! Joseph had a God-inspired dream of the sheaves of grain bowing down to his sheaf, and when this promise was fulfilled, it occurred right in the midst of a famine in which grain played a significant role. You can wholeheartedly believe God's word. No logic or intellect can ever stand against it.

However, the deceiver perverted the ordinances of God, and we can see how people have come under his influence throughout the ages. Instead of holding a holy reverence for the blood, humans started drinking blood as a cleansing ritual in many cultures and civilisations, and eating blood as a routine part of their cuisine (a practice that continues even in my country and state today). They offered unclean animals like pigs as sacrifices and even resorted to human sacrifices to their idols. Satan took something that was so pure and holy and corrupted it among deceived men. The patriarchs of the Bible knew the importance of the blood right from the beginning and reverenced it as sacred and holy.

The Table, for an old covenant saint, was meant to look forward to the work that would be accomplished by the Messiah. Whereas, for the New Covenant believer, the Table (the Holy Communion) is the declaration of His finished work. Lord Jesus magnified its importance when, on the same day that He was resurrected, He broke bread with His two disciples at Emmaus, following which **their eyes were opened**, and they recognised that it was the Lord who had walked and talked with them thus far. Does that enlighten you? **When we partake of the Lord's Table, our eyes are opened to discern Him, to know Him!** Because it is THE COVENANT God has made with us through His beloved Son. He is very serious about it!

The Holy Communion is "The Table" that the Lord has set before us in the presence of our enemies - poverty, lack, sickness, depression, oppression, pain, diseases, accidents, disasters, pestilences, famines, dangers, or anything that clearly falls under the definition of evil and death. The victory that overcomes all these is the death of our Saviour on the cross and His subsequent resurrection. Even death has been conquered by Him! Today, He is the King we serve. We are citizens of His kingdom, which is very much on this earth. It is not in heaven, far away. It is right here on this earth. He has given us the privilege of bearing His Name and the right to use the authority in His Name to silence our enemies. In truth, there is no place for fear, worry, despair, or hopelessness. When we partake of the Holy Communion, we are supposed to partake of it with this knowledge and understanding. None of our enemies can have a claim over our lives anymore. Satan hates The Lord's Table the most; it is an effective and persistent reminder to him of his eternal defeat, as much as it should be a reminder to us of our eternal victory through our Lord Jesus Christ. The reason our Lord Jesus fervently desired to partake of the last supper with His disciples was that our God Almighty, Creator of the universe, the King of kings, the Lord of lords, the Supreme Potentate, the Sovereign Lord, the Most High God, Possessor of the heavens and the earth, the Ancient of Days, has humbly looked upon desperate and hopeless mankind and made an outstanding covenant by exchanging His righteousness and inheritance for our filthy sins and their consequences.

This is our declaration every time we partake of our Lord's Table. It would take eternity for us to know the goodness of our God and fathom the depths of His love for us! The Father's love is ours through this covenant.

Paul was not present at the Last Supper with the Lord. Probably he was nurturing and building up hatred towards our Lord like all other Pharisees at that time. But upon his conversion, the Lord revealed to him the importance of His Holy Communion. In most of his epistles, he never omits to record the observance of it. Even today, when we partake of the Lord's Table, we read 1 Corinthians 11:23-26; some people continue the reading till verse 32 also. For many years, I partook of the table with a lack of this revelation. But I thank God today that it is no more that way. Today, it is a regular part of my life, and doing it "often," I declare His death till He returns and reap the benefits of doing so!

While reading this passage, the improper understanding of the words 'judge/examine oneself' and 'unworthy manner' causes a lot of confusion and hesitation. Further on, the mention of being weak and sick on account of partaking unworthily causes greater fear. All this happens because of a lack of revelation. Paul intends to say that the purpose of the Lord's Table is to declare the death of the Lord on our behalf and to cleanse us from all sin. If we judge ourselves as imperfect people and in desperate need of God always, let us come to the Table in order to obtain forgiveness and cleansing of our conscience. In this case, the Lord's sacrifice is appropriated to our need, and by grace, His strength is perfected in our weakness. If we judge ourselves righteous, then there is no need for the Saviour's sacrifice, isn't it? Then what is the need to come to the Table of the Lord? Knowing our weaknesses, let us come before Him and partake of His flesh and blood, obtaining mercy and finding grace to help in times of need! If we know that He has taken all our sicknesses and diseases, let us boldly partake of His flesh and blood and thereby declare that by His stripes we were and are healed! This declaration is made before the principalities and powers of darkness which are attacking us. It has a great bearing in the unseen realm, which then causes His deliverance to manifest in the physical realm. When we accept His perfect sacrifice and declare it often, we will see the manifestation of His healing in our bodies. We can stand before Him today because He has made us righteous and qualified us. Hence, because of His gift of righteousness, we can claim His forgiveness, healing, wholeness, help, strength, defence, and all good things that He has caused us to inherit. When we don't partake of His table with this revelation, we continue to be weak, sick, and lacking, not discerning the Lord's body (unworthy manner). I pray and hope that you will understand this and obtain this truth as a direct revelation from the Lord to your benefit!

In the days of old, even heathen people knew that the repercussions were severe for breaking a blood covenant. They took it very seriously since they feared losing their own lives if they broke it. How much more should we respect the covenant of our God when the Saviour's blood has been shed to seal this covenant of God to us?

If, as Christians, weakness, sickness, lack, or any negativity is still overruling us, the deficit is 100% on our side. We need to humbly accept that and not blame God or label it as 'His mysterious ways.' This can cause people who are influenced by us to go astray from the truth and miss out on God's best for them. Humbling ourselves in this manner may actually open our eyes to see where we are blocking God's power from flowing in our lives. In order to discern the Lord's body, we need to be meditating on the word of God until we are established in the truth. Then nothing can stop us from receiving God's deliverance. **This will cause us to 'KNOW HIM AND THE POWER OF HIS RESURRECTION AND THE FELLOWSHIP OF HIS SUFFERINGS BEING CONFORMED TO HIS DEATH.'** This will cause us to walk under open heavens here on this earth and to live in the fullness of our Lord Jesus Christ. We should not be ignorant of our inheritance, which was dispensed to us at a great expense.

The truth that David declared in this verse is as vital to us as the air we breathe! May our excitement in partaking in our Lord's Table continue to grow as we grow in this revelation. Do it boldly! Do it often! Put to flight the enemies who suck out your life! May your enemies tremble in fear and flee. It is between you and the Lord; let none stop you!

5(b) YOU ANOINT MY HEAD WITH OIL;

The word 'Anoint,' to most of us, almost always pertains to something holy or sacred. It is not a commonly used day-to-day word for people like us. Yet perhaps the clergy and other religious people may be using this word every day. "Anointing" basically carries the idea of applying/pouring a sacred concoction (oil/ointment) over somebody or something, which sets them much above the rest so that they/it cannot be labelled anymore as common.

In the word of God, this has been utilised in two ways: God anointing someone or man anointing something/someone. However, this was God's chosen word when He called His Beloved Son **"The Messiah," meaning "The Anointed One" or "Christ."** Following this, He graciously extended this honour to every human who believes in His Son for salvation. Hence we are called **"Christians - the anointed ones"!** It is a great unfortunate ignorance for Christians today to disown this precious title and label themselves with meaningless denominations and pride themselves in senseless divisions. Being called after our Master as Christians is such an honour and should never be forfeited or replaced by inferior titles at any cost. **Lord Jesus Christ is not divided.** The same should apply to the body of Christ, the Church, too (especially for those who senselessly follow denominations that divide). This should be our sole identity! Anything else is from the devil.

Many denominations that have been birthed thus far have severely crippled people's faith and belief systems. It has led men far away from the ways of God. Certain denominations (and churches who call themselves so) have even normalised abominations that are clearly prohibited in the word of God. Just look around, and you can very well see it. Being called solely as a "Christian" (to the exclusion of everything else) is priceless in God's eyes! This is the common ground for all those He called since we are all reconciled to Him through the Anointed One.

In the word of God, we see that the action of being anointed by God made a world of difference in a person's life. David noticed this clearly in his own life. After the prophet Samuel anointed him, he was set apart, consecrated, and sanctified for God's purposes. The same held true for the priests and other kings of Israel who were ordained by God through men. This anointing opened up the door to the supernatural for them. Now they could experience God live through them in all His power and glory.

Before the prophet Samuel anointed David, he was only the eighth son of Jesse who was faithfully and responsibly shepherding his father flock. He was small in his own eyes and most surely in the eyes of others also. But following the anointing by the prophet Samuel (after which the Spirit of the Lord came upon him), the drastic difference in his life and character was a spectacle visible to others. In 1 Samuel 16:18, a person bears witness of him before king Saul, testifying that David was a skillful musician, a mighty man of valour, a man of war, prudent in speech, a handsome person, and that God was with him! At this point in time, David had not fought any wars, nor was he even in the army. Yet he was called a man of war. This was because people saw David ferociously guarding his flock from lions and bears while the other shepherds in his place would have made good their escape, leaving their flock behind.

After the ascension of our Lord Jesus Christ, all His followers were called 'Christians'. This is indeed a gracious and honourable title bestowed by our Father God upon us. Just like our Lord Jesus, we are also 'the anointed ones'. But most of us do not understand the depths of it. We pride ourselves in false humility when we confess that we are ONLY humans as a ready excuse for anything and everything. If we were to renew our minds to the truth that we are 'anointed' just as our Saviour was, then akin to a small mustard seed, we would enlarge our potential exponentially for the Lord's kingdom here on this earth. Under the old covenant, the Spirit could not indwell a person like how He does in us today. The Spirit would come and then be lifted up. But for us today, His residence in us and with us is permanent by an everlasting covenant sealed with the precious blood of our Lord Jesus Christ. If David and the people around him could witness this supernatural potential unfold in his life, how much more should we? For this reason, David made sure to record the after-effects of anointing in this famous Psalm so that the future generations would be enlightened as they meditate on it.

God does everything with a well-defined and eternal purpose. In this case, even the anointing oil was special and set above any other similar preparation. The recipe for the preparation of this oil was dictated firsthand by God to Moses on Mt. Sinai, with a strict command to never replicate it for any other purpose or for common use. Even though Moses knew the composition of the oil, he did not know the technique for preparation. That was a secret that God revealed to Bezalel (whom He called by name) and Aholiab (Exodus 31:2, 6). God put wisdom in the hearts of all the gifted artisans in order to make every part of the Tabernacle and everything else in it. This included the art of perfumery. This sacred anointing oil was specifically meant to anoint the tabernacle and its elements to sanctify it, to sanctify and anoint the High Priest and his sons, and later on to anoint the kings of Israel. It was compounded in a unique manner, and hence, I believe that it was most desired (or coveted) by all. It held a special esteemed value that could only belong to the House of God, His priests, and His kings. It could never be used on common flesh. Its fragrance was unique, just for the fact that Almighty God designed it. To be anointed with it meant something profoundly special.

God Almighty made it a point to even record its components and the quantity of each. Studying the components of this sacred oil helps us to understand the essence of this practice ordained by God. Exodus 30:22-33 elaborates the specifications God gave Moses concerning the holy anointing oil. The ingredients were a combination of very expensive quality spices and the best oil. We shouldn't forget that they were in the wilderness at this time, and all these commodities were not easily available. I even doubt that anyone would have carried these things when they left Egypt. But they did come out with enough gold and silver articles which would have enabled them to buy these expensive ingredients from passing traders. The wilderness was frequented by merchants and traders who travelled in either direction to sell their wares at major cities like Egypt, Canaan, and Arabia. These travelling merchants had these commodities with them, and the Israelites had to buy them and then prepare the anointing oil. Each item was very expensive, and it was absolutely essential for it to be of the first quality.

While writing this section, I did a significant amount of research into the nature of the ingredients used and also the art of perfumery (followed for ages). You can straightaway believe me if I tell you that it is anything but easy. God's wisdom definitely takes the centre stage. Using essential oils and mixing them in a certain proportion is a piece of cake. But a perfumer of excellence would always start from scratch. He would start by acquiring the best quality raw materials, preferably from the place of its origin. Perfume industries that still practice this are top-rated in recent times and their perfumes are most desired and super expensive! After obtaining the raw material, the essence needs to be extracted from them. This was done by 2 methods: steaming with distillation OR soaking the crushed ingredients in a carrier oil like olive oil. This was time-consuming and needed expertise. It is important to mention that shepherding was the dominant occupation of the Israelites. Indeed, it is the wisdom of God that helped them accomplish this task of preparing the holy anointing oil! Bezalel, Aholiab, and their team of artisans were called by God to accomplish this very purpose.

Way back when Joseph's brothers envied him, they sold him to a caravan of Ishmaelites who were carrying spices, balm, and myrrh to Egypt. These people travelled through the wilderness and deserts to sell their wares, which were highly sought after due to their fragrance, culinary uses, and medicinal values. These were primarily carried as raw materials, which were eventually processed by the people who purchased them. This was the source of ingredients for the Israelites in the wilderness. However, after the Tabernacle was housed in the Holy Land, people offered these to the priests for the service of the Lord.

The holy anointing oil was one of a kind, and God commanded strict punishments for those who would dare to replicate it. Every Israelite was accustomed to its unique smell when they went to the tabernacle. The aroma was indeed heavenly! I believe many would have given anything to just have a drop of it applied on them. But that was just a dream unless it was a priest or a king (much later on). David had the privilege of experiencing an entire horn of this unique oil emptied on him by the prophet Samuel, and the obvious difference that it made in his life from then on. He also educated himself (renewed his mind) about the fact that he was on favoured ground, and the enemy's persecution only advanced him higher in fulfilling God's purposes. He experienced this even until he passed on. With this anointing came greater responsibility and exaltations. It made all the difference!

Each ingredient of the anointing oil was used separately for various purposes. It was burnt as incense, applied as ointment or cosmetic, used as analgesics (painkillers), antiseptics (preventing the growth of harmful germs), a flavouring agent in food and drink, to light lamps, used in gifting, embalming, etc. The authenticity of its value was time-tested. People in those days had learned to take God's selection seriously. If God mentioned something good for His house, they knew it had to be special. Maybe we should learn from them as well.

The ancient art of perfumery involved soaking the crushed raw materials in oil and leaving it for a period of time until it was necessary to get just the right amount of the desired extract. Specific protocols for extracting oil from olives were practiced. These required dedication and patience. From the very beginning, God certified the superior nature of olive oil, which science has validated now. Every ingredient of the anointing oil was fragrant. This speaks volumes. So when a person was anointed, it meant that he always smelled pleasant and inviting, like God. It gave him a presentable and decent appeal. I believe all of us would agree if I said bad odour repels, and fragrance attracts!

The 5 ingredients were as follows: 500 shekels of liquid myrrh, 250 shekels of cinnamon, 250 shekels of cane, 500 shekels of cassia, and one hin of olive oil. Each of these was a quality spice and very expensive. The specific proportions in which these were to be combined created a unique fragrance. Perfumers these days can confirm that even a slight change in the proportions can modify the characteristics of the final product, especially its fragrance.

Myrrh, named so because it is bitter, is a resin extracted from a thorny tree species when incisions are made into the sapwood. It flows out as a liquid but coagulates when exposed to air. Keeping it in the liquid form is indeed a challenge. Therefore, to obtain liquid myrrh, a steam distillation process has to be performed to extract its essential oil. For this, a larger amount of raw myrrh is used, and the entire process is time-consuming. Although myrrh has many uses, it is universally associated with death and mourning across all civilisations. One of its most valuable properties is that it prevents the growth of microbes that cause putrefaction. For this reason, regardless of the method of disposal of a corpse (cremation, burial in tombs, burial under the earth, mummification), myrrh was used by default in all of these practices. It not only masked the foul odour of decomposition but also substantially delayed putrefaction. Burning myrrh purified the air of septic aerosols. The Jews buried their dead in tombs, wrapped in linen cloth containing choice spices, including myrrh. This helped in air-drying bodies and allowing a tolerable decomposition, which permitted their relatives to return a year later and place their bones in a labelled storage box to be kept in a special room inside the same tomb, alongside the remains of many others. This was their custom since the days of Abraham. Queen Esther underwent a purification process in the Persian palace with essential oils and myrrh for 6 months, followed by sweet odours for another six months (totalling 1 year) before she could stand before the Persian king Ahaseurus. This symbolises the fact that myrrh was used to cleanse her, and the sweet fragrances were meant to endow her with a persistent aroma that pleased the king. It took her one whole year to reach this acceptable position.

Myrrh literally symbolises dying to oneself. As compared to the other ingredients, twice the quantity of myrrh was to be used, showing just how sacred and serious God's call is on the anointed ones. This is an essential foundation stone laid by our Lord Jesus Christ Himself. He left His glorious abode to accomplish God's will for His life and clear the way for us to the Father. He's called "The Messiah," "The Anointed One," "The Christ." To signify this, the wise men from the East presented the Child Jesus with myrrh. Mary, the sister of Lazarus, probably had a personal revelation of this and was the only one to **repeatedly anoint** the Lord with costly fragrant oil when He was alive (because she had no access to the holy anointing oil)! Denying oneself is the first step to follow His calling on our lives.

Equal amounts of cinnamon and scented cane (sweet-smelling cane) were used. Both these spices were expensive, aromatic, flavourful, medicinal (antiseptic and analgesic), and also used in embalming mixtures. The aroma and qualities of these ingredients were very inviting. Cassia was used in a proportion similar to myrrh (500 shekels). This was characteristically similar to the above ingredients. A combination of all these ingredients symbolised the strong godly virtue that His anointing imparted to His chosen. The best example set for us in all this is Lord Jesus Christ Himself.

Olive oil was God's choice as the base for this anointing oil preparation. Since God chose it, by default we can acknowledge that it is indeed very special. Its characteristics make it suitable for multiple purposes: the best oil for good health, for cooking, for lighting lamps, a base for ointments; it stands as a symbol of peace and the only oil chosen by God to light the Menorah. Today, it is scientifically proven to be the best quality oil and stands high above the rest. The olive branch is a symbol of peace, glory, and abundance. The land of Canaan had the best in store for the Israelites who were headed there. The harvest was ready, and they had to walk in by faith and enjoy the blessing. The dove that Noah sent out from the ark returned to him (the second time) with a freshly plucked olive leaf in her beak. The gap between the first and second trip was 7 days. The first time, she did not find any resting place for her feet (the waters had not receded enough to allow her to alight). The second trip was more fruitful because she returned with an olive leaf, a sign of life! This can mean one of only 2 things: the olive tree was not destroyed by the flood **or** it was the first to germinate and grow on dry land when the water receded. It symbolised peace and great joy to Noah and his family.

The protocol to extract oil from olives was streamlined from the beginning through the wisdom God gave to men. I would recommend you to go online and see the process for yourselves to understand the amount of hard work involved and the reason why it is so expensive. The first press of oil is known as extra virgin olive oil and is of top quality. A certain portion (like a tithe) of this was to be offered to God by the people and was used in the preparation of the holy anointing oil.

In conclusion, the Anointing oil, compounded by the instruction of God, was unique. All the (overlapping) qualities of its individual ingredients pointed to the attributes of God Himself. People anointed with it were set apart and had to portray the characteristics of God to the common people. **It was ALL ABOUT GOD!** The essence of this anointing oil is clearly explained in Acts 10:38 – **"How God anointed Jesus of Nazareth with the Holy Spirit and with power, who went about doing good and healing all who were oppressed by the devil, for God was with Him."** For all of us who are ignorant of the purpose of His anointing on us, this is the precedent. We are to acknowledge the tremendous responsibility given to us, know that we are set apart to do good, deliver those under satan's clutch, and be God-conscious always.

5(c) MY CUP RUNS OVER.

I believe that David wrote this Psalm in the latter part of his life, after having lived under the banner of God's faithfulness, mercy, and grace. Even though he lived during the Old Covenant period, he had an extraordinary revelation of the transition period and the New Covenant. He has beautifully prophesied regarding them in his Psalms. Based on his firsthand experience with God, he declares that God is the greatest giver, and none in the universe can ever compete with or out-give Him.

Being an insignificant yet responsible young shepherd boy, he experienced the power of anointing and God's blessing in every area of his life. He transitioned into many different roles - musician, armour-bearer, giant slayer, commander of a thousand, slayer of 10 thousands, and finally a wandering target of Saul before he was anointed as the king of Judah at the age of 30. 7 years later, he was anointed as the king of the Nation of Israel, and he ruled over all the tribes. He subdued all the enemies of Israel until there was none left, including Absalom and Adonijah, his own sons.

Even though his own sons tried to sabotage the throne, the Lord restored the kingship to David. David had not only tasted God's goodness and mercy, he had also digested it to such an extent that none could convince him otherwise. From probably having just a few or no coins in his wallet to having given an extravagant offering from his wallet to build God's temple at Jerusalem, David had indeed come a long way to see the Abrahamic blessing fulfilled in his life.

"Blessed to be a blessing" is the inheritance of every child of God. If we are not blessed, we CANNOT be a blessing. We would be too short-sighted to apply this only to money. Only if a cup has water, can one drink from it freely. Only if it persistently fills and overflows can it be a continual source of provision to self and to others. Only if we have, we can give to others. The cup running over speaks of a life that is so filled with the goodness of God that it has enough and more to spare! This is the life that God endorsed from the very beginning and established it further in the life of His Beloved Son, our Lord Jesus Christ.

While ignorant and legalistic believers blatantly speak against God's blessing of good health and wealth/prosperity, it will surely do such people greater good to just sit down for a couple of minutes and think about their damaging doctrine. I am not endorsing the love of money at any cost or the greedy preachers who preach on it just to fill their pockets for their gain. The Spirit of the Lord will surely grant us the grace to discern such people and stay away from their devious tactics. The word says that these people will be known by their fruits, and rightly so! They make it their calling to promote self above the rest and lure people into a life of lust and greed. But it is important for us not to be ignorant of the components of Salvation (total benefits) provided for us through the cross of the Lord Jesus Christ so that we can, in turn, benefit others. **IN OTHER WORDS, IF OUR GOOD HEALTH AND PROSPERITY ARE NOT BENEFITING ANYONE ELSE APART FROM OURSELVES, IT IS DEFINITELY ROOTED IN THE WRONG DOCTRINE AND WILL FAIL.** We are given the privilege to experience this blessing so that we can share the truth and enlarge the boundaries of the kingdom of God here on earth and increase the population in heaven later. Common sense is more than enough for us to realise that only if we are healthy can we minister to others or carry out our responsibilities on a daily basis. We can give to those who lack only if we have something with us first. How much can a sick or bankrupt person help another or spread the gospel? When one's cup is empty, how can he help fill another's? We cannot give away what we don't have, and this does not apply only to money!

David's declarations of God's character have helped millions like me today to understand, taste, and see God's goodness for ourselves. He was able to declare this because he lived a life where his cup overflowed constantly. Not only was he blessed, but he was also a blessing to many others, and God gave him the honour of being called 'The man after God's heart'!

The 'overflowing cup' type of life is a life that starts on the inside first when we hold fast to the finished work of our Lord Jesus Christ on the cross. It is then that our hearts can fully understand that we are filled with the fullness of God, and that we are complete in Him. At Salvation, our deadened spirits are made alive by the Spirit of God, and this life further diffuses into our soul and body. In order to know our sufficiency in Christ our Lord, it is necessary for us to know the word of God, believe, and confess it constantly even though our physical eyes may see things contrary to our confession. The more we hear ourselves say it, faith arises (Romans 10:17 - Faith comes by hearing and hearing by the word of God), and the provisions of God flow into our soul and body. This further refines our words and actions to impact the lives of those around us. This is the testimony that counts for eternity.

There are many who do a lot of good works and are big on charity. But when it does not have God as the foundation or at the centre of it, it all ends here on earth. It does not enter eternity because there is no saving of souls. This is the obvious difference between the true overflowing cup of a believer and the counterfeit overflowing cup of an unbeliever. There is no doubt that people are being helped by the generosity of concerned unbelievers. But it is only earth-bound and temporary. It is like building with wood, hay, and straw, only to be burnt up totally by the fire. We should make our generosity count by rooting it in the foundation of the Lord Jesus Christ. This has the potential of crossing over a physical barrier called death, into eternity. Remember! Every believer is blessed to be a blessing. It is not to (as one wise preacher said, and I quote) 'get all you can, can all you get, and sit on your can!'

It is absolutely essential for us to be connected at all times to the source from where we get our fill. If not, it is easy for us to get drained out! Lord Jesus, on multiple occasions, retreated to a personal one-on-one time with the Father to replenish Himself, in order to serve others. He also pointed us to Himself as being 'The Bread of Life' and 'The Living Water'. In John 7:37-39 the word says, "On the last day, that Great Day of the feast, Jesus stood and cried out, saying, 'If anyone thirsts, let him come to Me, as the scripture has said, out of his heart will flow rivers of Living Water.' But this He spoke concerning the Spirit, whom those believing in Him would receive (for the Holy Spirit was not yet given, because Jesus was not yet glorified)." This 'overflowing cup' life is what David is talking about.

The Source of Life is our Lord Jesus Christ, and He indwells us through the Holy Spirit today. He fills us with Living Waters, and it overflows from our lives into a dying broken world in order to save many souls by bringing them to the saving knowledge of our Lord. God's spirit in us sets our lives right so that we, being aligned with our Father God, can live as sons and daughters of the Most High God, having a healthy spirit, soul, and body. He uses all of it to minister to others who are lost and broken in order to transform them also into the image of His Son. Our Source is established, and we need to stay in constant communion with Him in order to impact our world for the glory of God. This up scales the necessity of spending a dedicated quantity and quality time in God's presence.

The word of God has the innate power to give us rest and refreshment. It is its virtue to provide us strength to live life God's way. This is called "Grace". But we need to go out wholeheartedly and receive it. When we do so, His power is materialised in this earthly realm, and bondages are broken. It makes a visible and tangible difference in our lives as well as the lives of others.

6(a) SURELY GOODNESS AND MERCY SHALL FOLLOW ME ALL THE DAYS OF MY LIFE.

The final verse of this beautiful Psalm establishes a beautiful truth in the life of every believer. It dictates the general kingdom principle and the unbreakable foundation of the path that our lives take when we receive salvation. God's words are 100% true. But when the Holy Spirit prefixes it with the word surely or assuredly, it means it is doubly sealed! So what was the certain doubly sealed truth revealed here? It is that the "goodness" and "mercy" of the Lord, the awesome virtues of our Almighty God, are bestowed on us as our inheritance.

David began this Psalm with the assurance that God goes before us and leads us in His righteous paths. This was followed by a clear picture of God being with us, right by our side, helping us to believe, understand, and receive all that He has paid for and made available to us. As he concludes this petit yet profound Psalm, David reiterates that Almighty God, in all fullness of His virtues, is close behind us as we walk through life.

Life can be lived in 2 ways. Either we live for God (glorifying Him by obeying His will) or we live for ourselves (glorifying ourselves and satan). There is nothing in between or otherwise. When we live for God's purposes, we do it 100% in His strength and grace provided to us for the same. That is "His goodness". When we fail, His mercy is right there! Just fall back into His everlasting arms of forgiveness, obtain mercy, and find grace to help in times of need (Hebrews 4:16). David experienced this strongly in his walk with God. Knowing that these 2 virtues of the Lord were at his disposal, he often declared God's hand doing the good on his behalf and the embrace of God's abundant mercy sustaining him from backsliding whenever he failed.

From the moment he was specially ushered into the Prophet Samuel's presence and anointed by him, till the day that he finally rested with his fathers, David steadily learned the true value of these virtues of God. While David's courage and wit stood out, he often struggled with lust and faltered in it to the point of cold-blooded murder of his own faithful,

God-conscious bodyguard, Uriah. It's not that lust just arrived out of the blue when he saw Bathsheba taking her "Mikveh bath". It started long ago when he could not be satisfied with one woman being his wife. David gradually grew in lust and finally graduated with a PhD! Despite strict orders from God in the book of Deuteronomy 17:17, where the kings of Israel were **ABSOLUTELY PROHIBITED BY GOD TO MULTIPLY WIVES AND HORSES,** David luxuriously married 13 women and had atleast 10 concubines over that. Certainly, his lust was uncontrolled! This set a very good precedent for his son Solomon, who way outdid him and landed up with 700 wives and 300 concubines, and not even one of them was Jewish! Added to this, Solomon also multiplied horses! Because of his moral failure, David could never admonish his sons (beginning with Amnon), who in turn had serious moral problems in their lives. It only got from bad to worse. Despite these failures, David learned how to embrace God's mercy and continued to fulfil God's purpose for his life.

If we are to understand the depth of this revelation, a good study of both the books of Samuel and 1 Chronicles is a necessity. After completing my study of these books, the Lord led me to highlight a few instances from the life of David to help us understand the meaning of this verse.

GOODNESS:

- ✡ David was a very responsible (youngest) son of Jesse. He was dedicated to taking good care of his father's few sheep, doing everything he could to keep them safe from the most dangerous predators. When the Prophet Samuel arrived at Bethlehem, the reason for his visit (anointing for kingship) was a secret between the prophet and God. No one else was let in on it, not even David or Jesse. Let me explain why I am saying this: when God told Samuel to stop his mourning over His rejection of Saul from kingship, to fill his horn with oil, and to go to Bethlehem to anoint the next king, Samuel was hesitant, knowing that Saul would definitely kill him if he got wind of it. He voiced this concern to the Lord. God commanded him to accomplish the task under the pretence (so to speak) of offering a heifer sacrifice to the Lord at Bethlehem and inviting Jesse's family to the sacrifice. Now this was not suspicious because the Prophet, having long settled in Ramah (his hometown), would often visit the cities of Israel, offering sacrifices and specifically inviting a select few to be a part of it. Not all were invited. Those invited could attend the proceedings and also partake in the feast that followed the sacrifice. If Samuel had publicised the kingship anointing before the Bethlehem crowd, the entire "Heifer sacrifice" deal would have been a total waste, as somebody would definitely bring the news to Saul, and he would kill David and Samuel together at the earliest! I believe that David's own brothers could have leaked the matter to Saul because they worked for him and obviously envied their little brother.

Anointing was always special. The most they all knew was that David was set apart for a special reason above all of them. On account of this, Eliab thought David was proud and insolent when he (David) wanted to fight Goliath (1 Samuel 17:28) instead of realising that the anointing prompted David's response. But the manifestation of this anointing soon showed up in David, so much so that the people witnessed a change in his personality. David did nothing to deserve this anointing and favour from God. In fact, God called him 'a man after His heart' in 1 Samuel 13:14, and this was years before he was even born! Come to think of it, none of us do! He knew that he was the prime recipient of the goodness and grace of God!

✡ After the goodness of God had anointed him for a special purpose, David witnessed a drastic change in his personality. Unlike his predecessor Saul, who did not advance in his anointing and purpose, David pursued his anointing by exploring it even while shepherding his sheep and warding off the predators. We can say that he grew into his anointing steadily. The step-by-step progress made by David is clearly depicted in the word of God. When he compared Goliath to the lion and the bear, it was not an empty comparison. The bears found in the wilderness of Israel average 9 feet in height when they stand up on their hind legs. So indeed, it was a matter of fact! He made good use of his anointing in everything that he did, perfecting his musical skills, slingshots, and strategies to keep the predators at bay.

He boldly acknowledged before King Saul that it was God who kept him from the paws of the wild beasts and that He wouldn't hesitate to give Goliath into his hands too. And God did!

- The victory over the giant propelled David further into God's will for his life. When David slew Goliath, Saul appointed him as his armour bearer. It was not a menial job. It was not all about polishing Saul's armour to make sure it dazzles or carrying it for him wherever he goes. David had the honour of protecting the King's life by being a bodyguard of high rank to Saul! That is the definition of an armour-bearer. During this period, David had to accompany Saul to war and was automatically trained in military strategies and the art of war. He excelled at it! Saul subsequently promoted him to higher leadership, making him a captain of a hundred and a thousand. Then he could go to war all by himself with his troop of soldiers. It is said that David behaved shrewdly and was well-loved by all. He was steadily climbing up the ladder of fame in Israel. It was at one such victory that the virgins of Israel, cheering David, sang a song declaring that Saul had killed thousands but David had killed 10 thousands. This elevated comparison sparked envy and jealousy towards David in Saul's heart immediately, and David's vagabond life began. David knew that it was God's goodness that had advanced him to this great level so that even Saul was jealous of him.

- Following his new status as a person who had killed 10 thousands, David was demoted by Saul and constantly targeted, so much so that he fled from his presence and became a vagabond in the wilderness of Judea for no good reason other than to be a victim of Saul's envy. Saul made it his calling to kill David because he saw him as a strong threat to his throne and his lineage. Saul did not even spare troubling David's parents and brothers on his behalf, because we see that even they all joined him in the wilderness later on. These were indeed times of despair. Instead of fighting the enemies of Israel, Saul was rounding up men to kill David! But David used this time to edify himself. While he was hiding in the cave of Adhullam, many (Jews and non-Jews) who were distressed, discontent, and in debt joined him. Initially, their number was about 400 and soon grew to 600. These people had messed up their lives, but by the grace shown to them, they became very efficient and came to be known as David's mighty men! They became famous for slaying giants and hundreds of enemies at once. They excelled in the art of war as swordsmen and archers.

It is important to mention here that under the leadership of Saul and David, the Israeli army mainly consisted of swordsmen and archers. There were no horses and chariots! These came in only during and after the reign of Solomon.

David had all the strength and reason to put Saul down. But he chose the fear of the Lord, knowing that God would avenge him and set him on the throne at the right time. Even though he wandered in the wilderness for no fault of his, he lived grateful for the fact that God's goodness provided him victory in every battle, the good and loyal companionship of 600 men, divine protection from Saul's threat, and an area of settlement (Ziklag) right in the enemy's territory with added favour from the king of Gath, Achish, for a period of 16 months. When Saul heard that David had fled to Gath, he stopped seeking him because he thought that the Philistines would do the job for him. **But God made David's enemies to be at peace with him (Proverbs 16:7).** Staying at Ziklag, David continued fighting and vanquishing Israel's enemies (the Amalekites, Geshurites, and Girzites) and gathered all the spoils. Ziklag was a city owned by Achish, king of Gath, which was the native city of Goliath, the giant whom David killed. Yet the goodness of God granted David favour in the eyes of his enemies and made them to be at peace with him!

David's stay at Ziklag is interpreted very differently by some. They have labelled this entire episode as David's disobedience to God, having fallen prey to discouragement. First and foremost, we need to understand that David was constantly running from Saul to save his own life. In doing so, he was not able to accomplish the task God had called him for, i.e., to vanquish the enemies of Israel, repossess the forfeited territory, and safeguard God's children (the Israelites). Added to this, his own people (the Ziphites and the people of Keilah) were more than happy to delivery him to Saul. God had called him to greatness, and David felt lost without accomplishing God's will for him. Instead of fighting the enemies of Israel, Saul was on David's tail, and both of them were running around in circles. To break this chain, I believe that David opted to trust God and approach King Achish of Gath. God granted David divine favour in the eyes of this gentile king (whose hero Goliath he had killed previously), and it solved both problems! Saul stopped pursuing David, and David resumed his calling to vanquish the enemies of Israel (the Amalekites, Geshurites, and Girzites), in turn enlarging the territory of Israel. However, he lied to Achish regarding the area he was attacking for obvious reasons. David would never dare kill his own Jewish brethren. But later on, he murdered Uriah the Hittite (his own right-hand man) in cold-blood and this wreaked havoc in his family. He lost 3 sons (Amnon, Absalom, and Adonijah), along with the grievous lifelong desolation of his beautiful daughter Tamar as a consequence. He had to pay a very costly price! God was watching, and certainly, he couldn't get away with that horrific, spineless act. And for the same reason, God certainly wouldn't spare him if he was killing his own Jewish brethren either!

✡ David feared God. He absolutely refused to take revenge on Saul. Saul came into his hands twice. As far as Saul was concerned, David passed every test with good integrity, even though the people with him tempted him to kill Saul. He respected Saul's life only for one reason: because he (Saul) was the Lord's anointed, and he firmly believed that the Lord would reward Saul for all the evil he did to him. In fact, one time he cut the corner of Saul's robe and was overcome with guilt for doing that! He never for once tried to crown himself king and waited on the Lord patiently to accomplish this task. Finally, on Mount Gilboa, Saul and his 3 sons were killed in a fierce battle with the Philistines, and God made the way for David to be first crowned king of Judah. He reigned for 7 years in Hebron while another of Saul's sons, Ishbosheth, ruled over Israel. But Ishbosheth was assassinated by his own army captains. After this, David was made king over the entire nation of Israel and ruled over it for another 33 years (totalling a period of 40 years). We often see David inquiring of the Lord before he ventured into something. He knew very well that the goodness of God went before him, was with him, and followed closely behind him. All he had to do was reach out and keep embracing it. And every time he did that, the Lord prospered him and made his name great.

MERCY:

Having spoken of how David embraced the goodness of God, let us have a look at how David constantly embraced God's mercy. A man of God aptly said, "The Christian life is not difficult; it is impossible!" Unless we constantly embrace both the goodness and mercy of God, we could actually end up living a life of constant self-righteousness and condemnation. Mercy never came cheap. The God of the universe paid a very costly price, and our Messiah paid for it with His life. It is His priceless virtue that should not be taken for granted. Coupled with grace and a progressively renewing mind, it is the most effective weapon against the weakness of the flesh. When we hold onto mercy, we can overcome the paralysis caused by condemnation and get right back on track with God's calling on our lives. God's mercy helps us repent and walk away from distractions, and grace steps in to rectify our actions so that our spirit overcomes our flesh.

- ✡ **David and the Ark of the Covenant:** David had a desire for the Ark of the Covenant unlike his predecessor Saul. Eli's sons foolishly accompanied the Israeli army by carrying the Ark to the battlefield without conferring with God. Israel lost the battle, Eli's sons were killed, and the Ark was captured by the Philistines. In order to display and celebrate their victory, the Philistines took the Ark of the Lord into the temple of dagon. The Ark robustly defended itself to such a degree that dagon lost his head and hands overnight, and the Philistines, along with their lords, were affected by tumours, and the land ravaged by rats! I believe that this was the bubonic plague in the days of old. A good 7 horrifying months passed before they finally decided to send the Ark back to its homeland. They hitched 2 milk cows to a new cart and placed the Ark on it with a chest beside it containing golden images of rats and tumours in it. The lactating cows, not turning aside to their calves and followed by the Philistine kings, walked right up the highway to reach Beth-Shemesh, a Levite city in Dan. When they got to the stone of Abel, the people of Beth-Shemesh gladly received it and sacrificed the 2 cows using the wood of the cart they pulled. Being satisfied with these signs, the Philistine kings returned home. But the people of Beth-Shemesh were struck with a plague, and 50,070 people died because they didn't reverence the Ark of the Lord. Fearing the loss of more lives, they requested the people of Kirjath Jearim (in the land of Judah, inherited by Caleb) to come and take away the Ark to their place. The men of Kirjath Jearim obliged, came over, and carried the Ark to the land of Judah, to Abinadab's house on the hill. There they consecrated his son Eleazar to minister before it. The Ark was there until David came for it (60-70 years).

Shortly after the Ark was housed in Abinadab's house, Saul was anointed king of Israel on the people's request. Saul showed absolutely no interest in the Ark. There was a time when he asked someone to bring the ephod and the Ark but shortly aborted the desire to consult it. The Ark of the Covenant is a picture of our Lord Jesus Christ. So in other words, Saul preferred to rely on his own wisdom rather than the wisdom of God. On the other hand, David's heart desired for Jebus (Jerusalem) and for the Ark in Kirjath Jearim. When he was crowned king of Israel, he wasted no time in acquiring these 2. Joab captured Jebus for David, and it became his capital city. Secondly, he built a tabernacle in Jerusalem (Mount Zion), right in front of his house and planned to get the Ark there. This tabernacle was unlike the Tabernacle of Moses.

While relocating the Ark of the Covenant from the house of Abinadab on the hill, David deviated from the Mosaic commandment for moving the Ark from one place to another (Numbers 4). He just took things for granted and tried to do it the Philistine way with some accompanying music. (This is a good example for us to learn not to do things the way the world does, when we know better). Nevertheless, the oxen stumbled; Uzzah put out his bare hands to balance the falling Ark and was struck dead. Frankly speaking, God did not have a personal agenda against Uzzah. Even David himself could have been struck dead if he did what Uzzah did. It was a known law that no one was allowed to touch the Ark with bare hands. It is equivalent to touching a live wire! The only way to transport the Ark (as dictated by God) was by bearing it on poles on the shoulders of the Levite priests. Uzzah's death was a consequence, even though his intentions can be justified. But Uzzah should have known better than touching the Ark because it was housed reverentially in his father's house for many years (about 60-70 years).

David was both angered and scared by this incident. He refused to proceed further, and as a result, the Ark was relocated to the house of Obed Edom. It remained there for a good 3 months, and the entire household of Obed Edom was bombarded with blessings! This reassured David that it was now safe for him to transfer the Ark to Jerusalem. However, this time he did it the proper way, having the Levites carry it on their shoulders and sacrificing after every 6 paces. David could have taken Uzzah's death as a bad omen and abandoned his desire for the Ark. Instead, he turned around and embraced God's mercy, accomplishing his heart's desire.

As much as believers depend on God's grace to fulfil His will for our lives, we must also rely equally on His mercy to rise when we fail. Only then can we effectively carry out His will for us. David had learned this lesson all too well!

✡ **Saul, David, and the priests at Nob:** Saul tried to kill David constantly. Fuelled by jealousy and envy, Saul made it his calling to destroy David. When David could no longer put up with this, he bade farewell to his dear friend Jonathan (Saul's son) and lived the life of a vagabond in the wilderness of Judea. On the way out, he stopped at the Levite city of Nob. Ahimelech, a descendant of Eli, was the priest in charge here. He was unaware of the issues between David and Saul. He knew that David was loved and favoured by all. So he granted David's request for some food (showbread) and a weapon (the sword of goliath that was kept in the tabernacle). At this time, Doeg the edomite (Saul's chief shepherd) was at Nob. He witnessed all these happenings, and David later confesses that he knew Doeg would use this to his advantage. Doeg did just that. When he got to Saul, he got into his good books by betraying this matter. Saul called for all the priests from Nob and confirmed the matter with them. But he did not believe their claim of innocence and got the entire congregation (85 priests along with their women, children, infants, and cattle) executed at the hands of Doeg (because Saul's men refused to touch the priests in the fear of God). Only one among them, Abiathar (Ahimelech's son), escaped and informed David in the wilderness of this horrific incident. Saul's jealousy, envy, and hatred literally turned him into a monster, so that he couldn't even differentiate basic right from wrong. When Abiathar broke this news to David, he knew that he was the cause of the loss of all those lives. How would you overcome the guilt if you were in David's place? It is hard, isn't it? Yet David turned around to embrace God's mercy and took Abiathar under his protection till the end (until he defected to Adonijah).

I would like to highlight here that Abiathar was from the lineage of Eli that bore a curse spoken by God, as said in 1 Samuel 2:31–33. Ahimelech, the father of Abiathar, was the son of Ahitub, who was the brother of Icabod, Eli's grandson, who was born when Eli and his sons died. Eli was a man who feared God but refused to correct his sons for their blasphemous behaviour. Even after repeated warnings by God through another man of God and young Samuel, Eli dripped honey while rebuking his sons, continued to ignore their wickedness, and ate from their abominations. Hence, the Lord cursed his lineage. This curse was in effect at the hands of Saul when he annihilated the priests of Nob. But I believe that both Saul and David were ignorant of the curse spoken over Eli's household. However, the Lord's word came to pass.

✡ **Polygamy:** Even though the Lord values His daughters highly and shouts it out from the pages of the Bible, satan has influenced the world big-time to be nothing but cruel and unfair towards women from the beginning. From the book of Genesis, God has made His stance on women very clear. God gave Adam one wife, Eve. They are God's perfect timeless design for marriage. But the fall changed this beautiful relationship into one with a high degree of self-centredness. Since God knows the end from the beginning, He made sure to pack His word with powerful instructions and truths to enable women throughout the ages to stand firm against atrocities (both big and small) carried out against them. As much as men failed to acknowledge God's standards concerning women, the women failed to educate themselves in the word and stand up for what is right. Satan made sure to keep literacy off from womankind for a long time. The ignorance of women has been and still is the single largest reason for the misery they encounter in life because they ignorantly forfeit their God-given rights.

Having raised a major point here, I would take this opportunity to encourage the women reading this book to go to the Word and find out for themselves. Knowing what the God of the universe has made available to us gives us grace to live lives that portray the goodness of God and help expand His kingdom here on earth while causing the kingdom of darkness to shrink and fizzle out. Women, who realised their God-given potential and rights as daughters of the Most High God, always stood out loud and clear as examples to all their contemporaries and also to us in these days. There is plenty to learn from them and go further in our relationship with our Lord and Father God.

Men who respect God will automatically respect His standards and commandments concerning women—**each one of them!** It is as simple as that! However, when we study the life of David concerning this, he failed this test repeatedly and terribly. 'Lust' was one very frequent visitor at the door of David's heart, and he entertained it almost every time it knocked. **The Prophet Nathan called lust a 'passing traveller '**. The probable root cause of the greatest pain that David had to endure in his life was lust.

Was David ignorant of God's standard for His appointed kings? I don't think so. God had given specific instructions to the future kings of Israel through Moses well beforehand in Deuteronomy 17. The instructions were crystal clear, with absolutely no room for doubt. Added to this, every king was supposed to make a copy of the Book of the Law (the first 5 books of the Bible) for himself when he was crowned, in his own handwriting, from the main one with the priests. So basically, each king literally became a scribe. Furthermore, this copy that he made had to remain with him, and he had to read it all the days of his life so that he would learn to fear the Lord his God and be careful to observe all the laws and statutes. In this very same chapter, the Lord commanded the kings very clearly regarding 3 things: they had to abstain from multiplying horses, wives, gold, and silver for themselves. David would have written this with his own hands. Though he kept away from the first and the last, he failed the test when it came to wives. God's esteemed standard for women is revealed very well here in this passage in Deuteronomy. If men chose to disobey these standards, it is not God's fault. One can say God could have given them a good punishment in order to warn others. If God had to strike every man who belittles women or every woman who disrespects men, not one person would be alive on earth today!

God's perfect standard for marriage is monogamy; not polygamy or anything else the world allows today. This was made very clear in the Garden of Eden. David, having written and read this passage many times, repeatedly broke this statute every time he married a new lady or acquired a concubine. This insolence would have broken God's heart much more than the indignation we ladies possess from reading about it. But every one of the ladies had the opportunity to refuse and stand against David if they wanted to! Even more outrageous than David's lust is the attitude his wives and concubines possessed and displayed. Abigail and Bathsheba showed absolutely no resistance to David's advance towards them. There is no record of any of his 13 wives or 10 (recorded) concubines standing against or rejecting David's proposal. Had they done it, I am sure that God would have made sure to record it for us, and He would have certainly stood by them and taught David a lesson through them. Sadly, these ladies (like Abigail) thought it was an honour to be the wife of the soon-to-be king. David was already married to Saul's daughter Michal when he proposed to Abigail, but she was not with him in the wilderness. However, this is absolutely no justification for David (according to God's standard) to seek another wife. Now, can we understand who needs to be blamed? Today, in most of our households, most parents certainly refrain from giving their daughters in marriage to a man who is already married. People in those days lacked that basic sense.

If only women knew God's heart for them and the high regard He shows for His daughters, their lives would be much better. **Proverbs 24:5 says, 'A person of knowledge increases strength'** and **Colossians 2:8 says, 'Beware lest anyone cheat you through philosophy and empty deceit, according to the traditions of men, according to the basic principles of the world, and not according to Christ'.** Every woman of God needs to have these 2 verses engraved on her heart. The traditions of men are rooted in the deception of satan. In my country, the marriage culture is absolutely biased. Even the 'Christians' have held onto these traditions, which are outright ungodly and against God's established standard of marriage. This is the reason why so many marriages get messed up in the church itself! When we, the daughters of the Most High, bend our necks and accept these harmful traditions, we become victims of our own making. By ignorantly and fearfully submitting to them, we make sure that such harmful traditions flourish! The cycle keeps repeating as we take advantage of this when our children (especially the son's) get married. So it is the need of the hour for women to sit with the word of God in our hands and study it to know and acknowledge God's love for us and the standards He has set for every area of our lives. Practicing the standards set by God **early** will prevent a mountain load of trouble and heartache later on. Secondly, we need to assure and convince ourselves that God is not a partner in crime with the men who reject His standards concerning us. The Lord will gladly bend the heavens to work on our behalf, dear sister, if we embrace His love for us and the glorious standard He has established in His Word. If we allow the detestable worldly tradition to shape our idea of marriage, then none of us have the right to blame God for the unfortunate things happening in our lives.

God is always good, dear ladies! Be assured of that. Be informed; acknowledge and accept His truth about you and the standards He has defined; DO NOT MISUSE HIS FREEDOM; submission to God and the standards He has set are of paramount importance; work with Him in obedience, and you will be a great witness to His restoration!

David's uncontrolled lust caused him much pain. At a point in time, even 13 wives and 10+ concubines were not sufficient for him, and he ended up committing adultery and murder! He was numbed by it for more than 10 months until God rebuked him through the Prophet Nathan. David finally woke up from his delusion and had to face harsh consequences. It was a series of heartbreaking events that spanned the rest of his life on earth. David could never set a moral standard for his family because he failed terribly in this area. He could not even say a single word to his sons in this regard, let alone rebuke them for their deeds. Incest and adultery tore down the lives of his children one after another. His son Solomon, the wisest king who lived on earth, faltered big time in this same area and went one step ahead to be the first king to establish idolatry in Israel, which is an absolute abomination before God. God requires fathers to teach their children and bring them up in the fear and admonition of the Lord. The mothers have their part in this too. David failed in this aspect. Yet he confessed his wrongdoing, embraced God's abounding mercy, and kept his heart on fulfilling God's purpose for his life. **He did not allow his**

blunders to cripple him; rather, he reached out to the gracious and merciful outstretched arms of the Father and went on to fulfil his calling.

Let me bring out the essence of Proverbs 31:3 here. David was 30 years old when he became king of Judah and reigned for a total of 40 years over Israel and Judah. He died at the age of 70 after he appointed Solomon to reign in his place. The word says that David died 'full of years'. I do agree that 70 years is a good lifespan. But today, we see people living beyond that. In the last few years of his life, David developed hypothermia, which could not be abated by any therapy. So his servants suggested that they get him a young virgin as a wife who could keep him warm through skin contact. It was a stupid advice, though, and we have plenty of well-wishers around us today who excel at such advice, pretending to be really concerned about us. But this just shouts out their ignorance concerning the simple commandments of God. This could have been done easily by any of his other wives or concubines. Even though David gave in, at least this time he had the sense not to lie with the young virgin Abishag, the Shunammite. His strength was all drained out. This is exactly what King Lemuel's mother advised him in this verse in Proverbs, saying: "Do not give your strength to women, nor your ways to that which destroys kings". David's strength was totally drained by the age of 70 because he gave his strength to women.

God made sure to record these details in His word for one reason: to serve as a lesson for us on how we can avoid foolishness and unnecessary pain. Never has God approved or supported such reckless behaviour. The consequences of their foolishness are well seen in the word, and I seriously doubt if we could handle such distress if we had been in their shoes. **God recorded the latter days of these kings to let us know His disapproval of their actions and the painful consequences that followed.** Although David embraced God's mercy and completed his days on earth, the same cannot be said of his son Solomon, who indulged his flesh big-time. Not one of his 1,000 wives and concubines was Jewish. That is the extent to which he disobeyed God. His successor, Rehoboam, was born to an ammonite princess, and Israel went downhill from there. All this stresses the dire need for godly parenting and setting good examples ourselves!

BATHSHEBA AND URIAH:

Having studied both the books of Samuel and 1 Chronicles with adequate background research into the Jewish culture of those days, I might be able to give you an interesting sequence of events that is important in the story of David, Bathsheba, and Uriah.

Uriah the Hittite was one of David's mighty men. He was probably a jewish convert due to his association with David. His character can be understood quite clearly from the little record of his words and actions in the Bible. It is understood from 2 Samuel 11:11 that he had a heart for Israel's rest, the Ark of the Covenant, and his commander Joab. His faithfulness to his king was well evident. He trusted David so much that he failed to question his crooked actions in the least. They did not have the luxury of news coverage in those days, as we have now. It was common for the king to be informed by someone who was sent from the battlefield, but it would usually be someone other than 'a mighty man' for that purpose. None of these things gave him the slightest suspicion! Uriah was one of the 600 people who had joined David in the wilderness when Saul was hunting him down. He had lived with him and proved his faithfulness to him.

Bathsheba was the daughter of Eliam, the son of Ahithophel. This Ahithophel was a highly respected councillor in the court of King David. 2 Samuel 16:23 says that the advice of Ahithophel given in those days was as if one had inquired at the oracles of God; so was all the advice of Ahithophel, both with David and Absalom. Eliam was one of David's 30 mighty warriors. They were natives of Giloh, a city in Judah. However, it is not known whether they were Jewish or not. But because Ahithophel was consulted for godly wisdom and Eliam was one of David's 30, we can presume that they were followers of Judaism.

David had built quite a magnificent house for himself on higher ground. He had a terrace that overlooked the entire city. It was made of cedar wood, presented by King Hiram of Tyre. During David's reign, only the southern half of the city was populated. It was later expanded by Solomon when he built the Temple of God and his own palace. However, there was a threshing floor in the northern part.

David had spent most of his life subduing and possessing the inheritance God had given the Israelites. He had enlarged the territory of Israel. He had also stationed garrisons in many cities in Philistia, Syria, Moab, Ammon, etc. They were his vassals' and paid tribute to him regularly. One such king was Nahash, king of Ammon. Following Nahash's death, his son Hanun ascended the throne. Since David had a good relationship with Nahash, he sent respectable men as messengers to offer condolences to Hanun. But inexperienced Hanun, giving heed to his foolish advisers, treated them badly, shaved off half their beard, tore their garments at the back to expose their buttocks, and sent them back in absolute humiliation. These men were embarrassed beyond measure and sent word to David. Now this took a turn for the worst, with David ordering Joab to destroy the ammonites. Ammon was a country with many cities. He requested the embarrassed men to stay at Jericho until their beards grew back and then to return to the city.

Hanun sensed danger and got the Syrians into a coalition by paying them big money. David did not go out with his army to fight this battle. I cannot exactly understand why David refrained from going, though it is possible that he thought that his able commander Joab and the competent Israeli army could finish the job well without him. However, this turned out to be to his discredit. It could also be that he got lazy with all the success God had given him or that he misjudged Ammon's strength. Only upon reaching there did Joab realise that the Syrians had allied with the ammonites. Nevertheless, being an able commander, Joab and his brother Abishai worked out a strategy to defeat the ammonites and the Syrians. While Joab rounded up all the mighty men and went against the Syrians, Abishai headed the army against Ammon. This arrangement was made so that the brothers could come to each other's rescue if needed. This war went on for months. The enemies would retreat, then come back again with a bigger recruit, and again get clobbered by Joab and his men. The country of Ammon had many cities. Hence, it took some time for Joab to subdue them.

While his commander, mighty men, and army were away at war, David had some good leisure. One evening, he arose from his bed and walked on his terrace. From the heights of his palace, he spotted a woman bathing. This woman was not bathing on the terrace of her house, as some people wrongly say. It's just that David's position on the terrace gave him an undue advantage to look down upon the houses and spaces of his subjects in Jerusalem. It so happened that Bathsheba was having her ritual cleansing after her monthly menstrual cycle (2 Samuel 11:4). This was called the "Mikveh bath". The period for this cleansing was anywhere between 7 and 14 days after the onset of the monthly period for women. Whether there was an actual Mikveh (a special room with a pool for this cleansing ritual) during this time is unknown. But certainly, it was the Jewish culture for women to cleanse themselves after every monthly period.

The guest (lust) already came knocking at David's heart. He got someone to identify her from there and was informed that she was Bathsheba, the wife of Uriah the Hittite (one of David's mighty men). Bathsheba was also the daughter of Eliam (another of David's mighty men) and the granddaughter of Ahithophel (David's councillor). At least at this point, David should have dropped the idea of any illicit affair. But his lust overpowered every sane reason. Any of his 13 wives or 10+ concubines could have quenched his lust, but he just had to have her! He sent messengers (not soldiers) to Bathsheba to get her. I believe that Bathsheba probably did not know the reason for the summons and went along with the messengers to David. But when she got there, the record of events sounds pretty smooth. The word says that she came to him, David lay with her, and she returned to her house! **Here is why I have a problem with this incident.** Later on, when I read about Amnon and Tamar (2 Samuel 13), verses 11–19 elaborated the reaction of Tamar (the sister of Absalom) all too well. The resistance she exhibited before, during, and after her violation is robust and is recorded for us to read. As compared to Bathsheba, Tamar was royalty and had good reasons to keep her mouth shut about the whole incident, as this truth would ruin her and her father David's house. Yet she exhibited such a high degree of remorse that she remained desolate in Absalom's house for the rest of her life! This behaviour is so contrary to Bathsheba's. Did Bathsheba's failure to resist result in a silent consent to David's advance? Maybe?

Added to this, let me raise another valid point here. David was the people's king. He wasn't a tyrant. People honoured and respected him from the beginning. Bathsheba could have just rejected him and threatened him on this basis if she wanted to. There is absolutely no record of her resistance. I am sure that this was no secret incident. Bathsheba had to come into the palace and walk out of the king's chamber. Messengers were involved at every level. There could have been an element of fearful submission, too. But she just kept quiet about it, even after getting out of the king's chamber. There is a marked contrast between Tamar and her behaviour. She had no willpower to fight injustice. The analogy between the ewe lamb in Prophet Nathan's story and Bathsheba only points to helplessness, as the rich man killed the poor man's lamb and fed it to his guest. But I still feel that the ewe lamb, which lay in the poor man's bosom, would have put up a good fight to get away from the greedy rich man as he dragged it away to kill it! Isn't it? Think about it.

This is the right place to speak about Uriah's character as well. With the little that is said of him (2 Sam 11:8–14), one virtue stands out loud and clear. He was sold out for Israel, for God, for his king, and for his commander Joab. He was so loyal to his country that he couldn't even think of settling down with his wife. Could it be that, due to his zeal for Israel's rest and the king's safety, Uriah had not consummated his marriage as yet (since Bathsheba was still menstruating and there is no mention of them having any children as a couple)? Maybe? He was not only talking about the present war but was also mindful of Israel's long-term, permanent rest from all wars. He yearned for Israel's rest and knew that until all the battles were fought and lands repossessed, Israel could not actually rest. His reply to David in verse 11 shows where his heart was. The Ark was his primary concern. He had made his king's desire the number one goal of his life. In doing so, Uriah was blinded to every deception that lay so open before him. Why would the king call out a mighty man from a fierce battle—that too with the Syrians? Why would he ask him to go home and send a gift of food behind him if he was only meant to be an informant? Why would he make him stay another day and get him drunk in order to make him go home? If he had even smelt the slightest stench of David's garbage, he would have opened the letter sent through his hand when he left back to the battle field, but he didn't!

There is a good lesson for us to learn from the character of Uriah, and that is to have 'godly discernment'. An audacious trust in man and a lack of godly discernment caused his death. However, Prophet Nathan's analogy highlights the love that Uriah had for Bathsheba. Indeed, this was a sad ending to a love so deep. This shows us the need for a strong personal relationship with God.

After this one-night stand, both David and Bathsheba went on with life until she conceived. At least it would have taken a month to confirm her pregnancy. She sent word to David, and in turn, David (the guilty man) hatched a plan to cover it all up! This part of the story is well known to all. David sent for Uriah from the frontlines of battle, and Joab sent him as the king commanded. After he arrived, David tried his best to get him to go home and sleep with his pregnant wife! I feel that in itself is top-notch cruelty! And then, when he failed, he sent a death warrant by Uriah's own hands, and he was slain in the battle field by betrayal (as the army withdrew) by the sword of Ammon. David not only contemplated Uriah's death, but he literally sealed it. Why was he so scared of what he had done? He was the king! He could have used his clout to silence them all if he wanted to. But David wasn't a tyrant. As said earlier, Bathsheba could have used this against David very easily if she wanted to, but she didn't.

Come to think of it: All this started with a simple condolence message sent by David to the new king of Ammon! I sometimes wonder "Was this message even necessary"? Would Hanun have even cared otherwise? This instructs us to be prudent in all that we do. If Uriah had kept his eye on God instead of David, he probably could have looked through the deception and remained alive. In these New Covenant days, we are called to look to the Lord Jesus Christ only and submit our loyalty to Him. Somebody else's calling doesn't extrapolate to us. God has a calling for each of us, and it is our duty to stick with it. It would do us a lot of good if we did just that. A one-on-one relationship with God is what all of us need, and that is more than enough to bury all deception and carry us through life.

During the final stages of the war (after the death of the child conceived by adultery and the birth of Solomon), David joined in and beat the Syrians. However, Joab knew that David's hand was involved in the death of Uriah. He used it to his advantage and stuck to his own strategies in the war. David could not question him in this regard. Upon hearing about her husband's death, Bathsheba mourned for the required period of time, and then David took pregnant Bathsheba to be his wife. She bore him a son when the gestation period was completed. There was no remorse or conviction in David even until this time (almost 10 months to a year). So the Lord sent Nathan the Prophet to spell out this blasphemous act as a parable before David. I believe that the concept behind this was for David to declare his own fit punishment. David immediately declared a death sentence for the guilty man along with a fourfold restoration since this was an act without pity. However, the Lord showed David mercy by sparing his life, but the child born as a result of this adulterous act died. Along with this male child, his 3 older sons, Amnon, Absalom, and Adonijah, died one after another. David indeed paid back fourfold, just as he decreed!

Nathan's parable highlights one very important truth. The rich man had flocks and herds, but there was no emotional connection between them. However, there was an ocean of love between the poor man and his ewe lamb. This is well related to the degree of love between the partners in polygamous and monogamous marriages. I would certainly say that the element of love is wrecked in polygamy. There are many examples of this in the Word to prove it. For the rich man, his wealth only remained as flocks and herds. But to the poor man, the little ewe lamb was like his "own daughter". That speaks volumes! When a man cares for his wife like a daughter, she is indeed blessed!

David had to pay a very expensive fourfold recompense that lasted for the rest of his life. The lives of his 4 children—the son born by adultery, Amnon, Absalom, and Adonijah—were largely affected. Added to that, his beautiful daughter Tamar's life became desolate. Had he not held onto God's mercy, there was no way David could have moved an inch forward in his calling. David had lost all moral authority and could in no way stop the consequences.

The same passing traveller, lust, caught hold of Amnon (David's firstborn). He brutally raped and destroyed the life of his own half-sister, Tamar. David's tongue was tied. Tamar grieved exceedingly and lived desolate for the rest of her life in her brother Absalom's house. Having to see his beautiful little sisters' reproach every day and the silence of his father, Absalom grew a bitterness so deep in his heart that it finally culminated in Amnon's murder 2 years later. Absalom absconded for another 3 years to his maternal grandfather's place (Geshur) until Joab coaxed David and got him back. After he returned, David still refused to speak with him or even see him for another 2 years. Finally, when they reconciled (after a total period of 5 years), Absalom started turning the people of Israel towards himself through deception, striving with all his might to be the next king, and finally proclaimed himself as king even while his father was alive. David did not defend himself but rather left Jerusalem with his faithful men following him.

Ahithophel, Bathsheba's grandfather, mindful of the wrong done to his granddaughter and her husband, sided with Absalom. He advised Absalom to set up a tent on the roof (the same place from where David had seen Bathsheba bathe) and engage in intercourse with his father's 10 concubines who were left behind, in full view of all Israel, before the sun! Absalom obeyed without any conviction. This entire saga culminated in a war between Absalom and David, incited by the former. Despite David's order not to harm Absalom, Joab killed him. God restored David to kingship through His mercy.

Shortly after this, David's son Adonijah followed in Absalom's footsteps. This prompted David to anoint Solomon as the next king, and eventually, he rested with his forefathers. Solomon later executed Adonijah because he lusted after his deceased father's young wife, Abishag. David's sons sank into disgraceful acts of incest and adultery, surpassing even that of David. The fourfold retribution was paid at a considerable cost. David navigated through all these consequences by holding onto God's mercy.

After so great a fall and a plethora of shameful happenings in his own family, David steadied himself and went on to put many things in order. He received instructions from God to build the glorious Temple at the threshing field of Araunah. The intricate details of the temple were given to him by God, and he recorded it all in writing. He further passed this on to Solomon and instructed him to strictly adhere to it. He also organised the Israeli army into a disciplined order according to rank. He ordained 24,000 soldiers on duty each month, and there were 12 such groups ordained to guard Israel for an entire year under an able leader for each month. He took a census of the Levites and rostered them for every service in the temple of the Lord. He made sure that the 24/7 praise and worship would continue at the new temple even after his death by appointing the musicians; he also rostered the gatekeepers. David accomplished a mountain of tasks close to his death because he embraced the tender mercies of God.

6(b) I WILL DWELL IN THE HOUSE OF THE LORD FOREVER.

Through the instances that I have previously mentioned, we can see how David constantly saw God go before him, walk beside him, and hedge him from behind and before. David constantly depended on God's goodness and mercy. God's goodness (grace) strengthened David to accomplish God's purposes for His kingdom, and His mercy sustained him in every failure. Proverbs 24:16 says that a righteous man may fall 7 times and rise again. This is clearly demonstrated in David's life. Because he had this clear understanding of God's priceless virtue, his final few years on this earth were purposeful and meaningful, impacting us even today.

God's purposes are not limited to a particular time or one generation. Beginning with Adam and ending with the last person born on earth, all the events form a huge puzzle. The only One who can see the complete picture of this puzzle is God. Every one of us fits into this puzzle somewhere, and it is enough for us to know that. Redemption was God's thought even before the earth was created, and He worked it out beginning from the Garden of Eden. 4000 years later, the Messiah came in person to fulfil all that was prophesied about Him. Now, 2000 years after His ascension, we are living in that astoundingly beautiful reality of God's promise. This will continue until He returns.

God's heart always beats for us with agape love. Proverbs 8:31 says that wisdom (the Lord Jesus) rejoiced in God's inhabited world, and His delight was with the sons of men. God is not only happy, but He is delighted to have a relationship with us. According to the good pleasure of His will, He has made us His sons through our Lord Jesus Christ so that we may display His goodness in this dark and cold world. He has flooded our lives with His grace and mercy. How much more can one demand from God to convince man of His love for him despite all the assurances from His Word? He never hesitates to commune with people who are open-hearted toward Him. When He delivered the armies of Israel from the bondage in Egypt, He wanted the entire world to see that "their God" was with them in a tangible way—a pillar of cloud by day and a pillar of fire by night as they journeyed through the wilderness. Shortly after their departure from Egypt, God divinely inspired Moses to construct the Tabernacle and the elements associated with it. When the people dwelt in tents, our God, who is the Creator of the universe, also lived among them in a tent. This is the humility of God and a sign of His love for mankind. **He identifies with us!**

The Tabernacle of Moses was all about the Messiah, the Lord Jesus Christ. Every small detail and element pointed people to Him. Whether it was the colour, material, metal, or design, the Lord Jesus was the picture behind it all. This tabernacle was a replica of the Temple in heaven (Hebrews 8:5). The most important part of this tabernacle was the Ark of the Covenant. Under the old covenant, only the high priest had the privilege of seeing the Ark with his eyes and only once a year, on the Day of Atonement. No other person could see it or even go near it. When the Ark travelled along with the people, it was always covered in multiple layers, consisting of the covering veil, badger skin, and blue cloth (by the high priest and his sons) and carried by the Kohathites (on their shoulders). This is very clearly mentioned in Numbers 4:1-15. I believe that when the wicked sons of Eli carried the Ark out to the battlefield, they had probably covered it. Or else, they would have certainly been struck dead then and there. But there is a good chance that the Philistines would have uncovered it and kept it at dagon's temple. Because of this, there was a terrible plague causing thousands to die. Finally, when they sent it back to Beth-Shemesh, it was probably uncovered. The Levites from the city offered sacrifices but probably forgot to cover it, and I believe that the plague at Beth-Shemesh was because the people saw the Ark with their eyes. Finally, the people from Kirjath-Jearim came and took away the Ark to their place, and none died. I would certainly attribute it to the fact that they might have done it the right way, by covering the Ark. That being said, for the same reason, I believe that David also brought the Ark into Jerusalem, covered. God had given them His protocol, and He expected the ones serving Him to obey and hallow it. When not respected, it always invited terrible consequences.

The Ark had always defended itself. Even when captured and kept in the temple of dagon by the Philistines, the consequences that ensued turned the land upside down. But this certainly taught them a good lesson, and they determined to send it back to Israel with a trespass offering. When Uzzah reached out his hand to steady the falling Ark, he was immediately struck by God. For this reason, I believe that the people of Beth-Shemesh were punished just because they **'looked at'** the uncovered Ark (not attempting to cover it), let alone trying to 'look into' it. There is no way one could even touch it with his fingers and not be struck dead. What more? Beth-Shemesh was a Levite city, and the inhabitants should have known better! The people of Kirjath-Jearim brought the Ark into the house of Abinadab on the hill, and the people consecrated Eleazar his son to keep the Ark of the Lord. 1 Samuel 7:2 records that the Ark remained there for 20 years. But it was there for more than that.

The first king of Israel was least interested in the Ark. Only once did he ask for the Ark to be brought into the battlefield, but the plan was aborted due to other distractions (1 Samuel 14:18-19). In comparison, David desired the Ark. In Psalm 132:6, he says that when he was in Bethlehem (Ephrathah), he had heard of the Ark and found it in the fields of the woods (Kirjath-Jearim-Jaar). It is possible that David went to Abinadab's house and worshipped before the Lord. There was a "connection" between the Ark and him. David had 2 important priorities to start with: the first was to capture Jerusalem from the Jebusites, and the second one was to bring the Ark into Jerusalem and build a temple for the Lord there, to finally rest the Ark.

As soon as he was appointed king over the entire nation of Israel, he got busy with his priorities and captured Jebus/Jerusalem from the Jebusites through the valiant act of Joab, his nephew. Then he set forth to bring the Ark from the house of Abinadab to Jerusalem. But he did it his way (without hallowing the set command by the Lord in Numbers 4). He was influenced by the Philistine way of transporting the Ark, as a result of which Uzzah died. The Ark was turned into the house of Obed Edom for a period of 3 months, during which his house was blessed! When David heard of this, he took the necessary steps to bring the Ark into Jerusalem the right way (with the Levites carrying it on their shoulders and innumerable sacrifices). He brought it into a tent, which he had erected right in front of his house. This tabernacle was very different from the one that Moses built. The Ark was kept inside and was surrounded by worshippers 24/7. It was different! The Mosaic Tabernacle was also functional at that time in Gibeon; but it did not have the Ark in the Holiest of Holies. However, the sacrifices as specified by the law of Moses were routinely performed there.

While David lived in his cedar palace, the Ark was housed in a tent outside his home, and this worried David. He desired to build a final resting place for the Ark in a grand temple on Mount Zion (Jerusalem). He expressed this unrest in his soul to the prophet Nathan. Initially, the prophet gave him a green signal to go ahead with the temple. But the Lord spoke to Nathan and instructed him to tell David that Solomon would build the temple. The reason why the Lord did not allow David to build the temple was that he was a "man of war". Now we need to understand why the Lord said that. David obediently strived to completely possess the Promised Land, which was the inheritance of the Israelites. In doing this, he had his hands full. In His foreknowledge, God knew that David would err in the case of Bathsheba and invite much turmoil from within his own family. He would have a good amount of trouble and turmoil to last a lifetime. With all this going on, David could never give the proper required attention to the supreme work of God—the construction of His Holy Temple. He could not afford to keep one foot in the work of the temple and the other in the battlefield. The Temple of the Lord was no small deal. It excelled in glory! So God needed one man (a king) to put all his heart and soul into the Temple work and prioritise it above everything else. There is a lot that we can learn from this. The Lord explicitly points out that a king who is at rest from all wars (Solomon) would accomplish this task. **EVERYTHING THAT WE ARE CALLED TO DO SHOULD BE DONE FROM A STANCE OF REST, BEING FOCUSSED ON THE VISION!** This needs to be embedded in our hearts.

When David was told that his son would be building the Lord's temple on Mount Zion, he did not get offended. He didn't argue with God, nor did he go ahead with his plan. On the contrary, in all humility, he accepted God's decision and began to do his part in preparing everything small and big that was needed to build the glorious temple. He also retained the Ark in the tent in Jerusalem, knowing that Mount Zion would hold the resting place for it in due course of time. David was known to spend much time in this tabernacle before the Lord, worshipping Him along with the Levites. He delighted in worshipping the Lord and expressed it in many of his Psalms. Even when he had faltered with Bathsheba and the child that was born to them became sick, he spent the whole time on his face, on the floor, in the house of God (Tabernacle of David). **HIS CONVICTION DROVE HIM TO GOD AND NOT AWAY FROM THE ONLY ONE WHO COULD RESCUE HIM.**

After the death of Absalom until the self-exaltation of Adonijah, David dedicated his life to the preparation work for the temple. All that he did is mentioned in detail in the latter half of 1 Chronicles. Not only did he sort out and organise all the wealth in the treasuries of Israel, he also donated a large amount of gold, silver, bronze, iron, wood, and precious stones from the wealth that God had blessed him with. He tabulated and scheduled the Levitical priesthood into 4 groups (the high priests, priests, singers/musicians, and gatekeepers) for the service in the temple that was to be built. He rostered them all well in advance. The Israeli army was excellently organised for each month under captains. He gathered together all the officials of his kingdom in Jerusalem and instructed them all in detail regarding their support and cooperation with his son Solomon in order to build the temple and complete it without any hindrance or objection.

The Lord had divinely instructed David by the Spirit regarding the design of the temple and everything associated with it, with perfect measurements. The place on which the temple would be built was also shown to David during the plague that he invited due to the census he had ordered. He saw the Angel with His sword drawn at the threshing floor of Araunah (Ornan) before the plague entered Jerusalem. Araunah had offered his own oxen and threshing implements to David, without any charge, to sacrifice to the Lord in order to keep the plague away. But David refused to take it for granted. He paid Araunah whatever it cost and sacrificed to the Lord there. Then the plague stopped. Then David knew that this was the spot for the Temple of God.

David was so dedicated to all the preparation work that he never left anything undone. He commanded and encouraged his son Solomon, saying "Be strong and do it", in the presence of all the people. Till the very end, David prepared all things (even iron nails) and made them readily available so that Solomon would not lag or lack anything for the work of God's temple. He did all this knowing very well that he wouldn't be alive to see the glorious temple with his own eyes. He was very satisfied worshipping the Lord in the tabernacle which he had erected before his house. And until the last minute, he prepared for the main temple. David literally dwelt in the house of the Lord all the days of his life. It was just a matter of time before he would go into the presence of God and spend eternity with Almighty God in His glorious heavenly temple! I believe that David meant this part too, in the last verse of this beautiful Psalm.

In all the Psalms that I will be covering in this book, I believe that Psalm 23 brings out the essence of "The Man After God's Own Heart" more explicitly. This is the reason I have positioned this Psalm at the beginning of my book. If we hold onto this revelation, we can also be men and women after God's own heart. It would certainly please God if we were after His heart, because the world would certainly be a better place than it is today. He can work out His plans and purposes more easily through us if we are mindful of His will. Let us draw on the grace, mercy, and goodness of our Almighty God and bring glory to His Name!

Psalm 22

INTRODUCTION:

This is an astoundingly accurate prophetic Psalm written by King David concerning the salvation that the Messiah would accomplish physically at the ordained time and how the benefits of this salvation would extend to all people under both covenants. The precision with which he prophesies the smallest details is just amazing! The event of the Lord's judgement, the crucifixion, and the way this would be appropriated in the lives of those who believe in Him are beautifully elaborated here. As we read through this Psalm, it is utmost important for us to know and understand that the Lord Jesus Christ suffered every ounce of God's judgement on our behalf; it was the entire load of punishment (an eternity in hell) that mankind deserved. Because He first loved us and because of the respect and honour He had for the Father's will, He established "The Way" to the Father for us.

I have divided this Psalm into 3 parts for ease of understanding: the first one consists of verses 1, 2, 6–21, which describe the sufferings of our Lord. Verses 3-5 describe the appropriation of His sacrifice to the people under the Old Covenant, and verses 22–31 describe the benefits extended to the people under the New Covenant till the last day that earth remains.

David usually sets the tune of his Psalms. This one was set to "The Deer of the Dawn". I don't think anyone today would have an idea about this tune, though. Since this Psalm is totally related to the Saviour, describing His suffering and His great victory, I believe that this tune probably starts on a minor scale but switches over to a major around verse 21. This Psalm has a good number of animals mentioned. Starting with the deer, he goes on to include bulls, lions, dogs, and oxen, giving vivid descriptions of each. Though deer live in the wild, they are very docile animals. Due to their nature, they were frequently kept in palace gardens and even used as pets. They are mild in character, herbivores, usually roam in herds, social animals, and almost always harmless. Due to the nature of their predators, they also adapt themselves to being active from dusk to dawn, being minimally active during the day, and usually feeding the most at dawn or dusk.

God is not restricted or governed by time; He governs it. The only place He was subject to time was when He came to the earth in the flesh as the Lord Jesus Christ. From times past, mankind has recorded everything in history with respect to His presence on earth as a human, whether before the birth (BC) or after the death (AD) of our Lord Jesus. I believe that this is no coincidence but divine ordination! The entire universe revolves around our Lord, having proceeded forth from Him. God is never restricted by time or space. Both belong to Him. Lord Jesus is the Lamb slain from the foundation of the world (Revelation 13:8). The physical manifestation of this happened when the Lord Jesus came to earth in the flesh. The benefits of this salvation have extended to all people before, during, and after His earthly ministry.

1. *MY GOD, MY GOD, WHY HAVE YOU FORSAKEN ME? WHY ARE YOU SO FAR FROM HELPING ME, AND THE WORDS OF MY GROANING?*

2. *O MY GOD, I CRY IN THE DAYTIME, BUT YOU DO NOT HEAR; AND IN THE NIGHT SEASON, AND AM NOT SILENT*

I believe that this is one of the most heart breaking verses in the Bible. I would have a sick feeling in my stomach every time I read it. After the Lord enlightened me on this, I came to understand that **"HE CRIED OUR CRY"**. The appropriation of God's judgement on our Lord began in the Garden of Gethsemane, continued in the house of the chief priest and Pilate's praetorium, and finally culminated after six agonising hours on the cross. This is well elaborated in all 4 gospels. But I believe that the prophecies concerning our Lord as spoken by David (Psalm 22) and the prophet Isaiah (Isaiah 52–53) are much more graphic, and they accurately describe His sufferings more than the gospels. The gospels confirm every prophecy regarding the Messiah's life, death and resurrection. The gospel writers quote these prophecies from the Old Testament when the Lord Jesus fulfilled them.

God created mankind in His image. We are a spirit, having a soul, and living in a body (tripartite beings). This is the actual hierarchy on the day man was created and is the blueprint for every human born thereafter. Our soul and body had to be led by the spirit within us. Unfortunately, this order reversed after the fall, and man got to be led by the desires of his flesh. His spirit died immediately because it was cut off from the life of God due to man's choice to be led by his own wisdom. This spiritual death ultimately led to death in his soul and body. However, we know that God punished our sin in His flesh (Romans 8:3), which means His suffering was totally in His soul and body. His Spirit remained completely righteous. Our sin could not touch or penetrate His righteous Spirit. Therefore, His suffering, which was in His soul and body, started with the travail of His soul in the Garden of Gethsemane and grew to include the excruciating pain in His body caused by the torture that was meted out to Him by the unbelieving Jews and Romans.

Why was it so painful for our Lord that night? Why did He sweat great drops of blood there? Why did He request God the same petition 3 times? Why was the last Passover so emotional and crucial? Let's try to understand a few points clearly before we get on with the answers to the above questions.

Shortly before the children of Israel were liberated from the bondage in Egypt by the hands of Moses, God instituted the Passover as an ordinance (an authoritative order). Their deliverance from Egypt followed only after the declaration of the death of the Messiah. They were still in the period of grace since the law had not yet been given. This ordinance of the Passover was the clearest and most understandable observance of the salvation that would be accomplished by the "Son of God- The Messiah". This had to be observed yearly, without fail, and signified the "Power of the Blood of the Lamb of God". However, the Israelites forgot to keep this ordinance many times, due to which they fell into a lot of trouble every now and then. It did not mean that God was punishing them. But rather, they failed to acknowledge and appropriate the deliverance that God had already provided for them by the observance of this ordinance. The Holy Bible has recounted the faithfulness of God despite the disobedience of the Israelites many times. The importance of keeping this ordinance was paramount in the Old Testament period.

The Lord Jesus kept every one of the Passover feasts during His lifetime, and the last one before His crucifixion was most valuable to Him. Why is that? This was because it was the starting point of the New Covenant, which the Father had prophesied through the prophet Jeremiah (31:31–34) and was going to be shortly accomplished by Him. Here is where He put a period to the Passover ordinance first instituted before they left Egypt. All these years, the Jews were required to keep this ordinance in observance of the work that the Messiah would complete. Now the Messiah was manifesting the reality of this ordinance and initiating the 'New Covenant' that would go into effect immediately and would be valid till the end of the earth, for many, many generations, until He institutes another one in the Kingdom of Heaven when we get there (Mathew 26:29). There begins another covenant for eternity.

The Holy Communion/The Lord's Table: The final Passover supper that the Lord Jesus had with His disciples in the upper room was very precious. The main components of the traditional Passover were the lamb roasted in the fire, the unleavened bread, and the bitter herbs. They were supposed to eat it with a belt on their waist, sandals on their feet, and their staff in their hand, denoting haste. The blood of the Passover lamb had to be applied to the lentils and doorposts of their houses. That night, after the Angel of Death had accomplished His purpose, the Lord would bring out His armies from Egypt.

At this last supper, the Lord Jesus instituted His Holy Communion while they were eating the Passover. It was a clear switch from the old to the new. He took part in this communion along with His 12 disciples. However, the main elements of this new table were 'The Bread' and 'The Wine'.

Our Lord repeatedly declared in various places and at various times to the people that He is the Living Bread and the source of Living Water that came down from heaven. Wine always had special importance (from ages) when people made a covenant with each other. The Lord Jesus was the reality of the Passover. He is the Lamb that was slain from the foundation of the world and who was manifested at this time. Now that He was going to fulfil this ordinance in a few moments, He made a new covenant with His beloved that would last till the end of the world. In a few hours, he was going to be flogged, ripped apart, ridiculed, despised, and crucified on behalf of every human in this world, beginning with Adam. He was going to represent mankind before God and receive every ounce of judgement and punishment from God that mankind fully deserved. In the Garden of Gethsemane, even as He said, 'Thy will be done', all the sin of mankind was transferred onto Him. To represent this truth, He took bread that night, blessed it, broke it, and gave it to His disciples. This bread represents the **truth** that His body was broken for us even as He carried not only our sins but also all its repercussions, like sickness, disease, depression, poverty, etc., onto His flesh. By partaking of the bread, we receive His sacrifice on our behalf and declare this truth to the physical and spiritual realm. We declare that He is always our perfect representative and wholly represents us forever, once and for all time and all people. He bore the full measure of punishment. No one in the history of this entire world has suffered as gruesome a death as our Lord. The gospels are restricted in their description of His torture (flogging, ridiculing, and crucifixion). But to understand the severity of it all, we need to research it further and also research the various types of capital punishments that have been practiced for ages for comparison. I will be sharing my research on crucifixion later.

After the disciples partook of the bread, the Lord took the cup of wine (His cup of wine). He said this wine signified His blood that would be shed even as His flesh was being torn apart, bearing the judgement on behalf of every human. It is very important for us to understand what I am about to say. Under the old covenant, sin was **'covered'** by the blood. However, under the new covenant, sin is **"removed"!** This is what His shed blood accomplished. Under the old covenant, on the Day of Atonement, a lamb was sacrificed, its blood collected in a basin, and the high priest would enter the Most Holy place with this blood, only once a year, and sprinkle it on the Mercy seat on the Ark of the Covenant. This was the only time man could stand before God, and that too not directly, but through the high priest who would represent all of Israel. Hebrews 9 gives a detailed explanation of what Lord Jesus accomplished by shedding His blood. Every drop of His shed blood washed us, cleansed us, made us white as snow, healed us, delivered us, and gave us abundant life in our spirit, soul, and body. Our sin is nowhere in sight; **it is removed!** Today, He stands before the Father as our faithful High Priest, having sprinkled His own blood on the mercy seat, which is a powerful, constant, effective reminder that we are His children.

Consider this example to understand the difference between sins being 'covered' and 'removed'. A thief who stands guilty of his wrongdoing will be punished by the court of law once he is arrested and presented before the judge. He serves his sentence or bears the punishment as ordained by the judicial system. After he serves his time in prison, he is released and cannot be again tried for the same wrongdoing (unless he repeats it or does something worse than that). However, his offence will be remembered because it is still a part of his past. Even though the punishment was served, the taint is not removed. This is similar to the concept of sins being covered. Under the Old Covenant, the sacrificial animal paid for the sin of man by its death. Its blood only covered the sin from the eyes of God. However, the sacrifice of the Messiah caused the sin to be removed by the power of His shed blood. Now, there is absolutely no remembrance of the sins of those who have obtained salvation through the Lord Jesus Christ. God will never hold our sins against us, and there is no more taint!

The Jews targeted our Lord out of pure jealousy and hatred. They knew their own intentions very well. They knew that He was the Son of

God (Matthew 21:33-46). On the other hand, Pontius Pilate and Herod also knew that our Lord was innocent of all the allegations levelled against Him and even declared His innocence. Right from the time of conception to His birth, His upbringing to the 3 and a half years of His earthly ministry, not one person could lay a finger on Him to harm Him. Such was the protection given to Him by the Father. The only time these wicked men got to touch Him was when His time came to be our substitute, and the Father allowed it because the Lord submitted to His will. This began at the Garden of Gethsemane. No sooner had He said 'Thy will be done,' that Judas Iscariot was right outside the garden with the armed goons to arrest Him.

Lord Jesus knew that the way to the Father, for all mankind, was only through His sacrifice on their behalf - ripping of His flesh and shedding of His blood. It is one thing to be forgiven. But at the same time, it's a totally different thing to be given divine help to repent and live an excellent life. This is what we who have believed in the Lord have received; forgiveness for all our sins and grace to live a God-centred life! After the last supper when everybody swore their loyalty and friendship to Him (Matthew 26:35), He took 3 of them with Him into the Garden of Gethsemane to pray along with Him. The least they could have done to keep their oath of loyalty was to have prayed with Him and for Him. He came back 3 times only to find them sleeping on all 3 occasions. They couldn't stay awake for even an hour to encourage the Lord. In the first place, they all never understood the seriousness of what was happening. This is the condition of every person who brags about accomplishing things in their own strength for God. They always fail. **One secret to having a successful relationship with God is to brag about His love and sacrifice for us and not vice versa.** We can't do the least if we are not empowered by His grace. There is no place for glorifying oneself.

Now, let us understand the magnitude of sin that He carried onto Himself when He submitted to the Father's will. It is the sins of every person, from birth to death, who are born into this world (beginning from Adam to the last person yet to be born). If we didn't have a Saviour, all of us would burn in hell for all eternity (eternity never ends). Added to this eternal measure of punishment are the consequences that we all see that are a part of the fall, which includes sickness, disease, pain, poverty, loneliness, depression, etc. All this was put on Him for about 18-20 hours. **When every measure of judgement of God was completely suffered by Him, He cried out saying, "IT IS FINISHED"!** In essence, there is no more judgement or punishment for sin from God remaining. **The only sin for which people will enter eternity in hell (after this redemption has been provided) is for the sin of rejecting salvation through Lord Jesus Christ (John 16:8-9).** Then He commended His Spirit into the hands of the Father and breathed His last. He is fully God and fully man. No one else could have provided like precious redemption as He did. The Father was right there with more than 12 legions of angels, standing by, ready to deliver Him if He asked for it. Yet the loving, obedient Lamb of God, our Lord Jesus Christ never backed off from establishing the way for mankind to the Father. He had the option to back off anytime, but never did (Hebrews 11:35). In the garden, I believe He prayed for grace even as He said, 'Thy will be done,' and an angel appeared to Him from heaven, strengthening Him (Luke 22:42-43); after all, the humans who swore their faithfulness to Him just moments before were fast asleep!

Hebrews 9:16, 17 says, 'for where there is a testament, there must also of necessity be the death of the testator. For the testament is in force after men are dead since it has no power at all while the testator lives.' Lord Jesus made the testament/New Covenant with all His disciples (us included) and then, to put it into effect, He submitted Himself to death on the cross. Hence, His covenant (declared by observing the Holy Communion) is perfectly effective in all our lives, and every time **we partake of it, as "often"** as we do, we remember His death on the cross and that we are already redeemed! It is a powerful declaration of His finished work and the victory He has won for us. It is a one-on-one covenant between the Father, Lord Jesus Christ, and us. No one else is given the right to intervene in this bond. Based on the revelation we receive and accept, **we get to define "often."** It can be once a year, once a month, once a week, or even every day! I pray that the Lord will enlighten you regarding this beautiful and powerful Covenant. I have found immense strength in observing this on a daily basis, declaring His finished work and the victory He has won for us!

Lord Jesus is the Beloved of the Father. There is not a chance that God would forsake Him anytime. Now that we understand the relevance of the New Covenant, it was we who were calling to the Father through Him - 'HE CRIED OUR CRY'. It was all our voices on the cross crying through Him. God would never abandon His Son. He was our representative on the cross! So one Man died and took the place of all mankind. He had no sin of His own. He paid the total price regardless of whether men accept it or not. But this salvation is effectual only in the lives of those who receive and confess His perfect sacrifice wholeheartedly.

What is the meaning of 'Why have You forsaken Me?' To understand this, we must understand the Holy and Just nature of God. God is Holy, Most Holy, thrice Holy! He is Just, very Just! Because of these 2 attributes of God, sin could not be swept under the carpet. It had to be dealt with, and it had to be punished. The only way this could be accomplished was by the shedding of sinless blood. There was no way Adam or his like could provide this blood because every person is born a sinner, even as a baby. David said 'In sin did my mother conceive me and I was brought forth in iniquity' (Psalm 51:5). This was our inheritance from Adam and Eve. However, the conception of Lord Jesus was totally different (the Word became flesh - fully divine), and He was birthed into this world through a virgin (fully human). Neither Joseph's sperm nor Mary's ova had any role to play in His conception. There was no transfer of blood or genetic material from Mary to Baby Jesus either. Very similar to the way God created Adam from the dust by His word, so was Lord Jesus conceived in Mary's womb by the same word! God Himself provided this requirement. Hence God was born in this world as a human - Lord Jesus Christ, the Son of the Living God. All our sins were carried onto His flesh (literal flesh), but His blood and Spirit were absolutely pure and hence it has the ability to cleanse every man who believes in Him from all sins. This is the cleansing tide for all humanity, and with this same blood, He entered the presence of the Father and sprinkled the heavenly tabernacle too. This was the ONLY WAY to make things right between God and man. This is the **WISDOM OF GOD!**

When our Lord requested that this cup pass away from Him, the Father could not oblige because there was no other way than this! The forsaking happened because sin had to be dealt with, and its power destroyed for all eternity. If only we all realised the awesomeness of this truth! We need to be ever grateful to God for accomplishing this redemption for us through our Lord.

Lord Jesus never addressed our Father God as God at any time except on the cross. He always called Him "My Father". The final desperate cry on the cross was the hopeless voice of sinful, suffering mankind verbalised through the mouth of our Lord. We should never forget, even for a moment, that Lord Jesus is 100% our representative on the cross, carrying 100% of our sins. He had no sin of His own. He was our substitute. So we cannot attribute any of His distress as being the result of an issue between Him and God. It was all our distress, hopelessness, and anguish.

Verse 2 mentions the words 'daytime' and 'night season'. Notice that both are singular. The sufferings of our Lord Jesus started in the Garden of Gethsemane as soon as He established the New Covenant with His disciples. Beginning at the garden (night season) to His crucifixion on the cross till 3 pm the next day (daytime), His assignment of being the propitiation for our sins was complete. During all this while, the Father and His angels were right with Him; but they could not change anything at that time as God's plan of redemption was underway through the wholehearted submission of our Lord. God, in His great mercy, condensed all the eternal damnation and punishments of mankind into one night and a day (18-20 hours), and our Lord bore the burden of it all.

6. BUT I AM A WORM, AND NO MAN; A REPROACH OF MEN, AND DESPISED BY THE PEOPLE.

7. ALL THOSE WHO SEE ME RIDICULE ME; THEY SHOOT OUT THE LIP, THEY SHAKE THEIR HEAD, SAYING,

8. "HE TRUSTED IN THE LORD, LET HIM RESCUE HIM; LET HIM DELIVER HIM, SINCE HE DELIGHTS IN HIM!"

The Psalmist and the prophet Isaiah elaborate on the sufferings of our Lord explicitly. They are very vivid and accurate in their description. The gospels confirm even the small details of their prophecies concerning the Messiah. The prophecies spoken by them run parallel and complement each other.

Our Lord was our substitute in all His sufferings, as explained above. He stood in the place that was rightfully and deservingly ours - the place of eternal wrath and judgement. Hence, every word spoken here concerns the state in which He hung on the cross, receiving our penalty.

Let me bring your attention to the word 'worm' here. This word in the Bible is almost always associated with destruction, decay, and hell. They are fragile, detestable, and dominate the area of putrefaction and decay - even hell! (Mark 9:44, 46, 48). Lord Jesus repeats a quote on worms 3 times in the same chapter, saying:

"Where their worm does not die,

And the fire is not quenched."

Even hell is not spared from these squirmy creatures. On account of our sins, Lord Jesus was reduced to this level of emotional agony on the cross. It was indeed the horrific punishment of hell itself that He suffered on the cross. It really interests me that a worm can indeed survive hell's fire. This needs some thought. The floggings, whippings with whips that had sharp pieces of metal and bone attached to their strings, the mocking, the ridiculing, the fatigue, the highest degree of physical, emotional, and mental pain - could never take Him down. Further on, the word says that every bone in His body was exposed to His sight, yet not one was broken. He hung on the cross as raw flesh and bones in the maximum measure of pain and humiliation possible. Still, He did not die under the effects of it all! I doubt if there is anyone who could have stayed alive having suffered even a tiny fraction of the agony He went through. It is humanly impossible. Yet in the midst of so great a suffering, Lord Jesus was alive as a worm in hell's fire. Only after He suffered/absorbed all the judgement and punishment from God, He committed His righteous Spirit into the hands of the Father and give up His life. The power to give up His life and take it back was vested in His hands (John 10:17, 18). Lord Jesus had received every grace from the Father to accomplish His calling.

He became the reproach of men and was despised by all the people because of their (the people's) poor understanding of the word and prophecies. People had watched Him do amazing miracles like none before. He was the express image of the Person of God. In His 3 and a half years of ministry, He demonstrated such excellence and miracles as no one had seen before. They had heard of great miracles being performed by prophets Moses, Elijah and Elisha, but nothing like this on a massive scale. They were so awed by His works and teachings that they forcefully tried to make Him king (John 6:15), but He withdrew, knowing what was in man (John 2:24); for some were convinced that He was the Messiah who was to come, while others followed Him for material gain. **It actually doesn't take long for the lips that flatter you to turn around and curse you!**

When they saw all the sufferings He went through, they did not understand, even for a moment, that it was mankind's burden of sin and judgement He carried. Rather, they thought God was angry with Him for blasphemy and due to that, He was going through the worst of all punishments (Isaiah 53:3-5). They were disappointed that having done so many wonders, He could not prevent this from happening. They were blind to His submissiveness to the Father's will. Even His disciples failed to understand this. Had they understood the prophecies, they probably would have stood by Him. People who despised Him from the beginning took advantage of this moment to make it worse for Him. The unbelieving Jewish lot had the audacity to outright reject Him and plot against Him all the time, despite knowing the scriptures and seeing the works being done before their eyes! Lord Jesus explained their stance very clearly in the parable of the vineyard and the wicked vine dressers in Luke 20:9-18. I fail to understand their deliberate rebellious behaviour, to have the nerve to outsmart God and try to get Him to back off! What were they even thinking?! That only shows how deeply absorbed they were in glorifying themselves all along. They would not allow even the Son of God to take away their glory and status! It speaks clearly about their attitude towards God and life. They had absolutely no intention to be the shepherds God had called them to be. No wonder He became a reproach; no wonder He was despised by arrogant men.

Today, most of Christendom fails to understand the gory nature of His death. There is no single word or even a sentence that can effectively sum up or describe His sufferings. This is largely because of the way ignorant people make cute crucifixes and paintings that depict a lean man, clothed with a garment on his waist, a halo around his head, wearing a crown of thorns, having his hands and feet nailed to the cross, and just 2 or 3 minor open bleeding wounds on his body. Most of the skin is intact, and he looks absolutely human. This bears absolutely no semblance to what David and Isaiah describe regarding His crucifixion. There is no difference between the knowledgeable Jews of those days and the hypocrites these days who have the privilege of having the entire written word of God in whatever dialect they wish and make such crucifixes. Man is ready to even go to the pit for money and take many with them too. Having seen such pictures in the early part of my life, I could never really fathom the reality of His sufferings. I got serious in studying God's word only in my late twenties. So when I heard sermons (thank God for preachers who preach the truth) and studied the prophetic scriptures in Isaiah 52, 53, and Psalm 22, the reality of it all slowly sank in. Let me list out some of the prophecies that would help dispel ignorance:

PROPHECIES REGARDING HIS PHYSICAL PAIN:

1. All My bones are out of joint (Psalm 22:14).
2. My tongue clings to My jaws (Psalm 22:15).
3. They pierced My hands and My feet (Psalm 22:16).
4. I can count all My bones; they look and stare at Me (Psalm 22:17).

5. His visage (appearance) was marred (impaired) more than any man (Isaiah 52:14).
6. And His form more than the sons of men (Isaiah 52:14).
7. He was wounded and crushed. Many stripes were on Him for our sakes (Isaiah 53:5).

PROPHECIES REGARDING HIS MENTAL/EMOTIONAL PAIN:

1. Being forsaken by God (as He was being judged in our place) and His own disciples - Psalm 22:1.
2. Being like a worm in hell's agony - Psalm 22:6.
3. A reproach of men and despised by the people - Psalm 22:6.
4. Being the target of all mockery - Psalm 22:7-8.
   - ✡ "All those who see Me ridicule Me."
   - ✡ "They shoot out the lip, they shake their head saying, 'He trusted in the Lord, let Him rescue Him; let Him deliver Him, since He delights in Him!'"
5. Many strong bulls surround Me and gape at Me with their mouths like a raging and roaring lion - Psalm 22:12-13.
6. I am poured out like water - Psalm 22:14.
7. My heart is like wax, it has melted within Me - Psalm 22:14.
8. My strength is dried up like a potsherd - Psalm 22:15.
9. Cry of distress for deliverance - Psalm 22:19-21.
10. He is despised and rejected by men - Isaiah 53:3.
11. A Man of sorrows and acquainted with grief - Isaiah 53:3.
12. And we hid, as it were, our faces from Him; He was despised and we did not esteem Him - Isaiah 53:3.
13. Yet we esteemed Him smitten by God and afflicted - Isaiah 53:4.
14. The Lord has laid on Him the iniquity of us all - Isaiah 53:6.

15. He was oppressed and He was afflicted, yet He opened not His mouth - Isaiah 53:7.
16. He was led as a lamb to the slaughter, and as a sheep before its shearers is silent, so He opened not His mouth - Isaiah 53:7.
17. They made His grave with the wicked, but with the rich at His death - Isaiah 53:9.
18. His soul laboured - Isaiah 53:11.
19. He poured out His soul unto death - Isaiah 53:12.
20. He was numbered with the transgressors - Isaiah 53:12.

This list is from only 3 passages in the scripture. There are plenty more!

Now let us review His life and His death. God, having spoken in the Garden of Eden and through His prophets, had announced well beforehand the coming of His Son, The Messiah, and all that He would accomplish. In order to make the people understand this better, He instituted sacrifices during the Old Covenant period, starting in Eden. At the fullness of time, Gabriel was sent to the virgin Mary with the proposal to bring forth the Son of God into the world. The moment she accepted the proposal, the Word became flesh in her womb. He moved the hearts of emperors for the sake of His prophecy and according to the prophetic word, the Lord Jesus was born in Bethlehem, in the land of Judah. They were put up in Judah for a minimum period of 2 years, after which they relocated to Egypt on God's direction. After the deaths of all those who sought to kill the baby Jesus, He was brought to Nazareth, where He grew up under subjection to His earthly parents and also must have worked as a carpenter along with His father Joseph. For all those 30 years, He was the most godly person, fulfilling every 'jot and tittle' of the law, keeping every single statute, ordinance, commandment, instruction, etc. He was sinless.

At the age of 30, He left home to begin His ministry and went to the river Jordan. He was water baptised by John the Baptist (His cousin). This defines water baptism very clearly. The Lord Jesus did not get baptised to wash away His sins because He was absolutely sinless. The meaning of water baptism is not to wash away sins. That is done by the blood of our Lord when we accept His salvation. **Baptism is the answer of a good conscience towards God (1 Peter 3:21).** John, who tried to prevent this, was told by the Lord Jesus Himself, "Permit it to be so now, for thus it is fitting for us to **fulfil all righteousness**". If the Lord Jesus Himself was water baptised (declaring to the world that His conscience was clear before God), we should not be judging whether it is necessary or not to be water baptised (as many do today and count it unnecessary). To fulfil all righteousness, He deemed it necessary to be water baptised, and we need to follow our Master. At this declaration, the Holy Spirit descended upon Him in the form of a dove and rested on Him. Following this, His earthly ministry began. Being empowered by the Holy Spirit, He was first led into the wilderness, where He had to overcome satan's deception and all the wild beasts (by the power of His word). He ate nothing for 40 days and 40 nights and still survived. Adam and Eve were given a garden loaded with the goodness of God, and yet they failed to trust Him over a cunning talking serpent. Here, Lord Jesus began His ministry in the wilderness, having fasted the whole time, in company with all the wild beasts and one persistently irritant pest called satan. Yet after 40 days, He emerged as the perfect victor.

After this, He went full throttle in the power of the Holy Spirit, emboldened by the strength of God, in all wisdom, knowledge, and understanding, portraying the glory of God and the express image of The Father to Israel and the surrounding regions every day for the next 3 and a half years. Apostle John said that if His work of those years of ministry were recorded in books, the world itself could not contain the books that would be written (John 21:25). So great are the number of His works and the goodness He has accomplished. Everything He did was to please the Father and help distressed mankind. Pleasing men was never on His agenda. This was one of the main reasons that incited the elite Jewish fraternity against Him. His works were all undeniably divine and done in their sight. Yet they sought to kill Him at every opportune moment in accordance with the prophecy spoken by Isaiah in chapter 53:1. They persisted in asking Him for a sign to prove Himself to them when all His miracles were glaring before their faces. But the Lord Jesus never obliged to their demand, not once. Having seen all His works, nothing was going to change the minds of these wicked men. They would not have believed Him even if He had pulled Himself together and come down from the cross towards them. At that point, these unbelievers would have thought that He was a sorcerer and would have even tried stoning Him. May we receive the gift to discern and stop wasting our time trying to prove ourselves to such people too.

Almost everybody thought it was the nails that held Him to the cross. But no! It was His heart of obedience to the Father's will and His unending love for us that kept Him there (Proverbs 8:30–31). After His resurrection, if He wanted, He could have just appeared in the temple in front of everyone to prove the truth. Even that would not have convinced the unbelievers, who were stubborn in their agenda and propaganda. He explained that very well in the story of Lazarus and the rich man (Luke 16:19–31) and in the hearing of the Pharisees. The bottom line was that these guys loved the world more than they loved God. Had they obeyed the voice of Moses and the other prophets, they would have exalted the Messiah, who was right before them.

For almost 400 years (after the last prophet, Malachi), there was no other prophet in Israel. After this period, John the Baptist arrived as prophesied (6 months prior to the birth of our Lord). He was endowed with the Holy Spirit in his mother's womb. He proclaimed boldly that he was sent to prepare the way of the Lord and that people should turn away from their sins. He attracted a huge crowd, and all those who repented were baptised by him in the River Jordan. Baptism was a prototype instituted by John the Baptist to denote that a person had confessed and repented of their sinful nature and acknowledged their need for a Saviour. It was probably a soul cleansing initiated by John, similar to the ritual body cleansing followed by the Jews in those days, called the "Mikveh". This prepared the baptised ones to receive the new Spirit, which the Lord would provide shortly. However, in 1 Corinthians 10 and 1 Peter 3, Paul and Peter talk about the counterpart of this baptism in relation to the Israelites passing through the Red Sea and about the flood at the time of Noah. John, having prepared the hearts of the people to receive Lord Christ, chose martyrdom after Lord Jesus began His ministry.

Lord Jesus came during this time, and as Isaiah says, "He grew up before God as a tender plant and as a root out of dry ground". He is 100% God and 100% Man. He came at the right time to proclaim the beginning of the acceptable year of the Lord, which is in effect even today for all those who would turn to Him for salvation. He brought hope to the hopeless and help to the helpless during the darkest times. It was the darkest time because the children of God who were called to a rich heritage were going about their lives in a worldly manner. It was all about food, clothes, shelter, selfish ambitions, etc., and not about accomplishing the will of God and bringing the world to the love of God. The elite group of Jews were busy getting all the name, fame, and honour while laying heavy religious burdens on the necks of the commoners. They had taken the privilege of interpreting the law on their own terms and made life hell for the rest. No wonder they wanted to get rid of our Lord, whose only intention was to make the heart of the Father known to His children. They made Him their perfect 'nemeses'.

Everything about the birth and the first 30 years of His life was seemingly ordinary in the sense that He had earthly parents, looked like any other human, was identified as the carpenter's son, was the oldest of a minimum of 6 kids, was a regular visitor to the temple and the synagogues, and probably worked along with His father Joseph in excellence. Yet this 'normalcy' became a hindrance to the people (in His hometown) who saw Him grow up. For all those who yearn to see the Lord Jesus in the flesh today, let me tell you that it is a far greater blessing to see Him in the word. God has spoken a greater blessing on those who have not seen Him in the flesh yet believe. People who lived seeing all His wonders could not accept the fact that He is God only because they saw His human appearance and vocation, which discouraged them and became a barrier to their belief. The latter part of Isaiah 53:1 says, 'He had no form or comeliness; and when we see Him, there is no beauty that we should desire Him'. I believe that though He may not have been the most handsome Person, He was the most elegant Being who walked the earth, with virtue radiating forth in His behaviour and mannerism. As a child, He grew up in wisdom, stature, and favour with God and men. The hearts of the elect are drawn to this loveliness.

When His time came to be crucified, the religious elite celebrated His sufferings and took advantage of the opportunity to mock and ridicule Him. For them, it was a victory they had longed for the past 3 and a half years. They could finally show the people that they were 'right' and our Lord was 'wrong', and hence God Himself had given Him this end. But the remarkable thing in all this is that none (neither Jews nor heathen) could even lay a finger on Him any time before this to harm Him. People who wanted to harm Him would spend days plotting to kill Him, and He would walk right past their plots. He had no fear of death and knew no one could touch Him until His time had come. Hence, He went about accomplishing the Father's will without any reservations. Persecution came His way many times through word of mouth. Yet none were able to harm Him physically. But when His time came to be crucified, these wicked men tore Him apart to the bones. They humiliated Him to the highest degree.

The Jews were not the only ones who were against Him. A whole lot of the non-Jews (Romans, Herodians, and Greeks) also awaited revenge on Him because their kingdoms were being destabilised by His works. The Romans never tolerated anyone who was a threat to their empire. They would mercilessly butcher them. But many among the heathen population were also turning to Him, and their faith amazed our Lord! I believe that He was the envy of the Jews, Romans, and Greeks. In Matthew 22:16, we see the herodians conspiring to arrest the Lord Jesus along with the Jews. To appease the Jews, Pilate had Him flogged. When they did not agree for His release, he delivered Him to be crucified, knowing very well that He was innocent.

Crucifixion was a package. First, the condemned person would be delivered to a centurion with his battalion of soldiers, who would conduct the proceedings as per their protocol. Firstly, the condemned person would be whipped (with 40 lashes) on his naked body. Then they would clothe him back, and he would have to carry the cross (usually the horizontal beam of wood) to the place of crucifixion (which was fixed). There he would be stripped of every cloth on his body (leaving him completely naked), his hands and feet would be nailed to the horizontal and vertical beams, and he would be hauled up. Death could occur anytime, from flogging (sudden death due to cardiac arrest) to even 4 days after being hung up. If the Romans decided to show mercy, they would break the legs of that person to speed up his death. Even their mercy was cruel! Men and women were subjected to this form of punishment. The Romans enjoyed conducting this manner of capital punishment on non-Romans. It was not common for them to crucify a Roman citizen unless he was convicted of high treason.

Our Lord had a double dose of whipping, owing to Pilate's false empathy. The event of this judgement even brought the 2 enemies, Pilate and Herod, into a good friendship. Herod happened to be in Jerusalem during this time, for the feast. Knowing that our Lord was from Galilee, Pilate sent our Lord to Herod to see if he could find something wrong with Him. Herod's ancestors tried to kill Lord Jesus when He was a baby! There was no way Herod had any empathy for our Lord. Arrows were directed towards our Lord from every direction.

Just reading about all this hypocrisy, betrayal, and all manner of wickedness condense on our Lord makes me feel sick. How much more the righteous soul of our Lord, our beloved Saviour, who bore all this even though 12 legions of angels stood by waiting for His word! All this, just to make 'The Way' for us to the Father! He never backed off from fulfilling the calling of God.

Asking for signs, these unbelievers were so blind that they overlooked the most undeniable signs displayed by creation that day. Midday became midnight from 12 p.m. to 3 p.m. Nobody in the history of the nation would have witnessed a total eclipse that long! When He gave up His Spirit, there was an earthquake, the veil in the temple tore into 2, the rocks were split, and the graves were opened. But all these signs caught the eyes of the Roman centurion who was put in charge of crucifying the Lord and all those with him, so much so that they feared greatly saying, 'Truly, this was the Son of God!' The unbelievers provoked even God the Father with their ridicule. Yet even if one of these repented at any time, our Lord made sure that salvation would be available to them when He prayed on the cross, saying, "Father forgive them, for they know not what they do". I believe that one such was Saul, later called Paul. Paul was in Jerusalem, being mentored by the famous Rabbi Gamaliel. There is no way anyone would have missed the show that day, especially not a pharisee like Saul. Would he have been one of those who ridiculed our Lord as He hung on the cross? Maybe! Was it worth our Lord praying to the Father and asking Him to forgive those who crucified Him? Of course! One of them just might have repented and written more than half of the New Testament, recording revelations that have blessed generations!

The unbelievers very well knew that God the Father had endorsed the Lord Jesus as His Beloved Son. All His works stood witness to that fact. God is indeed delighted in His Son. Following the ascension of our Lord, He continued to show Himself strong in the lives of His disciples, as we see in all the books that follow the gospels. Highly reputed Jewish Rabbis like Gamaliel warned their counterparts not to mess with the disciples of the Lord (Acts 5:35–39). To this day, God continues in His covenant with us and works through us.

9. BUT YOU ARE HE WHO TOOK ME OUT OF THE WOMB; YOU MADE ME TRUST WHILE ON MY MOTHER'S BREAST.

10. I WAS CAST UPON YOU FROM BIRTH. FROM MY MOTHER'S WOMB, YOU HAVE BEEN MY GOD.

The conception and birth of a baby into this world is nothing short of a miracle. God established this as a norm for every husband and wife. Indeed, this is one of the greatest gifts God has endowed mankind with from the very beginning. There are millions of these miracles happening in the world every day, and we need to stop and ponder this. Being a medical doctor, this was part of my academics, and I got to understand this process of conception and birthing very well. I doubt if I would have researched it otherwise.

Let me recapitulate this for you. After sexual intercourse, one out of the millions of sperms ejaculated by the male into the female genital tract, gains entry into the ova (egg cell) of the female. While there are millions of sperm in the ejaculate, there is only one mature ova released by the ovaries, alternatively, per menstrual cycle in the female. After sharing and combining their genetic material (DNA), they together form the zygote, which is a single cell containing the genetic material from both parents. After the exponential multiplication of cells within this zygote, an embryo is formed. At this stage, the precursor cells for every organ system of the body are established in 3 layers (ectoderm, endoderm, and mesoderm). From these 3 primary layers, further growth, differentiation, and maturation occur according to the signals issued from the DNA. Hence, every individual has a unique genetic makeup. The heart starts forming as early as 3 weeks of gestation and starts functioning in the early fourth week. A fully functional heart is picked up by ultrasound at 8 weeks and is an established sign of life. All the other organ systems develop according to the time ordained by our Creator, which is the same for all babies. A lifetime wouldn't suffice to appreciate everything accomplished by the wisdom of God! Not in a million years can man create something even close to this. The main programming for this miraculous process was done and finished in the first couple, Adam and Eve. Science has come so far to prove that these little humans in the uterus can hear and respond to sounds, feel our touch, and sense emotions as well. More research is underway every day to prove the excellence of God's wisdom.

This is followed by the phenomenon of birth. At the God-ordained time, the little one from within starts the journey to the outside world. The mother's body receives the commands necessary for the baby's safe exit and cooperates to birth the baby. Labour can range from a few minutes to 2 days. As the baby makes his way down, there is an awesome display of changes occurring in both the mother and the baby's body, with the appropriate hormones being poured into the blood stream from other organs like the pituitary and brain. The amniotic sac, which has held the baby so far, breaks open on time and helps in the smooth exit by lubricating the passage. Through a specific twisting and turning of the head, body, and legs, the little one comes out. Up until this point, the lungs of the child are not functional because the baby does not breathe inside the uterus. The exchange of gases takes place through the placenta. The first breath is taken when the baby is out. Due to the stretch of the lung tissue and the baby trying to take in as much air as possible to inflate it, the baby lets out 'the cry' that we all long to hear. At this point, the umbilical cord is tied and cut, and the baby is laid beside the mother for bonding after the routine resuscitation. Next, the placenta (the main path of nutrition and oxygenation from the mother to the baby) is delivered after it naturally separates from the uterine wall. There is never a mixing of blood between the mother and the baby in the womb.

For most, if not all, this intrauterine life cannot be recalled. We have hardly any memory of all this. But once the baby is out, he responds to the same stimuli he was exposed to while in-utero. This is proven scientifically. I don't think we can even remember many things from infancy or childhood. Frankly, at this stage, I don't think any baby would be seeking God; but not so with the Lord Jesus. He knew God the Father right from His conception. How can a child trust God on his mother's breast? I think mothers will be able to somewhat understand this feeling, having experienced their little ones cozying up physically and emotionally while being breastfed. I can personally attest that my children were not bothered by anything in the world when I breastfed them. They felt secure and satisfied in my arms! Even at this stage, our Lord had His trust in God as His All-in-all, and that had Him at the right place at the right time!

When we look at it in retrospect, we can understand that God does not force His will on anyone. He places the proposal before each of us. It gets carried forward only if we are willing to submit to Him. Similarly, Mary and Joseph were the only 2 people in the history of mankind who would have submitted to His will for the virgin birth of the Messiah. No wonder it took 4000 years from Adam to have the Word in the flesh. God blessed Mary and Joseph with abundant grace to accomplish this great work. I believe that Mary was a very modest teenager. She did not bother to rethink the proposal for the virgin birth, given the social stigma associated with it (more so then, compared to today). She did not even bother to discuss it with her fiancé, Joseph. I love that attitude! She believed that God would take care of all that, and she did not need to take things into her own hands. She made a beeline for the hill country of Judea and enjoyed boosting her faith with encouragement from Elizabeth, her relative, who was miraculously pregnant with baby John in her old age. Rightfully so, when she returned, God sent His angel to convince Joseph of the divinity of the Child that Mary carried. It is every engaged girl's dream to have an excellent married life without any unnecessary drama, insult, or disgrace. Yet Mary highly esteemed the Lord's proposal, readily said yes, and considered herself to be the most blessed. Now that's the perspective we believers should possess!

Since they continued staying in Nazareth for some time, how would they answer the relatives who saw Mary's abdomen bloating prematurely? What would they answer to people who would question the delivery of the baby within 6 months of marriage (considering that they got married as soon as she returned from Judea)? Would this have bothered them? All these questions would have bombarded most of us if God had placed the proposal before us, and most assuredly, we would have blocked God out. But this inspiring young couple belittled the insults and magnified God's purpose! God faithfully relocated the couple to Bethlehem shortly, saving them all the unnecessary criticism and getting them to deliver Baby Jesus there.

This passage reveals the truth about our status. Lord Jesus is the first fruit. If He had a relationship with God from His mother's womb, so do we. Though we were ignorant of this due to our dead spirit, which we inherited from Adam, God kept His part intact. He chose us and set us apart for His kingdom, even from our mother's womb! The same applies to our children. The prophet Jeremiah declares in chapter 1, verse 5, that God chose him even before he was formed in his mother's womb, and he was consecrated by God even before he was born. This is the doctrine of 'election.' Many of us seem to misunderstand this and get an image of God being partial. Having understood this by the Holy Spirit, let me put it forward to you.

God is omniscient - He knows everything from the beginning to eternity. He is the Alpha and the Omega. He is well aware of all the souls who will receive the truth of the gospel (Salvation) when it is put forward to them. Some would receive it immediately, while some would respond late. Yet He knows every soul. Out of the multitudes of people who existed before the flood, He knew that only Noah and his family would respond. Noah took 100 years to build the Ark. These 100 years of grace were provided for the unbelievers to repent and yet they did not. Among the multitudes of people who existed during the time of Abraham, God knew that only Abraham would respond by faith, while the rest were too busy getting deceived by satan. Hence, God elected Abraham. Likewise, Joseph, Moses, Joshua, Daniel, Esther, Ruth, Mary and Joseph, Peter, Paul, John, you, me,, and so on. He knew that we would respond to His call and fulfil it. The Bible labels these as 'The chosen' and 'the called according to His purpose' (Romans 8:28). We who have received His salvation are likewise His chosen.

Further on in verse 19-20, he says, "For whom He foreknew (the chosen), He also predestined to be conformed to the image of His Son, that He might be the First Born among many brethren. Moreover, whom He predestined, these He also called, whom He called, these He also justified, and whom He justified, these He also glorified." This is the doctrine of God's election. If you have received God's salvation or will receive it now, wholeheartedly, God knew that, and you are already onboard. It is not a surprise for God!

Not one person deserves anything good (including salvation) from God based on their merit. If the word 'deserved' has to be applied to us, it would by default mean 'deserving hell'. In fact, our sin qualifies us to receive the salvation of God. Hence, all of us, believers, are elected by grace that is made available through the salvation that is in the Lord Jesus Christ. This understanding of being elected by God even before we were formed in our mother's womb and being ordained even before we were born should bring us great joy and comfort. This is the fuel that should keep moving us in the path of righteousness, help us to enter into God's rest, and accomplish His will for our lives. He is our only hope for everything good.

11. BE NOT FAR FROM ME, FOR TROUBLE IS NEAR; FOR THERE IS NONE TO HELP.

12. MANY BULLS HAVE SURROUNDED ME; STRONG BULLS OF BASHAN HAVE ENCIRCLED ME.

13. THEY GAPE AT ME WITH THEIR MOUTHS, LIKE A RAGING AND ROARING LION.

The Lord Jesus was not an orphan. His mother was with Him even when He hung on the cross. On the contrary, nothing is heard of His father, Joseph, after Jesus was 12 years of age. He was mentioned last in the Passover feast celebrated in Jerusalem when our Lord was 12 years old. It may be possible that Joseph passed away sometime after that. After giving birth to their firstborn (Lord Jesus), Mary and Joseph went on to have a minimum of 6 more children (4 boys and at least 2 girls). Since our Lord was the oldest, I am sure that he would have stood up to the responsibility of helping His mother manage the home physically and financially. He probably would have carried on with His father's carpentry business, being excellent in His work and gaining the favour of men as well (Luke 2:52).

After His baptism, He totally committed Himself to the ministry. Multitudes followed Him. He chose 12 of them to always be with Him and called them His disciples (Apostles). A preacher whom I greatly respect and who deeply researches the word also said that all of His disciples were younger than Him (probably teenagers), and the oldest among them was Peter (probably in his early twenties). He very well knew the character of all His disciples because of His omniscience. He knew that Judas Iscariot was a thief who stole money from the money bag that he was put in charge of and would finally betray Him. Judas had 'Grace' living with him all the time and never bothered to take His help to rectify himself. Lord Jesus ministered to His family, His apostles, His other disciples, and multitudes of people who followed Him to show them the 'Love of God' and teach them the meaning of being associated with the One True Living God. Yet there was none who came to His help; no one was actually in any position to effectively help Him either.

The elite Jewish unbelievers, the Herodians, and the Romans stood stubbornly against Him always. They could never make peace with the truth about His divine Sonship. Keeping this fact aside, even none of His apostles or His family stood by Him when He was arrested. Peter, James, and John could hardly keep their eyes open after the Passover meal when He requested that they pray with Him in the garden. They were overcome by sleep and failed to do the least. Have you noticed how our flesh yearns to sleep when we want to spend time with God? But God gives us the grace to overcome this weakness if we are willing to receive it. Every one of His apostles promised Him their loyalty to death (Matthew 26:35), but they never kept their word. He went alone to the judgement, scourging, mocking, and to the cross to be crucified. All the men who swore allegiance ran away. But one point catches our attention in the gospels: the women who followed the Lord Jesus in His earthly ministry stood with Him, even on Mount Calvary! I believe that their physical presence there would have warmed the Lord's heart in some way, even though they were helplessly watching Him. Their hearty loyalty to the Son of God, in life and death, is well evident to the whole world today! They were the first ones to bring the news of the Lord's resurrection to the other disciples too! They showed their faith through their actions, not just empty words. They are an excellent example for us today. The only apostle who finally made it to the site of the crucifixion was John, the disciple who was conscious of the Lord's love for him. The rest who boasted of their love for the Lord absconded in fear! The unbelieving lot took absolute pleasure in tearing Him apart at every level, some very well knowing that He is the Son of God. These were the bulls—the strong bulls of Bashan—that encircled Him.

It is interesting to note the mention of Bashan here. Heshbon and Bashan were 2 cities east of the River Jordan that had 2 gigantic Amorite kings ruling them. These 2 lands were the land of the Amorites, and God had promised Abraham years ago that this land would be given to his descendants as a possession (Genesis 15:21). The land to the east of Jordan consisted of Edom, Moab, Ammon, Heshbon, and Bashan. But the Lord had strictly commanded the Israelites to keep away from Edom, Moab, and Ammon. To the west of Jordan were Canaan and Philistia. The entire stretch of land from the Nile to the great river Euphrates was promised to the descendants of Abraham by God (Genesis 15:18–21). As Israel ascended up from Edom, they requested the king of Heshbon (Sihon) to allow them to pass through his land, promising him that they would not put their hands on anything that belonged to him. Sihon did not oblige, but rather came for a battle against them and was defeated in this war. Everyone in Heshbon was put to death, including Sihon, and their land was taken as a possession. This land was later allotted to the tribes of Gad and Reuben by Moses. As they ascended further, Og, king of Bashan (a country with 60 fortified cities and many unwalled villages and towns), came against the Israelites for war at Edrei. God instructed Moses to fight him and that He would deliver him to them. Israel killed Og, his sons, and every person in Bashan until none was left.

Why did David mention Bashan here? Bashan was a land of giants. Satan got busy planting tares in and around the Promised Land, even before the time of Noah. The sons of God (the fallen angels) engaged in a polygamous relationship with the daughters of men, and their progeny were giants (Genesis 6:1–4). **There is one very important point we need to always remember.** Giants never came into being just like that. When a human (the daughters of men) consented and cooperated with satan's instrument (the fallen angels or sons of God), a giant was born. Women should have known better than to be sleeping around with demons! Today, people talk about many giant-sized problems in their lives, homes, countries, and the world. Did we even realise that humans ought to be blamed equally as much as satan and his instruments? We can be engaged in all types of prayers and fasting to rid the world of all giants, but as long as people gladly consent and cooperate with ungodliness, these giants will be around. Proverbs 6:27–28 says, "Can a man take fire to his bosom and his clothes not be burnt? Can one walk on hot coals and have his feet not be seared?" If today we are facing giants in our lives, homes, countries, and the world, we need to realise that there was a point where we humans consented and cooperated with satan and birthed these giants. And if these giants are to be tackled and destroyed, the first step is to declare the truth by preaching and accepting the gospel. The next step is for the people who are consenting and cooperating with satan to repent and renew their minds to the truth of the word of God. Following this, they need to take up their authority and boot out every satanic work from their lives. When this is accomplished in an individual's life, any giant can be tackled and destroyed with ease, no matter how big it may be. We cannot bring down giants if we start from the top and work our way down; it is impossible. We need to start at the bottom and work our way to the top. This is the way we tackle giants today.

In order to fight Goliath, God trained David first with the lions and bears. In order to lead the whole nation of Israel, God trained him to care for his father's sheep, followed by the 600 loyal men in the wilderness of Judah (when he faced Saul's threat). **David wholeheartedly practiced his anointing.** This gave him the upper hand to deal with Goliath with God-centred confidence. Towards the latter part of his life, he made sure to vanquish every living giant. To his credit, there is no more mention of giants after the last one was destroyed by his loyal men in 2 Samuel 21!

Even though the first lot of giants were destroyed in the flood, satan continued to adulterate the population on earth in the same manner after the flood in order to prevent the birth of the Messiah. Thanks to the massive cooperation he received from humans, the Promised Land was filled with these creatures. **Did it ever surprise you that there is no mention of giants in Babylon, Persia, Rome, or Greece? Why is that?** Because satan knew for sure that the Messiah would be born in this group of Israelites and not to some Babylonian, Persian, Roman, or Greek. These giants ('Nephilim') have been referred to as the Rephaim in Bashan, Anakim in Philistia and Canaan, Emim in Moab, and Zamzummim in Ammon. Goliath, Sihon, and Og belonged to this category.

Men of God like Moses, Joshua, Caleb, and David went after these giants boldly, fought against them, and destroyed them. In Deuteronomy 3:11, it is mentioned that Og slept on an iron bed which was 9x4 cubits (almost 13x6 feet), and he was the last of the Rephaim in that area. He was undoubtedly a seed of satan. But God gave a mighty victory for the Israelites there, and they killed him and all his people. Not one was left. Caleb voluntarily asked for Hebron, where the Anakim lived, and destroyed all of them, possessing the mountain as his inheritance at the age of 85. David took up 5 smooth stones from the brook in the valley of Elah when he went to face Goliath; and this wasn't because of insecurity. He knew that Goliath would go down with the first stone itself. He knew that Goliath had 4 more brothers who were giants (2 Samuel 21). This was no secret to the Israelites. So he stocked his sling bag with 4 extra stones just in case Goliath's brothers came out against him (David) when he (Goliath) fell. He never ceased until he killed the 4 brothers of Goliath after he became king. His mighty men killed all 4 later as recorded in 2 Samuel 21.

The mention of strong bulls of Bashan (referring to the unbelieving Jews) and their comparison to a raging and roaring lion gaping at Him with their mouths (again a reference to the seeds of satan as mentioned in 1 Peter 5:8) shows the dark forces at work in all the groups of unbelievers who ridiculed Him, despite the obvious signs, as He hung on the cross, nailed to it because of His love for us and also for the very people who ridiculed Him.

Lord Jesus is called the Lion of the tribe of Judah. He is the original. Satan loves to counterfeit and imitate Him at every level, every time. People who are unaware of this, fall prey to his deception. Proverbs 19:12 says that the king's wrath is like the roaring of a lion. This roar is what satan loves to impersonate (1 Peter 5:8) and make the children of God feel that God is persistently angry with them. This is the roar of condemnation that paralyses us. This deception takes place in the mind. This leads to more condemnation and going further astray. Condemnation has never helped mankind anytime, and no wonder satan uses it all the time. But conviction brings people to the love of the Father because it is the work of the Holy Spirit.

14. I AM POURED OUT LIKE WATER, AND ALL MY BONES ARE OUT OF JOINT. MY HEART IS LIKE WAX; IT HAS MELTED WITHIN ME.

15. *MY STRENGTH IS DRIED UP LIKE A POTSHERD, AND MY TONGUE CLINGS TO MY JAWS; YOU HAVE BROUGHT ME TO THE DUST OF DEATH.*

'WATER' is probably the most significant of all creation seen by its prominence in order and proportion when God created this universe. Rewinding to Genesis 1:1, we can understand that 'In the beginning, God **created** the heavens and the earth'. This means there was nothing before that in the whole universe. It was just empty space. Everything that exists today in the universe (earth, planets, sun, moon, stars, galaxies, etc.) was created by God in a phased manner, according to His wisdom. The word of God (the Holy Bible) given to us is tailor-made for those who inhabit the earth because we seriously won't be able to handle any knowledge more than that. In fact, it takes more than a lifetime to even understand the content given to us. From verse 2, we see God streamlining the details pertaining to this earth. In other places, as we read along, we also get an insight into the angelic realms, but it is by far limited compared to that about the earth. He is well able to give us information about the whole cosmos. But believe me, none of us will be able to wrap our brains around it.

For all the people who ridicule the word of God, I have one important thing to say: there is much more happening out there in the universe and in the unseen realms. Never judge the word spoken by God based on the things seen and the information that your tiny brain can handle. Knowing that none of us can handle even what is already given to us, He thought it best to keep the rest of the details aside and reveal them to those who gladly receive the truth.

Having stated that the universe was empty to start with, let us give a good applause to those guys who came up with the big-bang theory! They worked all their lives to prove Genesis 1:1. The only person they excluded from their theory was God. They did not want to give Him that credit. That's the mental makeup of advanced, intellectual human beings. Had they just believed what God had said, they could have used their time on earth fruitfully by being beneficial to others in many ways. The world speaks highly, applauds, and awards those who find it impossible to believe that there is a God and that He is good!

We must understand that much of history would have been passed down generations by word of mouth. Adam would have taught Seth, and so on. While passing this information, much would have also gotten lost. No one among the forefathers was actually bothered about literacy. Hence, we don't see Noah, Abraham, Isaac, Jacob, or any of his sons recording anything. Covenants were usually made by word of mouth and performing a sacrifice to seal them (blood covenant). They would eat and drink together when they made a covenant with each other regarding any matter. The spoken word was all, and the blood covenant was binding on both parties! These people valued their words highly, unlike today. For the benefit of humanity, God made sure that the next prophet, Moses, would get the best education and resources available at that time. And what place would be better than the Pharaoh's palace in Egypt? God has a purpose for everything. Amram and Jochebed (levites) hid baby Moses by faith and walked in the will of God. God honoured their faith, saved Moses from the slaughter commanded by Pharaoh, and made sure to get him into the palace as a prince! There is no match for the finger of God! Moses got the best education possible among all his Jewish brethren, and God used this to pass on information to succeeding generations—even to us!

In Genesis 1:2, God says that the earth was:

1. Without form (lacked shape and topography).
2. Was void (lacked inhabitants like people, animals, plants, etc.).
3. Was dark (lacked light).
4. Totally covered by water (lacked land).

Next, we see the wisdom of God creating light first among these 4 demands. However, the only matter that existed before that was water. There was water everywhere on earth. So water existed even before light. But God organised this water into compartments on the second and third days of creation. Water is a major component of every living being as well as the earth as a whole. Even primary school kids will be able to emphasise the importance of water. It is an essential component of life. The word symbolises water in a multifaceted manner. Apart from the fact that it is essential for life, the word emphasises its importance as a symbol for purification and also judgement. As far as the children of God are concerned, it is to purify them, but as far as the unbelievers are concerned, it is for judgement. It is a double-edged sword. During the time of Noah, all people, apart from Noah's family (a total of 8 members), were destroyed by the flood's water. Similarly, when the Egyptians attempted to cross the Red Sea, they all drowned. No one remained alive in both instances. Water was and still is the major component of purification for the Jews at the temple (for the priests) and at home.

In John 7, we read about the Jews celebrating the 'Feast of Tabernacles'. There were people at this feast who sought to harm our Lord. At this point, even the Lord's family members did not believe Him and ridiculed Him, daring Him to go up to the feast (to Jerusalem) to prove His calling. Having discerned the situation correctly, He went up to the feast in secret (not openly) because He was obedient to the law, which stated that all males should appear before God 3 times a year (Deuteronomy 16:16–17). This was the final feast of the year, the most grand among all, and a time of great joy and celebration. It was a harvest festival, and people set up temporary booths (tabernacles), symbolising the miraculous way God provided for, protected, and sheltered their forefathers in the wilderness and faithfully brought them into the Promised Land to enjoy the harvest there. They rejoice before the Lord, feasting and listening to the reading and teaching of the Torah. This was indeed a joyous festival.

An integral part of this festival was the final day, the 7th day, or the Great Day. Beginning from the first day of the feast, every day, the high priest would carry a golden pitcher (like a vase) and walk down with the other priests in a procession to the Pool of Siloam and fill the pitcher with water from the pool. This pool was an important source of water for the city of Jerusalem and was fed by a separate underground channel cut out from the Gihon Springs. Hence, it was considered pure and 'Life-Giving'. This pitcher containing 'Life-Giving' water was brought back to the temple in a grand procession. After they reached the temple, the priests circled the altar once every day from days 1-6 and poured this water on the altar. But on the seventh day, the priests encircled the altar 7 times while the great multitudes of people called on the Lord for salvation. It was believed that the measure of rain for the following year was sealed by God on this day. This water being poured out was very significant. On this same day, at the moment that the water was being poured out on the altar on the 7th day and the people were crying out for salvation, the Lord Jesus, who was teaching people in the temple, stood up and cried out, saying, '"If anyone thirsts, let him come to Me and drink. He who believes in Me, as the scripture has said, out of his heart will flow rivers of living water." This He said concerning the Holy Spirit. He is the source of living water. He said the same to the Samaritan women at the well (John 4:10, 14).

After the last supper, He washed the feet of His disciples with water. This incident has great significance. Sadly, some of them have converted this into a meaningless ritual in some churches today. Every Jew would come into their house and dine only after customarily washing their feet and hands. No one would miss this custom, especially while observing a feast like Passover. Hence, even though the disciples were prone to having dusty feet because they wore sandals and walked long distances, at the last supper, all of their legs were practically clean. Our Lord was not intending to clean the literal dust from their feet that day but was setting an example for His disciples regarding the principle of being His disciples. It symbolised the essence of 'servitude' and the importance of continual cleansing by the 'water of the word' that happens to us believers (Ephesians 5:26). Even though we desire to live a perfect life after being saved, we fail at times due to an unrenewed mind. Hence, this continual cleansing is a necessity and it is the work of the word. Hence, every time we fail, we are expected to go to the word of God and receive the cleansing of the word of God and the assurance that we can obtain mercy and find grace to help in times of need. This is the meaning of the answer the Lord Jesus gave to Peter when he asked Him to wash him from head to toe (John 13:10). That night, the Lord washed the feet of Judas Iscariot also; forgiveness was available to him also, but he did not receive it because condemnation in his own heart killed him. That is how damaging condemnation is.

Having elaborated on all this, we can come to the conclusion that water is for purification and salvation as far as His children are concerned. When the Lord Jesus died on the cross, He was being poured out for the salvation and purification of all mankind.

Did you know that the Lord Jesus was beaten unnecessarily an extra time before He was condemned to be crucified? I have already explained before that flogging was part of the protocol for crucifixion. But Pilate had Him flogged before he condemned Him, just to get Him off his hands. The Jews delivered the Lord Jesus to the Romans for the death penalty. But Pilate went in circles and had Him whipped with ghastly whips just to convince the Jews that adequate punishment had been served. The Jews were still not convinced, and finally, he gave the death penalty to Him. He never found Him guilty of anything wrong and even confessed this before the Jews, but to no avail. He compromised to obtain the favour of the people whom he governed.

David prophesied in Psalm 34:20, saying that "He guards all His bones; not one of them is broken". Likewise, not one of His bones was broken, and God did not allow the Romans to break His legs at any cost later either. The same was signified in the Passover lamb when the Lord commanded them not to break its bones (Exodus 12:46). There was no strength in His bones after all the scourging. I believe that with the way that He was handled that day, literally every joint in His body would have been dislocated. While I believe that this is possible, there is also another truth associated with it. That day, none of His disciples stood by Him. Everyone deserted Him. Ephesians 5:30 says, 'We are members of His body, of His flesh, and of His bones'. Every one of us has a part to play in the Body of the Lord Jesus Christ. We are the church. We are joined together at the 'Joints', very similar to the human body. That night, every disciple ran away, literally dislocating the Body of Christ. All the physical and emotional agony could not kill Him. The power to give up His life was in His hands. He waited for the ordained moment until the judgement from God was completed.

When He had suffered it all, He cried out, **'IT IS FINISHED'** and gave up His Spirit into the hands of the Father and died. Before the day ended, the Jews requested to break the legs of all the people who were crucified that day. But by the time the soldiers came to our Lord, He was already dead, and hence they did not break His legs (John 19:31–33). This was a deliberate attempt by the Jews to break the connection between our Lord and the prophecy concerning the Messiah. God made sure to foil their plans! Bones play a very important part in Jewish beliefs. I will explain the significance of this later on. It is an interesting study if you undertake it.

The Lord Jesus displayed an excellent spirit through His practical way of living. He was meek and compassionate, yet bold and firm. He demonstrated a perfect balance in character and set the perfect example for us. Nobody could fool Him, not even His disciples. He never bothered to please men or depend on their opinion at any time. If people close to Him got offended, He did not try to pacify them or explain Himself. He was so rooted in the truth and God's call on His life that numbers never mattered to Him. That is why He chose only 12 to be with Him always. This bold person softened His heart and humbled Himself all because of His love for us, so much so that He never used the 12 legions of angels who were on standby to fight on His behalf. That is the depth of His love for us!

The God of ultimate strength and power, who holds the entire universe in His hands, had no strength that day after all that He suffered. A piece of potsherd (broken pottery made of clay that has dried) is indeed dry and lacks moisture. That is the reason it breaks easily. Every bit of life was drawn out of Him so that we do not have to live dry and depressed lives today. That is how dry He was at the cross! Apart from all this, there was the physical pain that caused muscle spasms all over His body; this made His tongue cling to His jaw. Everything He owned, He laid it down that day! The God who lives forever had to taste death on our behalf that day!

16. FOR DOGS HAVE SURROUNDED ME; THE CONGREGATION OF THE WICKED HAS ENCLOSED ME. THEY PIERCED MY HANDS AND MY FEET.

The Jews have referred to gentiles as dogs from times past. Before we label them as racists for doing so, let us go back to creation and learn some things. All animals were created by God. Every species was created with the primary intent of glorifying God. At creation, every animal was a herbivore; all lived in harmony. After the fall, the status changed. Did you know that before satan got to Adam and Eve, he first managed to deceive the animal kingdom? Or else, how did he approach Eve in the body of a serpent? Hence, the first prey to satan's deception was an animal—the serpent—who was awarded the first curse by God. To date, they are one of the most despised creatures in the world. When Adam and Eve shook hands with the serpent, death set in in every cell of humans, animals, and plants. Creation took the route downhill, corruption dominated, and the countdown to the destruction of the earth began in the Garden of Eden. But because of the love God had for us, He made sure to make a way through the Lord Jesus Christ for those who believe in His goodness to spend eternity with Him. After this fall, animals changed from herbivores to carnivores, and mankind joined in. Even the plants were not spared. Various types of insectivorous plants exist even today. The world's peace was wrecked by the deceiver.

Similar to the way God has set aside His chosen, He has also set aside some animal and plant species, e.g., cows, oxen, bulls, sheep, goats, pigeons, turtle doves, grains, fruits, etc., as relatively clean. These are all remnants set apart to glorify Him. The animals and items mentioned above were used in offering sacrifices to God under the Old Testament law. Among all the animals, these remained very close to the way they were created, while the others defected to preying on other animals (usually weaker than them) and made blood an essential part of their meals. Their appetite ranged from flesh to blood to all manner of filth (putrefying animals and their carcasses). We can very well see today that even dogs belong to this category. The ones we rear as pets in our home are probably better-mannered than the stray ones roaming the streets. I have a pet beagle, and I love him. We brought him home as a little pup. In spite of all the training and teaching, he reverts to his 'dog nature' at times, and it disgusts me. Dog lovers may dismiss this as normal. But it is still disgusting and detestable. We give him good-quality food and clean water adequately as per his requirements, and still he defects at times! At the end of the day, that is who he is. No matter how much we can train him, he cannot be like a human. The nature inside him cannot be totally changed but can be controlled by training. The reason this is dismissed as normal is that 100% of the dogs show this behaviour. That only proves that they have all fallen. I have witnessed worse things done by stray dogs in my locality, and I certainly cannot label that as normal.

None of the Jews had dogs as pets in those days because they were classified as unclean (non-Kocher). They were not included in the list of clean (Kocher) animals. In the Bible, dogs are known to have eaten humans (2 Kings 9:35–37) and licked blood (1 Kings 22:38). They survive on their fallen natural instincts, which people today describe as normal. This is the reason why the heathen in those days (who lived according to their fallen natural instincts) were referred to as dogs. This was the title for the Gentiles. The Jews were kept in check by the law partially because they were commanded to keep away from all unclean things. God's standard for a moral life was handed down to the Jews through Moses because God had set them apart from the world. He showed them who man was created to be. However, the main intent of the law was to teach them that they could never depend on their flesh to be righteous before God because their flesh had already been corrupted. The law was given to make them realise the need for a Saviour, in line with the prophecies being spoken from the beginning.

The majority of the Gentiles were driven by their flesh rather than their inbuilt conscience given by God (Romans 1:19–20). Hence, they were considered to be nothing less than dogs. Immorality, adultery, self-centredness, wickedness, etc. was the rule of the day for these Gentiles and were more rampant than they are today. People murdered their own children by sacrificing them to idols! Thank God we live in better times where such abominations are punishable under law. Sadly, Israel also fell into these abominations after they occupied the Promised Land and suffered much because of their disobedience to God's commands.

Here, the Romans are referred to as dogs. These guys were stone-hearted, ruthless, immoral power-mongers who would do anything to stay on top. They were not ruled by their innate conscience. Their lives consisted of money, power, and pleasure. Finally, their era also came to an end, just as God had prophesied through Daniel. The remarkable point is that, even though they were in authority at that time, they could not lay a finger on Him until the Jews delivered Him to them. That was when the power of the dog was unleashed. How much more accurate can a prophecy get and the Jews not notice it?

17. I CAN COUNT ALL MY BONES. THEY LOOK AND STARE AT ME.

This is perfect evidence of the fact that not a single strip of skin was intact on His body by the time the Romans were done with Him. On the cross, His flesh and bones were exposed, and it portrayed us - the Church, since we are members of His flesh and bones (Ephesians 5:30). The skin is the most sensitive organ in our body. It has millions of pain receptors. Just imagine the skin being entirely ripped off from all the flogging! That is absolute pain! Even though all this was exposed, God made sure that none of His bones were broken. We are not meant to be living broken, depressing, oppressed lives. We are constantly expected to look up at Him just the way His bones stared at Him. This is what we practice by partaking of the Holy Communion.

18. THEY DIVIDE MY GARMENTS AMONG THEM, AND FOR MY CLOTHING THEY CAST LOTS.

The prophecy concerning the division of the Lord's garments and casting of lots for His robe during His crucifixion is accurate to the dot! This was fulfilled before the eyes of all the people there that day. I could not understand why the people were fighting over the Lord's clothes. In order to understand this better, I researched on capital punishments practiced so far, all over the world. In addition to that, I also researched on Jewish clothing in those days. Most of us wouldn't bother to go into the details of the crucifixion to understand His love for us. God draws us by His love into salvation. That would be more than enough for most of us to receive Him as our saviour. Most of us would be satisfied with just knowing that One Person cared enough to save us from the pit of hell and give us a wonderful life here on earth. This was my case, too. But ever since the Lord taught me to study His word rather than just casually read it, He has led me into profound truth, which has edified me massively and given me a fruitful perspective of life.

The research into capital punishments was very distressing, and it made me thank God that I live in better times. Man's heart has to be really cruel and beyond hope to even come up with the manner of punishments practiced by certain civilisations. The extent to which mankind has fallen is evident when we do the research into capital punishments, and I suggest that each of you go online and research it for yourselves since it is beyond the scope of this book. The Jewish law allowed capital punishment in 4 ways: stoning, burning, strangulation, and beheading. While the first 3 were restricted to condemned criminals, the last one was exclusive for non-Jews, especially Canaanites. Many times, the Israelites disobeyed God's standard of judgement and portrayed themselves as more merciful than God. As a result, they always ended up paying a costly price. Let me assure you of that. These capital punishments were the most humane among all the others in those days. It still surprises me that, in spite of the ghastly punishments practiced from age to age, man's heart could not be tamed enough to keep them away from evil! Even the law could not tackle sin. But both have been able to leash wickedness and sin to some extent. As compared to ages past, capital punishments practiced today are way more humane.

Here, I would like to restrict myself to elaborating on crucifixion. These are a few salient features:

- ✡ It was one of the main capital punishments practiced by the Romans.
- ✡ They learned this art from the Assyrians and the Babylonians and perfected it.

- ✡ This verdict was usually issued to non-Romans and some exceptional Romans who were convicted of high treason.
- ✡ Both men and women could be crucified.
- ✡ It would be conducted by a centurion and the soldiers under him.
- ✡ It involved maximum torture, a public display of their cruelty, and utmost humiliation.
- ✡ It was carried out in public view as an example to the rest of the population to keep away from disobeying them.
- ✡ The number of people crucified at a point in time would range from 1 to even 6,000. When the number was higher, the centurions and soldiers deployed for the same would also be higher.
- ✡ The first step in crucifixion would be to scourge the condemned person after stripping off his clothes. The person's hands would be tied above his head or to a post, and the entire back would be whipped with cords that had pieces of sharp metal, bones, and stones attached to their prongs. This would latch onto the skin and literally tear it apart to reveal the flesh and bones beneath. Some people would die of sudden cardiac arrest at this stage itself. The number of lashes would usually be 40. Then they would put his clothes back on him and make him carry the cross (usually the horizontal bar) and walk to the place outside (but close to) the city, meant for crucifixion.
- ✡ At the ordained site, the condemned would be totally stripped (absolute humiliation) and his wrists and feet nailed to the wood using 4-6-inch nails (usually rusted).
- ✡ Death could occur anytime from the time of scourging to even 4 days after crucifixion due to sudden cardiac arrest, asphyxia, and septic shock. If the centurion or the soldiers decided to show some mercy, they would break the legs of the person to speed up death.
- ✡ After the person died, if family members, relatives, or friends wanted to bury the body with their formalities, they had to approach a Roman judge and get permission to do so. If unclaimed,

the body would just hang on the cross as food for the birds and beasts.

- ✡ After the person was crucified, it was common practice for the Roman soldiers to share the items of the condemned (like clothes, sandals, etc.). This is very similar to the corrupt police officers these days who try to gain whatever they can from vulnerable people. These were either retained for their personal use, sold, or kept as souvenirs to display the number of people they had crucified. It probably worked out for their promotion!

John 19:23-25 confirms the fulfilment of this prophecy given in the Psalms. John records it in detail as compared to the other Gospels. He says, "Then the soldiers, when they had crucified Jesus, took His garments and made 4 parts, to each soldier a part, and also the tunic. Now the tunic was without seam, woven from the top in one piece. They said, therefore, among themselves, 'Let us not tear it, but cast lots for it, whose it shall be,' that the Scriptures might be fulfilled which say: 'They divided My garments among them, and for My clothing, they cast lots.' Therefore the soldiers did these things."

Based on Apostle John's account, I did some research on the manner of Jewish clothing in the days of our Lord. The minimum clothing of a Jewish man consisted of 3 essential items - a tunic (inner garment), a shawl or cloak over it (the shawl had tassels hanging from the 4 corners), and sandals (wooden sole with leather straps or entirely made of leather). Along with this, they would usually wear a sash or a belt at the waist and a head covering. Frontlets and phylacteries were texts from the Torah that were written and rolled up and worn using bands around the forehead and arm.

The tunic was their innermost garment, mostly made of linen, having long sleeves and reaching a little below the knees (ankle length for women). If found only in this piece of clothing, a Jewish man would be considered naked. However, fishermen would usually work wearing only this. Total nakedness (absolutely no clothing) in public was considered an abomination. In the least, a Jew had to wear a tunic. Over this tunic, a cloak or shawl would be worn that covered the shoulders and back, being open in the front. The tassels at the edges were a reminder of the commandments of the Lord. The cloak could either be sleeveless or may have sleeves. This served many purposes. The length varied according to the socio-economic status of the person; the rich ones wore a longer cloak/shawl. The tunic and outer garment would be held together at the waist by a belt for the sake of convenience.

When we consider the Lord's garment, we can understand that it must have been totally drenched with blood, at least the tunic. The interesting point to be noted here is that the tunic the Lord wore was seamless. The Romans, who were a greedy lot, thought it was better that they cast lots and one person takes the whole thing. Why would they think like that if His tunic was not expensive? The bloodstain was not an issue; it could be washed off later. This in itself speaks volumes, and John took special care to notice and record it. The blood-soaked tunic went to one soldier, and I am sure when we get to heaven, we will be hearing how that tunic would have forever changed that soldier's life! John clearly mentions that His garment (outer clothing) was divided into 4 parts, and each soldier took one (meaning, it was probably torn into 4 parts and divided). So we can conclude that there were 4 soldiers in charge of our Lord that day.

Very contrary to the belief that Lord Jesus lived like a beggar on the street, I would love to impart the revelation God gave me through the study of the word. I really believe that this needs to be said. People in the days of our Lord had various occupations - fishing, agriculture, shepherding, carpentry, merchants, etc. This is similar to being a doctor or engineer or banker, etc., these days. Carpentry has been an industry right from the start. All occupations were respectable, and the occupants were respected. We cannot judge their socio-economic status based on the modern-day standard. I believe that our Lord was excellent in His work when He worked with His father in the carpentry shop. His excellence would have made their carpentry business do very well. He worked with the same material that would be used to crucify Him one day. Does that speak to your heart? Why was He not born into a shepherd's or a farmer's family? After all, David was a shepherd, and He came from that lineage. Why was

He not born in a Levite family? Moses was a Levite and prophesied that One like him would come in the future, and everyone had to obey Him (Deut 18)? Every word in the Bible is significant and written for a reason. Don't you think that the wood in the workshop would have constantly reminded Him about His calling? Definitely!

If we want to understand the times during the birth of our Lord and the circumstances He was born in, we need to go back and understand the world in those days. It is indeed regrettable that the birth of Lord Jesus Christ has been masked by so much tradition and legend about Christmas that it is hard to let the Bible speak for itself. Let me show you how. Mary and Joseph came to Judea for the census much before the birth of the Lord. **When they were there, Mary's days were fulfilled for her to be delivered (Luke 2:6).** This is contrary to what is portrayed in most videos showing Mary and Joseph reaching Bethlehem when she was in active labour, in so much pain; and directly being rejected by all the innkeepers, they resorted to a stable for their stay!

The census was a time of massive relocation. There were thousands of people who had to move from city to city to get their names registered, and it was not an overnight deal. Unfortunately, they lacked the technology we have now (like computers) to store information from the previous census. Everything was recorded by hand, and in order to get them all registered, it would have taken days to even months or a couple of years. During all this while, they had to lodge wherever they could get space. Their inns (rather guest rooms in relatives' houses) were no comparison to our modern-day hotels and lodges. They were just houses that were extended to accommodate a certain extra number of people (virtue of hospitality was a norm of the Jews). They were served food from a common kitchen, and it is possible that the rooms could have been like dorms where many people occupied one room and shared it. Those who had relatives may have stayed with them.

While staying there, since Mary went into labour, it would have been easier for the couple to move out to a private place rather than all the other occupants vacating the room for them. Most if not all the people, owned animals in those days. They were used as the most common mode of transport, apart from being used for animal husbandry. Therefore, similar to having garages for parking cars (like us), they had a stable to house them in. Being the only available private space during a chaotic time, Mary and Joseph would have shifted there for privacy. According to historical accounts, the stables in houses in those days were maintained very neatly by regular cleaning. The word does not say that Mary and Joseph "could not afford an inn." It clearly says that there was **"no space for them at the inn"** (Luke 2:7). If we compare those days' conditions with the present-day luxuries for childbirth, we will end up believing the worst-case scenario.

After a safe delivery, Mary wrapped the little Baby Jesus in swaddling clothes (a usual practice of those days) and laid Him in a manger (the only comfortable bed available for the Baby). When I gave birth to my children, it was usual for us to bathe them, feed them, and put them in a safe place like on a bed or a cradle. This is exactly what Mary and Joseph did. But this particular event had greater importance and was a **sign for the shepherds** to whom the Angels revealed the birth of the Lord. What are the odds of finding a newborn child that same night, wrapped in swaddling clothes and lying in a manger, in a bustling city? Probably one in a million! The shepherds were given the privilege to share the joy of the birth of the Lord; not the Pharisees or King Herod or the Roman Emperor. The Lord loves 'hanging out' with commoners. If you are no one important, it is absolutely fine; the Lord takes much pleasure in giving you company! He even said He is the Good Shepherd, and He wanted the shepherds to share in the joy of the Saviour's birth. These shepherds were 'watching over their flocks by night.' The Lord wants His shepherds (Pastors, preachers, teachers, etc.) to watch over His flock (the Church) at all times (Matthew 24: 45-51); especially at night because they are more vulnerable to the predators in the open fields, outside the city.

For a period of almost 2 years, the family of our Lord stayed in Bethlehem of Judea. How do I say this, you may ask? Remember the wise men from the east? These men (non-Jews) were astronomers from the land of Persia. They studied the stars. We all know now that stars don't move. These people knew that fact well. A moving star caught their attention, and they knew it was the star of the King of the Jews! God led them to follow the star, and they came over with many presents to honour and worship this new King. They travelled thousands of miles and came to Jerusalem. Instead of continuing to trust the star to lead them to the exact location where the Baby was, they preferred to ask Herod. Now, why would Herod like it if someone was born to replace him? So, he inquired with the wise men regarding the 'time' of the appearance of the star. This was very significant for him to specify the cut-off age of the babies to be put to death. Then he confirmed the matter with his 'wise men'. Having obtained the necessary information, and being very angry that the wise men did not come back to him to reveal the location of the Child, he got into action to annihilate all male children less than 2 years of age (Matthew 2:16). It's not that he randomly picked the number 2 just because it was his favourite! He calculated the approximate age of the Baby with all the information provided to him. Hence we can confidently say that Baby Jesus was about 2 years old when the wise men came. And yes, the number of the wise men who visited Him is also not given in the Bible. The number 3 came into the picture because of the 3 gifts that are mentioned. The reason that these 3 gifts are mentioned is not to give the number of the magi; but rather to denote something important. Gold declared His royalty; frankincense portrayed His Priesthood, and Myrrh denoted the bitterness He had to go through for the salvation of the nations! All 3 were expensive gifts! This is an excellent example of how the Father provided for the Lord.

Shortly after the wise men departed by another route, Joseph was warned by God to leave for Egypt with the mother and Baby, that same night; and he did. After Herod and all those who sought to harm Him had died, God brought them to Nazareth where He grew up being submissive to His parents.

The most common reason people think that Lord Jesus was very poor and destitute is because of Luke 2:24 (the customary offering for cleansing after birthing a child), 2 Corinthians 8:9 (though the Lord was rich, yet for our sakes He became poor), and Luke 9:58 / Matthew 8:20 (foxes have holes and the birds of the air have nests, but the Son of Man has nowhere to lay His head). Having understood the meaning of these passages by His guidance, let me place it before you in a proper sequence:

- ✡ **2 Corinthians 8:9 - "For you know the grace of our Lord Jesus Christ that though He was rich, yet for your sakes He became poor, that you through His poverty might become rich."** One essential point we have to remember when we study the word of God is to read it in its context. The entire chapter 8 deals with the 'grace of giving,' the best example being our Lord Jesus Christ. Paul intends to emphasise the priceless nature of the Lord's sacrificial giving of Himself here. He begins by appreciating the people of Macedonia who abounded in this grace despite their great trial of affliction. These Macedonians were persecuted for their faith in the Lord. This persecution was welcomed by them, and the abundance of their joy, coupled with their deep poverty, made them richly liberal. If someone was in deep poverty, what could they give? This is a logical question. Paul goes on to further say that they gave what they were able and even beyond their ability (verse 3). We would describe deep poverty as lacking essentials. Then how did they give beyond their ability? The Lord has always encouraged us to give what we can; not borrow in order to give. Paul calls this attitude of giving as Grace. This is very true. None of us would budge from the smallest measure of our wealth if it were not for the grace of God that helps us to give. David worded this beautifully in 1 Chronicles 29:14.

  Now, let us understand what Paul meant by saying this. He says that the Lord Jesus was rich. When and where was He rich? Was it before or after He came to earth? The answer is evident. It was before His birth and after His resurrection. He owned the universe and still does. The only moment of poverty was when He stepped into the earth in the flesh. A song that I love and listen to often elaborates on this point very clearly. It says the 'Lord came running' from heaven with mercy in His eyes and stepped down from a throne of endless glory to a cradle in the 'dirt.' He was restricted in every aspect when He was birthed into this world. **The very fact that He left His heavenly throne and came to the earth made Him poor.** This is the poverty that Paul has attributed to our Lord. I hope you are getting this. Out of a wrong understanding, people literally equate His life here to that of a beggar on the streets. That is not true! Lord Jesus was always provided for by the Father, and He provided for those who followed Him. He wasn't a millionaire, but He certainly was not a beggar! **He had enough and more to bless others.**

The Macedonians also displayed this same sacrifice. Even though they could have escaped the persecution, they chose to go through it for the Lord's sake and at the same time continued to be a blessing to others. If they had 2 garments and gave away one to help someone else, then that would be considered very good giving. But if they gave away both, it would be something done beyond their ability! This involves an extreme degree of sacrifice and dying to our flesh. This is also very well understood by the story of Nehemiah (in chapter 5 of the book of Nehemiah) who gave up his rightful demand on the governor's provision because the bondage on his people was huge. The King of kings and Lord of lords stepped down to earth for us. This in itself made Him poor.

✡ **Luke 2:24 - "and to offer a sacrifice according to what is said in the law of the Lord, 'A pair of turtle doves or 2 young pigeon'".** This passage that Luke has quoted is from Leviticus chapter 12. When a woman gave birth to a child, she would be considered unclean for 7 days for a male child and 14 days for a female child. On the 8th day, the male child had to be circumcised. There is no requirement for any sacrifices or offerings to be made at this point. There was no specific procedure to be followed for a female child. The lady would have to continue in the blood of her purification for 33 days for a male child and 66 days for a female child. Her days of purification would end on day 40 (7 days + 33 days) for a male child and day 80 (14 days + 66 days) for a female child. The first 7 or 14-day period would be the time when the woman would be totally unclean, and everything that she would touch would be unclean. In the later 33 or 66 days, she was relatively clean, but she was not allowed to touch any hallowed thing or go into the sanctuary. I basically see this period of uncleanness as God's plan of much needed post partum rest for the mother.

After this stipulated time of 40 or 80 days, she had to bring a lamb of the first year and a pigeon/ turtledove OR 2 pigeons/ turtle doves if she could not bring a lamb. This offering was to be made on her behalf to testify that she is pure from then on. Luke says that they went to Jerusalem to present the child to the Lord and, along with that, to offer a sacrifice for Mary's purification. Luke merely quotes this law from the book of Leviticus but does not say that that is what they offered. Even if we assume that Mary did not offer a lamb but limited herself to offering the birds, it could have been because they had to travel from Bethlehem to Jerusalem with the Baby and buy a lamb at exorbitant prices from the crooks who traded in the temple premises. We need to remember that they were in Bethlehem for the census when all this happened, and a prolonged stay would have made them offer something that they could afford at that time with the finances they had.

✡ **Luke 9:58 / Matthew 8:20: And Jesus said to Him, "Foxes have holes, and birds of the air have nests, but the Son of Man has nowhere to lay His head."** If we read this verse in context in the 2 gospels where it has been recorded, we can well understand what the Lord is saying. A scribe (v19) happened to tell the Lord that he will follow Him wherever He goes. Most scribes were opposed to our Lord and they partnered with the chief priests and Pharisees in plotting to kill the Lord. Most of these individuals were wolves in sheep's clothing. They always wanted to show off their self-righteousness and pretence holiness. The Lord knew them very well. These scribes would look for a secure and insured life with all comforts guaranteed. Lord Jesus answered right to the point to him. In Luke's account, we get to know why He answered this way. Luke says, that His time had come to be received up (v51), and hence He set His face steadfastly to go to Jerusalem. He was very eager to preach the gospel to as many people as possible, and hence He sent out messengers before Him. He was travelling from Galilee to Jerusalem. However, a village of the Samaritans did not receive Him. Further on the way, this scribe asked Him this question. The Lord's reply was basically a question back to the scribe if he was willing to go all the way without any material security. He did not prevent the scribe from following Him, though.

With this clarification and the evidence written in the Word, I believe that God took excellent care of His Son and provided for Him sufficiently when He lived on earth. Though many intended to harm Him before His time, God the Father did not allow it. Our Lord Himself said, 'if your heavenly Father feeds the birds of the air and clothes the lilies in the field so excellently, why wouldn't He take care of us, His beloved creation?' He practiced what He preached, and the Father bore witness by providing everything He needed. I bet He never wasted a moment worrying about provision at any time.

19. *BUT YOU, O LORD, DO NOT BE FAR FROM ME; O MY STRENGTH, HASTEN TO HELP ME!*

20. *DELIVER ME FROM THE SWORD, MY PRECIOUS LIFE FROM THE POWER OF THE DOG.*

21. *SAVE ME FROM THE LION'S MOUTH AND FROM THE HORNS OF THE WILD OXEN. YOU HAVE ANSWERED ME.*

Lord Jesus was God in the flesh. He felt pain, shame, exhaustion, reproach, betrayal, loneliness, etc., through all that He suffered, beginning from the Garden of Gethsemane. His Spirit was and is always spotless. The sin of mankind that He carried could never penetrate His righteous Spirit. Our sins were condemned in His flesh (body and soul). He always openly acknowledged that it was the Father at work within Him, and He did not do anything on His own; God was His strength. When His time came to be crucified for the sake of our salvation, He submitted to the Father's will, refused the help of more than 12 legions of angels who stood by, and hence God stood back until the work of redemption was done. But He accomplished all this with the grace and strength provided to Him by the Father.

Lord Jesus is the perfect embodiment of grace. Grace is the Person of our Lord Jesus Christ. He is the source of grace to all those who believe in Him. This grace enables us to do the difficult and the impossible. His earthly ministry is the perfect example of the heights we can reach when we are empowered by His grace for the benefit of the kingdom.

The painful ordeal that the Lord suffered lasted for about 18-20 hours. It began in the evening (after twilight) at the Garden of Gethsemane and ended the next day at 3 p.m. on the cross. It would have seemed like forever while He went through the torture, though. During the time of His earthly ministry, there were many who spoke blasphemous words to Him. But since He never allowed the opinion of men to bother Him, He was not affected by it. In the final 18-20 hours of His life on earth, He was literally taken through hell - the place rightfully meant for us. Hell is an eternal place of absolute misery meant for those who are separated from God in this life because they have rejected His salvation. I believe that **this eternal load of punishment that was meant for mankind was condensed to 18-20 hours of the worst suffering ever, for our Lord on the cross.**

In this passage, our Lord asks God to save Him from 4 things - the sword, the power of the dog, the lion's mouth, and the horns of the wild oxen. Each of these is very significant, as we will see further on.

In Zechariah 13:7, a prophecy was spoken, saying, '"Awake, O sword, against My Shepherd, against the Man who is My companion," says the Lord of hosts. "Strike the Shepherd and the sheep will be scattered."' Lord Jesus was the Tree of Life in the midst of the Garden of Eden. When God drove Adam and Eve out of the garden, He placed Cherubim at the east of the garden and a flaming sword that turned every way to guard the way to the Tree of Life. Lord Jesus (the actual Tree of Life) came to earth, having crossed this sword without being struck by it. But when He had to ascend back up, because He carried our sins, this sword struck Him. This was the sword of judgement prophesied by the prophet Zechariah.

He is the Good Shepherd and God's Companion. This sword struck the Shepherd on that day, and indeed the flock (His 12 disciples) scattered; all His disciples deserted Him at that moment.

I have previously spoken in detail about the power of the dog. The Jews considered the heathen – Romans, Greeks, and Egyptians as dogs. Only at the time of crucifixion, their power was manifested. Lord Jesus told Pilate in John 19:11, **"You could have no power at all against Me unless it has been given to you from above."**

"The third point mentioned is the lion's mouth. The lion holds an important place in the world as the king of the beasts. It is often mentioned in the Bible too. It is first mentioned by Jacob when he blessed Judah, his son, as a prophecy regarding the Messiah in Genesis 49:8-12. He calls Judah a lion's whelp (cub) and that the Messiah (Sceptre, Lawgiver) would come from him. The first prophecy concerning the Messiah was given in the Garden of Eden. Starting there, satan kept looking for more clues and how he could thwart God's plan because he knew that the Messiah would surely crush his head. We can say that satan paid more attention to the prophecies than the Israelites did! Satan also loves to impersonate God. That was the main reason for his downfall. After hearing this particular prophecy, he gladly pursued impersonating the Lord in this aspect. However, his intention has always been the exact opposite of God's character. Whenever God says something, satan gets busy corrupting it (like impersonating or counterfeiting) or making it look insignificant (through distraction and deception).

The Lord Jesus is the Lion of the tribe of Judah. The lion is always used as a positive symbol in praise of its majestic stature, walk, and strength. Examples of some animals used with negative symbolism include the fox (cunning), serpent (cunning and subtle), wolf (deceiving), etc.; satan corrupted the symbolism of a lion among the people on the earth. Rulers of various civilisations used lions to devour condemned prisoners. Nero used these majestic creatures to martyr the early church disciples, falsely blaming them for burning Rome. Lions have targeted men of God like Samson and David and lost to them. Daniel was supernaturally delivered from the lion's mouth when he was thrown in for disobeying the law to worship the king. In all these instances, satan lost. While these great men of God were delivered, the martyrs in Rome chose to give up their lives (Hebrews 11:35), not accepting deliverance.

As we see in all this, satan used this personification to imitate and twist the real symbolism of a lion. As believers, we should be aware of this. The roar of the lion can be heard at a distance, cautioning everyone. Its magnificence, supreme strength, stately walk, and kingly nature are used to describe the nature of our Lord. However, after the fall, this animal also defected, and its nature now is detestable at times, being indulgent in hateful and self-centred virtues. This perfectly describes satan. After the fall, lions became carnivores and are experts at hunting in the night (because of good night vision) and attacking their prey from behind, giving them a very painful death. Many times they start feeding on the prey even before it dies. Doesn't this perfectly match satan's character? However, the lion exhausts its energy very fast. He cannot pursue a prey for long. His attack is characteristically short and powerful. This is very similar to satan. That is why faith and patience are desirable virtues for all God's children in order to overcome him. These 2 virtues are satan's antagonists and make him flee from us. The animals that are preyed upon during the daytime have a good chance of escaping from the lion because the conditions are contrary to the latter. Similarly, a believer who lives in the light of God's word has the advantage to escape satan more easily. The verbal accusations heard by our Lord on the cross in the physical realm included the voice of satan too. Satan could not understand that his time was coming to an end; rather, he thought he was victorious and was rejoicing at that. The deceiver himself got deceived!"

"The wild oxen mentioned here are aurochs and are extinct today, but they existed in the days of our Lord. Most of the heathen idols replicated this form. These were huge creatures with characteristic deadly horns that were stocky, long, and curved outwards, typically built for killing. They were symbols of power, sexual fertility, and prowess. They were herbivores. The single most powerful part of their bodies was the horns, which they used for protection and dominance - a reason for pride. These turned out to be blueprints for heathen idols like 'moloch,' to which children were commonly sacrificed as worship. Even the Israelites participated in this abomination following their marriage with the Canaanites. A mixed population came into existence, and these people were not cut off from the Jews because no one enforced the law of God effectively. They prided themselves in this - they exalted their horns of pride.

When the Lord was condemned on our behalf, He was struck by the sword, caught in the power of the dog, the mouth of the lion, and being sheared by the horns of the wild oxen.

After all this cry of travail, He ends verse 21 on a note that makes faith arise on the inside of us. He says, **'You have answered Me.'** His cry for deliverance was answered after the Father's judgement was completely absorbed by Him on the cross. Having suffered all judgement and punishment from the Father on our behalf, He cried out, 'IT IS FINISHED,' and committed His Spirit into the Father's hand and died. An eternity of punishment was borne by our Saviour in 18-20 hours from the Garden of Gethsemane to the Cross of Calvary.

The Father did speed up the entire process, and His Beloved Son rested in His bosom after that. In 3 days, His uncorrupted body was resurrected by the re-entry of His Spirit which He had committed into the hands of the Father. This body bore the marks of crucifixion and the spear mark on His side (souvenirs from ungrateful mankind on His glorified body). When He was resurrected, He became unstoppable. No sword or dog or lion or wild oxen stood a chance before Him. None of these could prevent His resurrection, His appearance to His disciples, or His ascension into heaven to the right hand of the Father."

22. I WILL DECLARE YOUR NAME TO MY BRETHREN; IN THE MIDST OF THE ASSEMBLY I WILL PRAISE YOU.

In view of all that has been explained until now, including the purpose and process of His death, one thing becomes very clear. God the Father loved us from the beginning. Even though man refused His love, He never took a stand against us. He loved us so much that He prepared a way well beforehand for us to go back to Him and know His true nature. He never abandoned mankind because Adam and Eve sinned. For that matter, He never allowed sin to be a permanent barrier between us and Him. This barrier was broken forever when the Lord Jesus died for us on the cross. The benefits of this extended in both directions from the cross - towards the old covenant people as well as us, the new covenant people. But the intention behind this was the same for both people - to make the Father and the Son known to all - even the way it was carried out was different under both the covenants. Salvation (forgiveness of sin, healing, deliverance, prosperity, wholeness) was available to every person born since the beginning.

In the Old Testament, God revealed His name as 'I AM' to Moses and the Israelites. I have previously elaborated on the Names of God. They were so separated from Him because of their own sin conscience that they thought themselves unworthy to even verbalise the name YAHWEH. They considered it a great sin if anyone would refer to God calling Him by that name because of their unworthiness. In times such as these, Lord Jesus came calling and revealing God as 'our Father.' This infuriated the religious people. But Lord Jesus wanted to break this barrier of guilt that separated us from Him and be blessed by having a wonderful relationship with the Father.

The rest of this chapter, as well as verses 3-5, show how this salvation was appropriated to the people of the new and old covenant, who believed and now believe in Him."

3. ***"BUT YOU ARE HOLY, ENTHRONED IN THE PRAISES OF ISRAEL.***

4. ***OUR FATHERS TRUSTED IN YOU; THEY TRUSTED AND YOU DELIVERED THEM.***

5. ***THEY CRIED TO YOU AND WERE DELIVERED; THEY TRUSTED IN YOU AND WERE NOT ASHAMED.***

23. *YOU WHO FEAR THE LORD, PRAISE HIM! ALL YOU DESCENDANTS OF JACOB, GLORIFY HIM, AND FEAR HIM ALL YOU OFFSPRING OF ISRAEL!*

24. *FOR HE HAS NOT DESPISED NOR ABHORRED THE AFFLICTION OF THE AFFLICTED; NOR HAS HE HIDDEN HIS FACE FROM HIM; BUT WHEN HE CRIED TO HIM, HE HEARD.*

The goodness of God and the appropriation of the benefits of His salvation can be seen beginning at the Garden of Eden where God sacrificed the first animal and clothed the couple who tried to hide their nakedness with leaves (works of the flesh/self-righteousness). I believe that it did not happen as quickly as we may think. God hides treasure in His Word for us, and one such treasure is the part regarding clothing Adam and Eve with tunics of skin. How did they get tunics of skin in the garden? It had to be from an animal. Therefore, blood was shed there, and I am sure Adam and Eve witnessed this first sacrifice firsthand. God the Father would have taught them the meaning of this sacrifice and asked them to observe it regularly, declaring their faith in His redemption through the Blood of the Lamb - the Messiah. I say this because we see Cain and Abel observing the same thing later on.

The sacrifice of the Saviour puts both the old and new covenant people on level ground. They declared His upcoming work by faith in performing the animal sacrifices, and we declare His finished work by faith by observing the Holy Communion. Neither of us has witnessed His death with our physical eyes except for those who were the contemporaries of Lord Jesus. This is witnessed so strongly in our spirits by His grace. Prophets like David and Isaiah witnessed this so strongly in their spirits that they accurately defined all that the Saviour would suffer and accomplish. Prophesying to their degree requires massive guts!

The benefits of this redemption and salvation have extended to the Jews as well as the Gentiles. Abraham and his descendants constitute the Jewish lot; the non-Jew category consists of people from Adam to Terah,

Job, Ruth, heathen kings like Nebuchadnezzar and Cyrus, the Shunammite widow, Naaman the Syrian, the Roman centurions during the time of the Lord, the Syrophoenician woman whose daughter was delivered from demons, the Gadarene demoniac, us, and the rest of us who believe in Him. Both categories are totally undeserving of the goodness and mercy of God. It is 100% His mercy and grace that caused Him to rescue us from destroying ourselves. What made all this possible? It was the Lord's obedience to the Father's will even before the foundation of the world was set (Revelation 13:8 and 1 Peter 1:19-20).

It is beyond the natural ability for any man to approach God through the law or any other way. Those who try always end in failure. The only way we can stand before God today is through faith in the redemption and salvation offered by our Lord Jesus Christ. Abraham was declared righteous by faith, and this was before the law was given. God never forsakes anyone who comes to Him in faith. The Word is loaded with examples of His faithfulness to people who never deserved it.

Our God is the King of the universe. Heaven is His throne, and the earth is His footstool. No man can build a throne worthy of His person. Moreover, God is not looking for a (rather far inferior) physical throne or temple to sit in on the earth. God has always desired the 'throne of the heart' in all mankind. This belongs to Him when we receive His salvation and submit to Him in every area of our lives. When we do so, we give Him worship that originates from our righteous heart, and this is called worshipping Him in spirit and in truth.

There is a heavenly realm that exists from the beginning, which is more real than the earthly realm that our physical eyes see. The earthly realm will one day come to an end, but the unseen spiritual realm is eternal. This realm has real power. The spoken word by God (which is invisible to our eyes) brought forth the hosts of the earth which we see today. The unseen holds the real power. Our praise and worship of God (mostly done by words) cannot be seen. But this has enormous significance in the spiritual realm; or else why would satan covet this praise and worship from mankind to God. This is the main reason he defected. When we praise and worship God, He is exalted in the spiritual realm, and His victory is appropriated to us and abounds in our salvation; and the demons flee.

Ephesians 6:12 clearly says that 'we wrestle not against flesh and blood, but against principalities, against powers, against the rulers of the darkness of this world; against spiritual hosts of wickedness in high places.' Demonic forces will oppose us when we are walking in God's will, while most often our own stupidity and carelessness pose an opposition to us when we are not following God's will. Hence we have no business blaming God when we haven't committed our lives totally in obedience to Him. The simple solution in these instances would be to rectify ourselves and submit to Him. On the other hand, we can effectively overcome the opposition of satan by praising and worshipping God (Psalm 8:2). This puts him to flight as he sees God being enthroned in our hearts. When we praise God, it literally paralyses satan and his troupe.

What does it mean to praise and worship God? Rather than just mouthing the phrases 'I praise You' and 'I worship You', we have to proclaim God's ability, His power, magnificence, and majesty. After finishing the sermon on the mount, as the Lord came down, a leper came to Him and **worshipped,** saying, 'Lord, if You are willing, You can make me clean'. Here it says that the **'leper worshipped saying'**. He merely spoke what the Lord was capable of, and this is labelled as worship. When we exalt God's ability, power, and magnificence, then we open the door for God's finished work to be appropriated in our lives because it makes God bigger and our problems smaller. His word automatically takes over, and victory manifests. Being thankful and recounting God's faithfulness in our lives is also worship. When this praise and worship flows from our hearts, our soul and body also line up and express themselves, like lifting up our hands, falling on our knees, prostrating before God, etc. When we worship God **out of a sense of having been made righteous before Him, we are said to be worshipping God in spirit and in truth;** it most often involves speaking in tongues as well. Anything other than this is meaningless and useless. This is the reason God objected to the manner in which the old covenant people offered the sacrifices, just as a formality. God abhorred such sacrifices.

The word brings out the clear fact that God never overlooks the cry of a frantic, desperate, and sincere heart. He is all ears to their cry and always answers them by delivering them from their distress. God's provision is always perfect and readily available, provided we do things according to His will. We suffer lack only when we defect from His will. But even in that, He will correct us and show us the way out.

Man's pride makes him forfeit the goodness, provision, and protection of God. Mankind finds it too hard to understand the simple truth of 'Ask and you shall receive'. They always took the route of grumbling, complaining, and griping during times of want. Today, in my part of town, church leaders force and encourage people to bawl and cry. That never works out because it is the tendency of the flesh and never materialises. The best thing to do is to simply "ask God", knowing that He always provides, and thank Him for it, knowing that He will give it. That is faith! The Lord Jesus explained this when He spoke about the birds of the air and the lilies in the field. David has also elaborated on this beautifully in Psalm 104:20–22 and 27–28. Much of his early life was spent in the wilderness, where he faithfully shepherded his father's sheep and also when he was hiding from Saul. This experience taught him many things, even as he observed things on earth and in the sky. That being said, it is not wrong or unreasonable to pour our burdens before the Lord when our hearts are heavy. He is the only true Comforter. But we should keep away from portraying God as being harsh and deaf to us.

God's faithfulness to the Israelites is declared by Joshua in Joshua 21:44–45, saying, "The Lord gave them rest all around, according to all that He had sworn to their father's. And not a man of all their enemies stood against them; the Lord delivered all their enemies into their hands. **"NOT A WORD FAILED OF ANY GOOD THING WHICH THE LORD HAD SPOKEN TO THE HOUSE OF ISRAEL. ALL CAME TO PASS".**

All the books in the world wouldn't suffice to declare the goodness of God to all His children. If we would just study the lives of the saints in the word of God, it is more than enough to boost our faith in God's goodness.

Having known and tasted the goodness of God, the Israelites were reminded again and again to praise and glorify God. His faithfulness was taught to the subsequent generations by the priests and by parents to their offspring. Why should we hold onto this? It is because we have to constantly remember that our sins were judged in the body of our Lord. The Father heard His cry of affliction; He saw His seed and the labour of His righteous soul and was satisfied (Isaiah 3:10–11). The Lord Jesus poured out His soul unto death and was numbered with the transgressors; He bore the sin of many and made intercession for us (Isaiah 53:12). He did everything that was needed and demanded for our justification—to present us holy and blameless to the Father. **The salvation of mankind cost God everything He had—it is priceless!** For this reason, we have to receive this priceless gift, magnify His finished work, rest in His goodness and promises, and live an abundant, victorious life. Our Father will never look away from us.

25. MY PRAISE SHALL BE OF YOU IN THE GREAT ASSEMBLY; I WILL PAY MY VOWS BEFORE THOSE WHO FEAR HIM.

26. THE POOR SHALL EAT AND BE SATISFIED; THOSE WHO SEEK HIM WILL PRAISE THE LORD. LET YOUR HEART LIVE FOREVER!

Every single day of the ministry of our Lord, recorded in the Gospels, shows the manner in which He exalted God. He constantly spoke about the Father everywhere. His goal was to make the Father known to mankind. By the time He arrived in person, the religious people had made havoc of the image of God by adulterating His laws, statutes, commandments, and judgements. They had misinterpreted most of it for their profit and laid heavy burdens on the people. However, they never bothered to keep any of it, becoming hypocrites of the highest order.

The primary work our Lord did was to undo the wrong perspective of God that these individuals had instilled in the hearts and minds of people. At the ground level, He demonstrated the true nature of God, preaching the word and establishing it with signs and wonders before the eyes of all the hypocrites and the people who had been deceived by them. He came revealing "The Father" to a guilt-ridden, sin-conscious world that could not even call God by the Name revealed to them - YAHWEH. This infuriated the hypocrites who could not digest the fact that one Man was actually calling God His Father.

In the Old Testament, God revealed His Name to Moses as "I AM." There was a time when I just couldn't understand why God did not complete that statement. The Egyptians had a battalion of gods and goddesses for every aspect of life (very similar to the culture practiced in Asian countries today). However, they did not have one who had the power over all or who was in charge of everything that concerns life. When God revealed His Name to Moses, it had a very deep impact on him as well as his brethren. **The Name was 'all-encompassing' and meant that "He is everything to every one of His children."** The Israelites did not have to approach a separate deity for each problem. They did not have to run from pillar to post looking for deliverance from an innumerable list of gods and goddesses. They had the Creator of the Universe declaring His relationship with them through His Name! He was their All-in-All! He was their protector, healer, provider, deliverer, strength, hope, refuge, etc. Whatever the need, He was their answer. Likewise, **HE IS TO US today**! But they never understood this perspective. Sadly, this went on until the time the Messiah entered into His ministry, declaring His Name as 'Father.' Now this was a word they understood because almost every human had an earthly father, and this relationship of love was well experienced by most if not all. This is a good example for people then and now also.

The same manner in which Lord Jesus glorified the Father is the same manner in which we should live. When we have received His love for us, it becomes necessary for us to share the truth of God's love with everyone whom God brings into our path. When we do so, we must remember to exalt God to the supreme place and stick with John the Baptist's declaration: "He must increase, and I must decrease." This ensures that the attitude of our hearts is right, and our conscience is clear. In all we do, we should seek to glorify God (1 Corinthians 10:31) and keep Him always in high esteem.

God the Father had explicitly stated a vow in the book of Jeremiah 31:31-34. This promise stated that the Old Covenant would be annulled, and a New Covenant would be introduced and established. God said that the days were soon coming when He would make a New Covenant with the house of Israel and the House of Judah, not according to the Old Covenant that He made with their fathers when He brought them out of Egypt, which they broke despite God's perfect faithfulness. Unlike the old one, which was recorded in the book of the law and on stones, God promised that He would put His laws in our minds and write them on our hearts. He swore that He would be our God, and we would be His people. The relationship between Him and us would be so perfect that no more would any man teach his neighbour or his brother, saying, 'Know the Lord'. This was because all would know God, from the least to the greatest. Unlike the old covenant where sin was just covered under the blood of the sacrifice, here, sins would be totally done away with because God would forgive our iniquities and remember our sins no more!

This was the promise/vow of the New Covenant that God spoke through His children and recorded explicitly in the Word as a witness to the whole world. This held the assurance of personal guidance from God to us. Lord Jesus came to fulfil this vow through His perfect sacrifice. There is no doubt that He lived a perfectly holy life from conception to death. He paid this vow with His life and instituted the Holy Communion as a visible gesture of this covenant just hours before His death.

Throughout His earthly ministry, there were multitudes that followed Him. There were a good number of faithful followers who were with Him most of the time, including women who ministered to Him. But among all these, He chose the 12 to be with Him always. Certainly, our Lord would have enjoyed their company, but the beneficiaries were definitely the 12. These 12 disciples were the privileged ones who partook first in the institution of the New Covenant. They were given the responsibility to carry this remembrance forward, and they did. After His resurrection, He appeared to 2 people on the road to Emmaus and broke bread with them. Following this, their eyes (which were previously restrained from knowing Him) were opened up, and they knew it was the Lord. Furthermore, the Apostles and the disciples continued to observe the Holy Communion with all reverence.

The Apostle Paul had a personal revelation regarding the Lord's Table directly from the Lord, and most of us read this passage (1 Corinthians 11:23-26) before we partake of the Lord's Table today. All of us who are saved have confessed that we are poor in spirit and, with all diligence, partake of the Holy Communion. This is indeed a powerful declaration of the death of our Saviour for us and has a great bearing in the spiritual and the physical realm. This satisfies us perfectly because we know that He carried all our sin, its consequences, and gave us the benefits of salvation as co-heirs with Him, He being the first fruit among all the brethren. We who partake of the Holy Communion declare the Lord's death till He returns. We are given the spirit that lives forever despite a physical body that has to be done away with through physical death. The minute we physically die, our spirits are clothed with the glorified body that lives forever with God. This way, our hearts live forever, and we will always live a life of praise, acknowledging every good thing the Father has accomplished for us and given us.

27. ALL THE ENDS OF THE WORLD SHALL REMEMBER AND TURN TO THE LORD, AND ALL THE FAMILIES OF THE NATIONS SHALL WORSHIP BEFORE YOU.

28. FOR THE KINGDOM IS THE LORD'S AND HE RULES OVER THE NATIONS.

29. ALL THE PROSPEROUS OF THE EARTH SHALL EAT AND WORSHIP; ALL THOSE WHO GO DOWN TO THE DUST SHALL BOW BEFORE HIM, EVEN HE WHO CANNOT KEEP HIMSELF ALIVE.

30. A POSTERITY SHALL SERVE HIM. IT WILL BE RECOUNTED OF THE LORD TO THE NEXT GENERATION.

31. THEY WILL COME AND DECLARE HIS RIGHTEOUSNESS TO A PEOPLE WHO WILL BE BORN, THAT HE HAS DONE THIS.

It is interesting to note the constant mention of 'eating' and 'remembering' in these passages. Time and again, the Lord's Table and its significance are well emphasised in the Word of God. When I read this passage, I could very well relate to it. My day usually starts at 6 am with my personal time with God for about an hour, consisting of prayer, declaration of His word over my loved ones, and reading a chapter from the book of Proverbs. Following this, I tune into God TV for about one and a half hours for my daily feed. Then I go about my work for the day, attending to my husband and children. This was my routine in the lockdown due to the pandemic. Before the pandemic, I would do most of my Bible study when my children were off at school. But watching God TV, I understood the essence of the first verse in this passage. There is no point in denying the impact of the powerful sacrifice of our Saviour. One would be unjust to refute this claim. The truth has impacted billions of people worldwide, to this day. People are learning the true meaning of the Holy Communion and partaking in it on a regular basis. Dedicated, God-fearing preachers and teachers are teaching people the relevance of the Lord's Table! The remembrance of our Lord's sacrifice is no longer restricted to once a year when people celebrate Good Friday and Easter. Times are changing for the better as the Lord's love is drawing our hearts to know His truth. I thank and glorify God that every part of His body, the Church, is busy following God's calling.

I am most grateful to The Father for God TV. This channel came as a beacon of hope in my life at a point of deep despair. At that time, I did not have access to the internet or any form of social media; the television was my only source of information apart from the sermons I heard at church. The programmes on this channel have greatly helped me at every stage in my life. I wouldn't be exaggerating if I tell you that certain programmes have been tailor-made for me in challenges that sprouted up. God never ceases to feed me to this day through this channel apart from my personal time with Him. When I watch the programmes on this channel, the enormous and astounding work of God can be seen - so many lives touched and changed for the better; so many lives saved and having an assurance of being with God in eternity instead of hell; so many people going forth teaching, preaching, making disciples, and evangelising the whole world and bringing the gospel of grace to all people. This prophecy is unfolding before our eyes! We see people from all nations, belonging to different ethnic groups, cultures, and occupations forsaking their vain pursuits, receiving salvation, and pursuing God's will for their lives.

Lord Jesus Christ is ruling and reigning today on earth because all authority is vested in His hands (Matthew 28:18). Satan continues with his deception, having absolutely no authority, and there are people who continue to choose to follow that deception rather than accept the love of God. But the beloved flock of God continues to hear His voice and is kept by Him.

This passage clearly states that the prosperous of the earth shall eat and worship, and also those who go down to the dust will bow before Him. This is delineating 2 categories of people: the first one consists of those who are saved (those who partake of the Holy Communion), and the other group are the unsaved (those who reject the salvation of God). God describes success and prosperity very differently from the way that the world defines it. A good understanding of these 2 related words can be obtained from Genesis chapters 24 and 39. In the first instance, it concerns the oldest servant of Abraham's house when Abraham commissioned him to find a bride for his son Isaac from his native land. The second speaks of Joseph when he was purchased by Potiphar to be his slave. In both instances, these words clearly refer to the presence of God in their lives being so evident that what they wanted to accomplish (according to the will of God) came to pass. This was even seen and appreciated by the people around them. Genesis 39:2 (KJV version) says "The Lord was with Joseph, and he was a prosperous man."

Though many may think success is an outcome, it is basically the fact that God's presence in our lives causes us to rise higher and live more meaningfully. Joseph was not rich at this point. In fact, he had just been bought by Potiphar from the Ishmaelites and was probably not even properly clothed, let alone having gold, silver, or his own house. He was in submission to his Egyptian master in such a godly manner that his master could see that 'The Lord was with him and that The Lord made all he did to prosper in his hands' (Genesis 39:4). For Abraham's servant, as he went seeking a bride for his master's son, success was to find that one beautiful young woman among many others to oblige his request for a drink from her pitcher of water and also offer voluntarily to draw water for his 10 camels. This was a sign he had requested of the Lord when he got to the native land. Furthermore, God went one step ahead and made sure that she was a direct close relative of Abraham (his brother Nahor's granddaughter). This was both success and prosperity for him. We would all be much better off in life if we stick to the definitions of words given by God. The world organises the best and biggest rat race to define success and prosperity, and even Christians fall prey to that. It is really sad indeed!

Those who are saved must and will remember the sacrifice of the Lord. But what about those who are not saved? The only basis on which people will be thrown into hell is because they reject the salvation offered by God through the Lord Jesus Christ (John 16:9). People will not enter hell because of the sins of lying, adultery, stealing, etc. **"Dust you are, and to dust you shall return" was the curse pronounced by God on Adam after the fall (Genesis 3:19).** Man was created from the dust of the earth by the hand of God. The woman was made from one of his ribs (a bone!). The bones of humans are highly significant in the Bible. Both Jews and Christians have the habit of burying the body after death; the Jewish custom is a little different. We bury the body underground after placing it in a casket. The Jews, however, from times past, would wrap the body with preservatives and perfumes for a certain period of time and keep it in the tomb meant for this purpose. This would be shifted to different rooms in the tomb based on the level of decomposition. Once the decomposition of the flesh and organs was complete, all the bones would be collected carefully, sealed up in a wooden box, labelled properly with the person's name and family details, and placed in a separate room that contained many such boxes. This was the final step in the burial, which would be carried out over a minimum period of one year. For some reason, people showed faith in the preservation of the bones of their loved ones. Joseph specifically commanded his brethren to carry his bones out of Egypt when the Israelites left for the Promised Land. Ezekiel records the most famous vision of how a great army emerged from a valley of dry bones in Ezekiel, chapter 37.

It was prophesied that not one of the Lord's bones would be broken (Psalm 34:20), though His flesh would be ripped apart. It is well known that bones are the last to decompose, and many don't. Archaeologists have dug up the bones of humans that are thousands of years old. Does this hold any relevance? This has encouraged me to research more and study God's word more in this aspect. I encourage you to do the same. When the Lord Jesus died, many graves were opened. These were not soil graves. Rather, these were the boxes that contained the bones of many people who had died. After His resurrection, many saints rose up, went into the holy city, and appeared to many! This runs parallel with Ezekiel's prophecy of the valley of dry bones.

Having said a few important and interesting points, I would also like to draw your attention to the well-known practices of most heathen religions. Most of them follow cremation, burning the dead body to ashes. This way, even their bones are burnt to ashes, and truly, the saying comes to pass: 'dust you are and to dust you shall return'. These are almost all who have denied our Lord's salvation. But even these will bow before the Lord one day. This pandemic has just about taught everybody one bitter truth: No matter how rich a person is, when it is time to go, it is time to go! Money is never a factor that can change that fact. Monarchs, business tycoons, famous singers and actors, etc. have succumbed to sickness and diseases. Did money save them? No! Every one of those who rejected the love of God will also bow before the Lord one day. This definitely includes atheists and agnostics as well.

There can never be an end to the kingdom of God. God has already established His kingdom, and whether anybody likes it or not, it will continue into eternity. Man has no say in this matter. There have been many people who have tried to wipe out Christianity from ages past, and many more will rise up in the future to do the same. As such, it has been a waste of a good life. They have never succeeded in the past and will never succeed in the future either. Christianity continues to flourish; the Bible is still the most printed book and best seller! From generation to generation, people have accepted salvation and taught their successive generations about it. This is the posterity that will serve the Lord. It will never have an end!

Psalm 1

1. *BLESSED IS THE MAN WHO WALKS NOT IN THE COUNSEL OF THE UNGODLY, NOR STANDS IN THE PATH OF SINNERS, NOR SITS IN THE SEAT OF THE SCORNFUL.*

Mankind longs to live a blessed life. The book of Psalms and Proverbs instructs us greatly on how to do that. A blessed life, in turn, blesses others. If it does not, then it is a selfish life characterised by stagnation and unfruitfulness.

As long as we are in this world, we socialise with many people. Some are temporary participants in our lives, while others stay on for a long time. In the midst of this crowd that is more than willing to advise us on how to live life, we need to exercise godly discretion to stay safe and alive. The only way to have a blessed life is to be constantly and consistently **'in'** God's word and meditate on it day and night, no matter where we are or what we are doing. Our minds need to stay with God. This verse particularly instructs us concerning the things that we need to **keep away from** if we want to be blessed.

I would like to refer to this verse as the 3/3/3 secret to being blessed. It consists of 3 day-to-day actions, 3 people, and 3 aspects that we should keep a watch on in order to have a blessed life.

- ✡ 3 actions: walk, stand, and sit.
- ✡ 3 aspects: counsel, path, and seat.
- ✡ 3 people: ungodly, sinners, and scornful.

The daily life of man consists mainly of 3 actions when we are awake. Added to this is the fourth action of sleeping, which is dependent on how well we carry out the 3 actions when we are awake. Every man is in the constant company of other humans. Our thoughts, intentions, actions, and attitudes are the aspects of our lives that determine the course and outcome of life.

An ungodly person is a person who is devoid of the knowledge of God and says everything opposite to what God says in His word. He may even call himself a 'Christian' and live according to worldly standards of right or wrong and derives morals from the traditions of men. He may be a good man in the eyes of the world, but he does not always consent to Biblical morality. We see plenty of these today.

The world's standards are highly influenced by the local culture. Most of the cultures of the present-day world are totally opposed to God's word. From large nations to individual homes, laws and rules are made for their jurisdiction under the influence of their major religious culture and practices. When such counsels, rules, and laws are imposed on us, we need to have godly knowledge and discretion to decline them and actively resist them. An excellent precedent was set for us by Daniel and his 3 friends, which demonstrates the faithfulness of God to carry us through such instances of persecution. God does not want us to submit to ungodly morals and principles, no matter who they come from. By studying the word of God meticulously under the guidance of the Holy Spirit, we learn the morals and standards of God. This saves us a lot of trouble by helping us to resist ungodly counsel. In turn, we can live a blessed life.

'Standing in the path' of sinners is not difficult to understand. It is called 'consideration or contemplation'. It is the step before 'walking in the path' of sinners. Sin is obvious to most of us, except for those who have seared their conscience so much that they can hardly do anything good. To stand in the path refers to thoughts that we may have prior to taking any step in that direction. It's contemplating sin more than committing sin. This is exactly the reason why God doesn't want us to take any vengeance on our enemies. If we return the act when people wrong us, we are also doing wrong. We have taken the path of sin when we pay back evil for evil. We need to think twice about settling scores. Leave it to God. He is the God of justice, and He will settle it in justice. Guard your thoughts. Don't contemplate anything sinful because you will just end up doing it. **"You can't be tempted by something you don't think about,"** said a wonderful man of God.

Sitting in the seat of the scornful is to be thoroughly established in prideful and biblically immoral principles. This type of person doesn't even consider the righteous path. A scornful person is a haughty and proud person. He will not entertain any suggestions of getting his heart right with God. He is so blinded by his pride that what God says absolutely doesn't matter to him. God cannot have His way with a person who resists Him. God's presence and man's pride repel each other. Pride will bring a person down, and God knows how to work that. But if a person is repentant (like King Nebuchadnezzar) and wants to humble himself, God is more than willing to mercifully forgive and grant him the grace to live.

Hence, we need to keep away from **walking by** the counsel of the ungodly, **standing (contemplating life)** in the path of sinners, and **sitting (being established)** in the seat of the scornful. These are the 3 important negatives that we need to keep away from in order to be blessed. This is indeed a part of everyday life. Similarly, Proverbs 8:13 says, 'The fear of the Lord is to hate evil; pride and arrogance and the evil way and the perverse mouth I hate.' Hence, **living a godly life is the sum of 'doing the right thing' and 'keeping away from the wrong'.**

2. BUT HIS DELIGHT IS IN THE LAW OF THE LORD AND IN HIS LAW HE MEDITATES DAY AND NIGHT.

After instructing us on things we need to avoid in order to stay blessed, we are being instructed on what we need to embrace to be blessed - The Lord's law/word.

David lived under the old covenant. Hence, the law that he is referring to here is the laws written in the Torah. For us, the New Covenant people, the law here is the general law of God, which we know as the commandments that the Lord Jesus gave. In other words, it's the WORD OF GOD. When we are saved, God gives us the grace that attracts us to the word of God. The flesh cannot, by itself, get attracted to God's word. For any person who is not saved, the Bible appears to be just a book with lines that are hard to understand. At the most, it may seem to be a storybook with good morals. It doesn't look attractive to the unsaved. On the contrary, they may find it offensive.

Let me point out something very interesting. John 1:14 says, "and the word became flesh and dwelt among us." Lord Jesus Christ is The Word that became flesh. The latter half of Isaiah 53:2 says this regarding the Messiah: "He has no form or comeliness; and when we see Him, there is no beauty that we should desire Him." Can you see how these 2 verses are connected? To the eyes of an unbeliever, Lord Jesus has no beauty that they should desire Him. Since Lord Jesus is the Word in flesh form, the word also looks unattractive to them. The word of God comes alive to us only when we study it with the help of the Holy Spirit. He is the one who guides us into all truth and opens the eyes of our heart to see the awesomeness of God. There needs to be a great emphasis on "studying the word" instead of just reading it as a religious routine (which is useless).

This verse instructs us to prioritise studying the word of God. Ideally, every day should be started in the presence of God, giving Him thanks, praise, and glory, as well as being still before Him to receive wisdom and strength to live each day for His glory. The primary way God speaks to us is through His word. So when we sit and study the word every day, prioritising it over everything else, we will attract blessings. Meditating on the word implies that we are mindful of the word we study and apply it in our daily life. The Lord gives us the desire to do this faithfully every single day, and it is indeed delightful to walk with God in this manner. Work your schedule around studying God's word and prioritise it. When we seek first the kingdom of God and His righteousness, the rest of the things will be added to us. In other words, every aspect of life falls into place as we give God the first place in our lives every single day.

3. *HE SHALL BE LIKE A TREE PLANTED BY THE RIVERS OF WATER THAT BRINGS FORTH ITS FRUIT IN ITS SEASON, WHOSE LEAF ALSO SHALL NOT WITHER; AND WHATEVER HE DOES SHALL PROSPER.*

The definition of 'being blessed' is given very clearly here. The Lord gives us an excellent comparison here, as He likens us to a tree. Many times, God gives us profound revelations using the host of creation. The Lord Jesus did that quite often in the parables.

Let us ponder about a tree. It has roots underground to start with, followed by a thick trunk, branches, leaves, flowers, and fruits. It is a habitat for many animals and birds. It is of much use to mankind, providing him with air (oxygen), food, and wood for various purposes. The importance of trees is very well acknowledged from the beginning. While almost every part of the tree is useful to man, the leaves are more useful to the tree itself since they are the place where it prepares food for itself. Though every part of the tree is important, the leaves play a very important role in nourishing all the other parts of the tree. The fruits and flowers are of good use to others. The roots are the foundation of the tree, and the trunk is the main support.

The banks of rivers (channels) are an ideal habitat for any tree. There is an inexhaustible supply of water and nutrients for this tree. It never lacks any provision to nourish itself. The rivers of water refer to the living waters of God's word. In other words, it's a never-ending supply of His wisdom, knowledge, understanding, grace, and mercy. God's river will never run dry. It is always abounding with life-giving water. The roots are strong and healthy because of this, and they are always supplied with the best nutrients.

The leaves speak of our relationship with God. There are many types of trees that God has created. Each of them adapts to its habitat. Deciduous trees, evergreen trees, coniferous trees, etc. are some examples of the broad classification of trees. Some trees are known to shed their leaves in autumn and get new growth in spring every year. Here it talks about a tree whose leaves never wither! They never wilt and fall off! So this blessed man's relationship with the Lord is evergreen. **It is our relationship with God that sustains our lives. It is His love for us that keeps us alive and not our love for Him.** The 'leaves never withering' indicate a vibrant relationship with God that provides us ample energy to feed every part of our lives. So God promises that if a man delights in the word of God and lives according to it consistently, his relationship with God will always flourish, and he will always be blessed and favoured.

Everything that this man does prospers. The flowers, the fruits, the trunk, the branches, the roots—all are blessed! A tree never eats its own fruits. It provides fruit as food for animals and mankind; the flowers are not only used for aesthetic purposes but also for many other things; the trunk and branches provide wood and sap, etc. Every part of this man's life is a blessing to others. This tree lives a very long time, always being fruitful. Similarly, this man lives a fruitful life on earth that continues into eternity in the presence of Almighty God.

This blessed life starts with a relationship with God through the Lord Jesus Christ, His son. It depends on forsaking the evil and clinging to the good.

4. *THE UNGODLY ARE NOT SO, BUT ARE LIKE THE CHAFF WHICH THE WIND DRIVES AWAY.*

5. *THEREFORE THE UNGODLY SHALL NOT STAND IN THE JUDGEMENT, NOR SINNERS IN THE CONGREGATION OF THE RIGHTEOUS.*

These verses describe the life and the end of the ungodly man. The life of an ungodly man is empty (weightless) like the chaff. Though many unsaved people have great accomplishments, it does not carry any weight in the sight of God. It is all wood, hay, and straw, which are easily burnt up by fire. When his spirit leaves his body at physical death, it automatically gets blown into hell. There is no place for a man who has lived the best moral life on earth without accepting Lord Jesus as his Saviour, to even have a second chance to stand before God on the day of judgement. No Jesus, no heaven. There is no hope for a sinner who rejects salvation to enter the kingdom of heaven.

The word of God makes it very clear that the citizenship to heaven should be first acquired on earth while we are still breathing. Once the heart stops beating, there is no way to get that citizenship. Proverbs 1 brings this out very clearly. It starts here and continues into eternity. God is long-suffering, and He gives plenty of time for every man to repent and turn to Him. So nobody can complain about God's righteous judgement.

6. *FOR THE LORD KNOWS THE WAY OF THE RIGHTEOUS, BUT THE WAY OF THE UNGODLY SHALL PERISH.*

The path walked by a righteous man is ordained by God. Every single step has a purpose. Every person he comes in contact with is known by Him. God commands doors to be shut or opened for him. Every part of his life is under the vigilant eye of God. Being omnipotent, omnipresent, and omniscient, God guides him, empowering him with all grace and dealing with him in mercy. Nothing can come as a surprise to God. That should be so comforting to us! If we understood the magnitude of this truth, we would place our entire confidence in God alone.

The way of the ungodly always leads to death. Any life that is devoid of the saving power of the Lord Jesus Christ is doomed to end in destruction. Though it may seem that they lived problem-free and died peacefully, it is never the end because eternity has just begun for them, and it is horrific in hell. Every point along the path of the ungodly spells destruction. Just that they are blinded from seeing it.

Psalm 2

1. WHY DO THE NATIONS RAGE, AND PEOPLE PLOT A VAIN THING?

This is the sad reality of the world since the fall of man in the Garden of Eden, and it continues to this day. The Lord Himself testified in Genesis 6:5 and 8:21 that the thoughts and imaginations of a man's heart are continually evil from his youth (birth). To date, there is no man who can make himself righteous before God by any of his works, except our Lord Jesus Christ. The day mankind relied on 'self', his spirit was separated from God. Thereafter, by default, his every thought and action became contrary to God. Even an infant displays this behaviour very well, though initially in ignorance, but continues the same selfish attitude even after growing up. Proverbs 20:11 says, even a child is known by his doings, whether it is pure and right.

A believer who walks with God consistently knows the futility of man's selfish ambitions and the vanity of the world's rat race. Plotting against God and getting angry with Him is absolutely vain. The only One who can actually help us is God! All said and done, once we leave this earth, there is an eternity in heaven or hell depending on whether we have accepted or rejected the salvation given to us by God through our Lord Jesus Christ. We may strive and be very ambitious in accomplishing things for our own benefit and pride. But in the end, it has absolutely no eternal value. Remember that eternity never ends. Our earthly life is just like the blink of an eye when compared to eternity. Hence, stop living in vanity;

stop all retaliation and rebellion to the word of God. It is always wise to respect and obey the standards that God has commanded in His word. They are meant for our good and His glory.

2. THE KINGS OF THE EARTH SET THEMSELVES AND THE RULERS TAKE COUNSEL TOGETHER, AGAINST THE LORD AND AGAINST HIS ANOINTED, SAYING,

3. "LET US BREAK THEIR BONDS IN PIECES AND CAST AWAY THEIR CORDS FROM US."

This is seen so often in the word. Satan has made himself God's enemy. His main intention is to always steal, kill, and destroy (John 10:10). He works through people in causing havoc everywhere and every time. Being the master deceiver, his tactics are well described in the word of God. Every time he plotted against God, he was defeated big time. God also works through people. When God's people come up against any opposition from satan (working through his followers), God stands up for His children and delivers them faithfully if they put their trust in Him. He always has!

Even today, men are openly fighting for ungodly rights such as homosexuality and abortion in epidemic proportions. They are so hell-bent on it that they want legislations to be passed to fight God! This is so insane and self-destructive. Marriage is not hallowed by many, and pre-nuptial agreements are the norm just in case things don't work out. Live-in relationships are wholeheartedly embraced, and people idolise celebrities who do that and follow their example. Finally, people don't understand the reason why such rich and famous idolised celebrities commit suicide one fine day! And everyone lights a candle, march in silent processions, and text RIP all over social media. How can a candle symbolise a person who chose to put off their light/life? How can their soul rest in peace when they have rejected the only way to peace? All they did was resist the love of the One who truly loved them and wanted their good.

Citizenship to heaven has to be acquired here on earth, while we are alive. Once we enter the kingdom of God here, after we close our eyes (in physical death), we just continue the same citizenship in the kingdom of God in heaven for eternity. This is the truth. If we don't receive it here, we cannot get there. This is obtained only by believing and accepting the redemption offered by God through Lord Jesus Christ. It is impossible to fight against the morals and principles laid down by Almighty God and have a good life on earth even though it seems contrary to the eyes of some people. Remember, only God knows the heart of man. Every misery in their life is before Him. Men may hide it from other men, but nothing can be hidden from the eyes of God. One day, our eyes also will see the misery of the ungodly, wicked, and rebellious man (Psalm 91:8).

Our Lord Jesus Christ suffered much opposition from the Roman leaders, Jewish leaders, and the common people. There was constant plotting happening against Him from every corner of Israel. Finally, He was betrayed by His own disciple, who happened to be a thief all along. The Lord very well knew that He would be betrayed and crucified. He also conveyed this many times to His disciples. The only reason Judas Iscariot stayed on was because of the long-suffering nature of God. Besides, God's will for Christ had to be fulfilled. There were more than 12 legions of angels (Matthew 26:53) standing by to protect Lord Christ. Yet He thought of you and me and never used that opportunity for deliverance. He did not owe mankind anything. He submitted Himself to God and went to the cross for our sake. Nevertheless, the Father resurrected Him on the third day, and He appeared to His disciples before ascending to the Father. Now He is seated at God's right hand in absolute glory and authority! Stephen saw the heavens open, and the Lord Jesus standing at God's right hand (Acts 7:55) to receive his spirit into eternity with Him. This is what matters. Every martyr is given grace to go through what they go through. I believe that strongly. It is no surprise that they are so strong in the spirit!

Be wise. Take God's side. You will never regret siding with God and living according to His principles.

4. HE WHO SITS IN THE HEAVENS SHALL LAUGH; THE LORD SHALL HOLD THEM IN DERISION.

5. THEN HE SHALL SPEAK TO THEM IN HIS WRATH AND DISTRESS THEM IN HIS DEEP DISPLEASURE:

These 2 verses have been explained beautifully by a parable spoken by the Lord recorded in Luke 19:12–27. There was a certain nobleman who went into a faraway country to possess a kingdom and return. Before he left, he gave a mina to each of his ten servants (totalling 10 minas) and asked them to do business with them till he returned, and he left. But his own citizens hated him and sent a delegation after him, saying they didn't want him to rule over them. But that didn't matter a penny to the nobleman. He went and received the kingdom that he went for and returned to his own country. Upon arriving, he first called his servants, to whom he had given the mina, to know what they had done with it. The first servant gave his report of how his mina earned 10 more minas. The master was very pleased with this servant and gave him authority over 10 cities. The second said that his mina had earned 5 minas. Likewise, his master appreciated him and gave him authority over 5 cities. Then another came and showed no profit from the mina given to him. Moreover, he misunderstood his master's character all along. He falsely accused him of reaping what he didn't sow! This servant was immediately reprimanded by his master, and the mina was taken away from him and given to the first servant, who already had 10 minas.

Now is the climax of the parable. After taking into account the returns obtained by his servants, the master then commanded to bring the rebels (who had sent the delegation) who had refused to be ruled by him and slay them. They were the last ones on his agenda! They were not even worth his time. The nobleman was more interested in his servants than the rebels.

The interpretation is as follows: The nobleman is the Lord Jesus Christ. The far country is heaven. He will return to this earth again. We are His servants. 'One mina each' signifies God's impartial distribution of grace and spiritual gifts to each of His children. The rebels who did not want the nobleman to rule over them are the unbelievers (ungodly, wicked, and rebellious people). It doesn't matter how much people put themselves against God. He has ascended to heaven to prepare a place for us, and He will return one day. On that day, we, His children, have to be accountable for the grace and gifts given to us. Accordingly, He will reward us. He holds us accountable for whatever He has given us. We need to use it for His glory and to profit the Kingdom of Heaven. The Lord faithfully rewards us exponentially. The believer who buries his mina in the ground all because he doesn't have the right understanding of God's character will be at a total loss and will incur the wrath of his Master. The mina will be taken from him and given to the one who used it well. That's the principle on which God's kingdom works. It's not vice versa, as so many Christians believe.

Use your gift well for the glory of God. God has commanded us to be the salt and light in this world. Our flavour and radiance, which are from God, have to go forth (2 Corinthians 2:15). The least the servant with one mina could have done was to have invested it! Finally, all the rebellious, pompous fools who were strutting around in their own arrogance for their ungodly rights were put to death right before the eyes of the Master. Did you notice the fact that not an ounce of their rebellion affected the master in any way? True! Nothing of the ungodliness happening in today's world affects God's person. He is always enthroned on high. He is always the High and Exalted One. Every knee will bow before Him one day and confess His Lordship. That day is not far away.

As long as man stands in opposition to God's word wilfully, he is harming only himself. If he repents and turns to God, He is just and able to forgive him and accept him as His son.

6. *"YET I HAVE SET MY KING ON MY HOLY HILL OF ZION."*

This is a prophetic Psalm of David. Even though there were prophets like Nathan and Gad who prophesied God's word to him, David was inspired by the Holy Spirit to write many prophetic Psalms concerning Lord Jesus Christ and His life.

As explained earlier, God Himself testified that there was only wickedness in the heart of every person from his youth. This is an established truth. But there was only One person in the whole world who respected and honoured God all His life: Lord Jesus Christ. He was the only person who loved God perfectly with His whole heart, mind, and soul and lived a perfect sinless life on earth.

So this is a declaration from the mouth of the Messiah spoken prophetically by David. Lord Jesus declared this continually by His words and actions when He walked on earth. He honoured God like no other and esteemed the will of His Father above all things. Even though He faced strong opposition to the point of death on the cross, He never backed down or avenged Himself. He exalted the Father by doing His will in all things, at all times. By His obedience, He proved that the Lord is always enthroned.

David also witnessed the futility of disobedience to God in his lifetime. Whether it was someone else or he himself, they were no match for God. As much as he could, he tried to live blameless before God.

7. "I WILL DECLARE THE DECREE: THE LORD HAS SAID TO ME, 'YOU ARE MY SON, TODAY I HAVE BEGOTTEN YOU.

All through the earthly life of our Lord Jesus, we can witness this declaration in action. He lived and did everything with absolute authority. Since we see this prophecy regarding the Messiah being spoken by David, apart from the other prophets, it is once again affirmative that the Lord Jesus Christ was chosen to be the Lamb of God from the very beginning. Staying in accordance with God's solemn call on His life, Lord Jesus accomplished the will of His Father even to the death on the cross.

'Declare' is a very important word that we need to understand in Biblical terminology. When God declares something, He is making that permanent or established. There is no backing off once a declaration is made. The birth of Lord Jesus was a virgin birth. The seed was the word of God spoken by the Angel Gabriel to Mary. This word became flesh in Mary's womb and was birthed as the Saviour of the world - our Lord

Jesus Christ. Hence, He is the Son of God and the Son of Man. He was formed from the spoken word and was birthed through a human. That's what makes Him fully divine and fully human. Neither Joseph's sperm nor Mary's Ova had anything to do with His conception or birth.

Lord Jesus held on to this good confession till the end. Even when Pontius Pilate questioned Him, He was steadfast. Let us learn from our Lord to hold fast to everything that our Almighty God has declared over our lives till the end. His decrees regarding us begin in Genesis and go into the book of Revelation. To know this, we need to study His word with all diligence. A lifetime wouldn't suffice to cover it all.

8. *ASK OF ME AND I WILL GIVE YOU THE NATIONS FOR YOUR INHERITANCE, AND THE ENDS OF THE EARTH FOR YOUR POSSESSION.*

9. *YOU SHALL BREAK THEM WITH A ROD OF IRON; YOU SHALL DASH THEM TO PIECES LIKE A POTTERS VESSEL.'"*

These verses declare the absolute power that Almighty God has bestowed on His Son, Lord Jesus. All authority, power, might, and dominion are given into the hands of our Lord, just as David has prophesied here. Lord Jesus Himself declared this when He was taken up into heaven after He was resurrected (Matthew 28:18). His actions of healing the sick, raising the dead, and countering the hypocritical Pharisees demonstrate this authority.

When Lord Jesus took the place of mankind on the cross, He literally asked for the world as His inheritance. We are all absolutely and totally indebted to Him. The earth and everything in it belongs to Him. For those who don't accept this truth, the harsh reality of verse 9 will inevitably be evident.

The Apostle Paul, while writing to the Romans, speaks about the potter's vessels for honour and dishonour in Romans 9:21. The truth remains the truth no matter who rejects it. All authority is given into the hands of our Lord Jesus. He is the Head over all things to the church. He is ruling and reigning right now in the whole universe. Those who resist Him will have the same end as was described in the parable of the nobleman explained earlier in this chapter.

10. *NOW THEREFORE, BE WISE, O KINGS; BE INSTRUCTED, YOU JUDGES OF THE EARTH.*

11. *SERVE THE LORD WITH FEAR, AND REJOICE WITH TREMBLING.*

12. *KISS THE SON, LEST HE BE ANGRY AND YOU PERISH IN THE WAY, WHEN HIS WRATH IS KINDLED BUT A LITTLE. BLESSED ARE ALL THOSE WHO PUT THEIR TRUST IN HIM.*

This is an excellent conclusion to all the truth declared in this Psalm. It is indeed futile for a man to fight against God, no matter how influential he may be in this world. There is no use in coming together and plotting against Him either. It doesn't affect Him. The truth is, those who fight Him end up losing. By saying it plainly, the Lord is instructing us to keep away from the foolishness of rebellion and trying to outsmart God. He is Supreme!

This is not only a command to the ungodly and sinners. It holds good for those who call themselves Christians but are poor witnesses, as well as for believers. Revelations 1:6 says that the Lord Jesus has made us kings and priests to His Father. It's a robust advice for mankind.

Our call is to serve the Lord with fear and to rejoice with trembling. The word fear here indicates a solemn reverence for God that arises from an intimate relationship with Him. When we live to serve God and desire to do His will, He always fills our hearts with His shalom peace, and unspeakable joy. This rejoicing arises from within our hearts, as opposed to the circumstantial joy that enters from the outside. Certain materialistic things may make us happy, but this joy doesn't last long. The joy that flows from within is not affected by external factors. It is the fruit of the spirit deposited in us at salvation. Have you ever trembled when you were happy? Trembling usually accompanies fear. When do we tremble in happiness? It is when our expectations are met beyond our imagination! Our God is the One who does exceedingly and abundantly above all that we ask or think, **according to the power at work in us** (Ephesians 3:20). The reward for serving God in fear is a rejoicing so great that we cannot fathom it.

True wisdom for a man is to believe and obey the One who created him and to accept the salvation He has offered through the Lord Jesus Christ, His Son. The result of rejecting this priceless sacrifice is eternity in hell. Therefore, submit to the Lord Jesus. He has only good thoughts for us—thoughts that give us hope and a future filled with His goodness. Lord Jesus made that very clear in Matthew 21:44, saying, 'Whoever falls on this stone (the cornerstone, i.e., Lord Jesus) will be broken. But on whomever it falls, it will grind him to powder'. Can you understand the increase in severity between being broken and being ground to powder? Many live broken lives on earth, ignorant of the fact that wholeness is found only in Christ, our Lord. But after physical death (when His wrath is kindled but a little), the only reward for rejecting the Lord Christ is being ground to powder (an eternity in hell). When the Lord is being so clear in emphasising the truth, we should not take it lightly.

There is a sure reward for everyone who believes in the truth, trusts in God alone, and walks in obedience. They are blessed!

Psalm 3

INTRODUCTION:

This Psalm was written by King David when he fled from Absalom, his son. Here's the story.

David was anointed to be the next king of Israel (after Saul) by the prophet Samuel as a young shepherd boy (probably a teenager). After the anointing, the Lord's Spirit rested on him, and he soon came to be recognised as a fine young mighty man, prudent in speech, handsome, and skillful in playing the harp (1 Samuel 16:18). So he was sent for by Saul, on the recommendation of his servant, to play the harp for him when he was distressed by the evil spirit. Saul actually appointed him as his armour bearer. Shortly after this, he slew Goliath. He soon rose to fame with the people of Israel, and they all loved him. It did not take very long for Saul to envy him and seek to kill him. Yet David made up his mind, in fear of God, to never fight against the Lord's anointed, even though he had the opportunity to. He had to resort to the wilderness and spend approximately 13 years hiding from Saul. During this time, along with all the distressed, indebted, and discontent people, even his father, mother, and brothers came to him at his hideout and stayed with him because Saul probably targeted them also.

After a long time in the wilderness and in the land of the Philistines, he became the king of Judah at the age of 30, following Saul's death. He ruled Judah for 7 and a half years (during which Saul's son Ishbosheth ruled Israel until he was executed by his own men) before he was appointed King of the entire Nation of Israel. While David was in Hebron (Judah), he had 6 sons from 6 wives—Amnon being the oldest and Absalom the third in line. When David ruled the Nation of Israel, his sons were chief ministers (2 Samuel 8:18). David had never suffered any trouble within his family thus far.

After David became king over all of Israel, he fought many wars and won great victories. But at one point in time, when kings had to lead their armies out to battle, David stayed back in the palace and let Joab head the battle against the ammonites. This was at the peak of his success. Long story short, he ended up committing adultery with Bathsheba, the wife of Uriah the Hittite, and murdering him stealthily after discovering that Bathsheba became pregnant due to the act. He thought that he had handled the matter quite well and took Bathsheba into his palace as his wife. But the Lord revealed David's sin through the Prophet Nathan and reprimanded him severely. The Lord received the child conceived by this adulterous act to Himself. Solomon was the second child born to the couple later on.

Shortly after that, the real trouble began within his family. Since David stepped into the life of another man and committed adultery with his wife, sin wrecked his house. He repented before God and received His forgiveness. However, the consequences of his foolishness showed. His oldest son Amnon fell madly in love (rather lust) with his stepsister Tamar, Absalom's own sister. He probably could have married her. But he chose to listen to deceitful advice given by his cousin, Jonadab, and ended up defiling Tamar after calling her to his house to serve him under the pretence of being sick. After satisfying his lust, he despised her and sent her back home in a shameful manner. Absalom was very angry with Amnon because of all that he did to Tamar, but he did no obvious harm to him immediately. David heard of the matter but did nothing **because he was not a good example of morality himself.** For a period of 2 years, Absalom remained silent, breeding bitterness in his heart to the point of contemplating murder. After 2 years, he lured Amnon into a plot and killed him. David was broken! Absalom fled to his maternal grandfather,

Talmai, king of Geshur and stayed there for 3 years. David's heart yearned for Absalom, even though he was angry with him. Noticing this, Joab, the commander of his army, worked out a plan to get Absalom back from Geshur and succeeded. But still, David would not look at Absalom's face, despite repeated requests from the latter for 2 years. However, Absalom finally worked on a plan to meet David through Joab, and they reconciled. But this reconciliation was just an eye wash.

Absalom cunningly began recruiting the people of Israel to himself by winning their hearts and pretending to be a kind and caring person. He worked really hard (through deception) to win the heart of Israel and almost succeeded for a time. At 40 years of age, Absalom went up to Hebron under the pretence of paying his vow and declared himself as the new king (while his father David was still alive and well). His main adviser was Ahithophel (Bathsheba's grandfather). His advice was considered as the oracle of God. But because David had violated his granddaughter, Ahithophel yearned vengeance. So he partnered with Absalom and went to Hebron with him to overthrow David.

When David was informed of this, he did not retaliate. He humbled himself, knowing that this was the consequence of his wrongdoing that had destroyed the family of his loyal mighty man Uriah. He did not seek vengeance, nor did he justify himself. Rather, he immediately gathered his family and close aid (about 600 people) and fled to the plains of Jordan and crossed over, lest Absalom attack the entire city and kill all his subjects. He left behind his 10 concubines to take care of the house. He still pursued God with a broken and contrite heart, waiting on Him to justify him and bring him back to the land and kingship if the Lord willed. He never attempted to justify himself before Absalom or God.

Long story short, since Absalom overlooked his advice to rally all Israel and pursue David to kill him the same night, Ahithophel went back home and hung himself in shame. The Lord made Absalom reject the counsel of Ahithophel, and he ended up fighting David much later (giving David some time to recuperate) and was killed in the battle by Joab. Finally, David was brought back by the nation of Israel and reinstated as king. More details of this incidence will be included in the explanation of the verses.

1. LORD, HOW THEY HAVE INCREASED WHO TROUBLE ME! MANY ARE THEY WHO RISE UP AGAINST ME.

2. MANY ARE THEY WHO SAY OF ME, 'THERE IS NO HELP FOR HIM IN GOD.' SELAH.

Having read the story, one can understand David's distress and the cause of it. Not only did Absalom betray his own father, he cunningly and successfully recruited many of David's loyal subjects to himself. People definitely judged David for the sin he committed with Bathsheba. Certain people thought that he deserved this and even more. By the turn of events, the people would have thought for sure that God was not with David anymore and was punishing him for his sin. Counsellors like Ahithophel, who gave godly advice to David, also turned against him to such an extent that he went public with his odious advice. Ahithophel advised Absalom to pitch a tent on top of the house (David's palace) and go into (rape) all 10 of his father's concubines in the eyes of all Israel to assure his supporters that David would certainly hate him. Absalom diligently obeyed this counsel of Ahithophel, even without thinking twice. Absalom pulled away large crowds of common people and the army to himself.

When we speak about "vengeance", God has made it very clear that it is never a man's job to avenge himself or anyone else. This was established from the very beginning in the case of Cain. God said in Genesis 4:15 that "whoever kills Cain, vengeance shall be taken on him sevenfold". A judgement rested on Cain's head for killing his brother Abel. That vengeance belonged to God. But for any man who would take it into his hands to punish Cain, the judgement would be sevenfold! Here we see Absalom taking a stand against David (very subtly) in order to punish him for his sin against Uriah, his attitude of silence towards Amnon's wrongdoing, and the desolation of Tamar. David's sons were young men when David committed adultery with Bathsheba and would have been absolutely embarrassed by their father's shameful act. Yet it was not Absalom's right to take vengeance on David.

Absalom rallied the army of Israel to fight David upon the advice of Hushai, who was actually David's spy in Absalom's camp. But Hushai did this to buy some time for David to cross over the Jordan and secure himself. This advice was chosen over that of Ahithophel's, who suggested that they should attack David the same night he fled, immediately after they returned to Jerusalem from Hebron.

David knew he was in deep trouble. He knew that his enemies were greater in number and strength. He humbled himself and cried out to God for deliverance. He knew he had invited all this misery because of his reckless act with Bathsheba and Uriah. He knew the futility of going by his wisdom without God in this matter. He left it in God's hands to deliver him from his son Absalom, whom he still loved. This is the hallmark of a character that depends on God. David lived through all this distress because he believed in the merciful and gracious God of hosts. He laid his concerns only before God and not before any man. He sought direction and deliverance from Him alone. He believed and was confident that he was already forgiven by God for the mistake that he had made. But he knew that the consequences of his foolishness had to be dealt only with God's help and mercy. He never displayed the attitude that God owed him anything. He made his request known to God and waited patiently on Him for deliverance with an obedient heart. This pleased God the most, and He acted on his behalf.

3. *BUT YOU, O LORD, ARE A SHIELD FOR ME, MY GLORY AND THE ONE WHO LIFTS UP MY HEAD.*

From where do you think David got this revelation? From God's promise to Abraham in Genesis 15:1, where God declared to Abraham that He was his shield and exceedingly great reward. God spoke these blessings to men not because men had lived right or deserved them. When we study the story of Abraham, his shortcomings stare us in the face. The Bible is very candid. By exposing us to the reality and fragility of humans, the Holy Spirit teaches us and gives us excellent counsel through the examples of others. Moreover, He opens our eyes to see the excellent attributes of our

Almighty God. Concerning the words of blessing spoken to the saints in the Bible, the onus to personalise them to our lives is on us. David did that here.

When God spoke about instructions to be given to those who were going to be appointed as kings over Israel in Deuteronomy 17:16–20 (much before there was a thought to appoint kings), they were given specific instructions. They were not to multiply wives or horses. David had greatly failed at the first one. He had a total of 8 wives and at least 10 concubines. This in itself would have battered his conscience before God. Yet he believed that God had forgiven him, but he had to deal with the consequences. So he never justified himself in any aspect. He always depended on the mercy of God and looked to Him for deliverance. The kings were commanded to make a handwritten copy of the Book of the Law for themselves and meditate on it all the time when they were appointed as kings in order to be godly rulers. So David had studied the scriptures that were available at that point in time and was aware of God's promises to the ancestors. He never hesitated to personalise those promises to himself.

David had a revelation of salvation by grace through faith (the New Covenant). Many of his Psalms describe this vividly. He knew the futility of animal sacrifices offered without true conviction or repentance. Hence, he boldly declared this and lived it. He was assured of God's unconditional love for him and declared that God was his shield. David stood strong and acted on the covenant that he had with God. He firmly believed in circumcision (since he was under the old covenant) and also rested in the New Covenant (since he had a revelation from God about it). Circumcision was an external sign made in the flesh of man, declaring he had faith like Abraham. It was meant to remind man that his faith should be in God and His work alone. The physical sign of circumcision was itself very personal.

David was very sure that God would not only deliver him from his adversaries but that He would honour him before them. David had learned this truth from all that happened in his life. He was one of those who constantly meditated on God's goodness in his life, time and again.

When David wrote this Psalm, he was in great distress—climbing up the mountain, barefoot, and weeping with his head covered. All those who followed him were deeply distressed to see him in this state. Yet he encouraged himself (his hallmark) by embracing the Lord's promises from the word of God. He never uttered a curse on himself. He declared the righteous acts of God even before he saw them come to pass. He was assured in his heart of the Lord's mercy and faithfulness.

Needless to say, most of our distress arises because of our foolishness. But how often do we possess the attitude that David had? Most of the time, we justify ourselves in our own conscience, fret against God, go hard after the person who offends us, and refrain from seeking the Lord to justify us. Let us learn to maintain a good attitude through all that we go through.

4. *I CRIED TO THE LORD WITH MY VOICE, AND HE HEARD ME FROM HIS HOLY HILL. SELAH.*

5. *I LAY DOWN AND SLEPT; I AWOKE, FOR THE LORD SUSTAINED ME.*

When David and his loyal men left the city, the priests Zadok and Abiathar carried the Ark of the Covenant along with them and followed David to the banks of the Jordan. But David forbade them to follow him and commanded them to return to the city with the Ark. The Ark was symbolic of the Lord's physical presence with the people in those days. For David to tell the priests to take the Ark back was a step of humility and great faith. He waited only on God to justify him and declared that if the Lord was pleased with him, He would bring him back to the city and to His Holy place to worship before the Ark again.

David declares that God heard him when he called out to Him. When he declared this, he was well outside Jerusalem. Yet he declared the end result he was praying for rather than declaring his actual condition. **This is the language of faith.** He wasn't in denial and chose not to be carnal either. He believed strongly in the mercies of the Almighty.

The Holy hill is Mount Zion, also known as the Mountain of Grace under the New Covenant. David was very radical in his thoughts. He believed that the only way to God was through the Messiah (Grace) and not the law. So when he says that God heard him from Mount Zion, he is declaring that God was answering him according to His grace. God's mercy protects us from the punishment that we so rightly deserve, and His grace gives us access to His goodness (which isn't a reward for our works). Nothing that we do can qualify us to receive His mercy and grace apart from an acknowledgement and confession of the love and sacrifice of our Lord Jesus Christ from our hearts. So even when the Ark was not with him, David was assured that God had heard his voice. 'Hearing' implies that God has granted his request and delivered him from all trouble. It is an 'active' hearing.

How could David be so confident that the Lord had heard him? For 2 obvious reasons: first, he says he lay down and slept; he awoke the next morning because the Lord sustained him. Most of us often lose sleep over trivial matters. We allow a tiny offence to take away our peace to a great extent. Yet at this point, David was able to lie down and sleep. Can you imagine the extent to which the peace of God ruled in his heart? Then he rose up the next morning. This was the reason he believed that God had heard his prayer because it was only God who would have granted him sleep and sustained him through the night so that his enemies wouldn't kill him while he was asleep and also woke him up the next morning. In fact, Ahithophel had advised Absalom to pursue David the same night and kill him. David was not hallucinating regarding the danger that could come his way. Most of us would overlook a fact (that he slept and woke up again) which seemed so significant to David. It's these things that we also need to be sensitive to and that will magnify the work of God in our lives.

Secondly, when David heard that Ahithophel had sided with Absalom, he prayed that God would turn the counsel of Ahithophel to foolishness and saw it being answered when Absalom gave importance to Hushai's advice over that of Ahithophel's. Hushai kept David informed of everything happening in Jerusalem. Following this insult and shame, Ahithophel went home and hung himself. Definitely, this rejection of Ahithophel would have come to David's ears, and he knew that God had answered his prayers.

6. *I WILL NOT BE AFRAID OF 10 THOUSANDS OF PEOPLE WHO HAVE SET THEMSELVES AGAINST ME ALL AROUND.*

What a statement! How many of us can declare this? Most of us are praying to keep off from trials and persecutions. It is true that peace is very much necessary in our lives. But trials and persecutions bring us to the place when one day, even we can declare this truth boldly like David. And when we finally reach that place, satan is totally disarmed because his main aim is to make us stumble by arousing fear in us.

David had been in this position several times. Starting with lions and bears that he had to fight off while guarding his father's few sheep, he had learned to depend on God and be confident in the fact that His spirit rested upon him. **He practiced God's anointing.** When he had the encounter with Goliath, he remembered the victory God had given him over those ferocious animals. Similarly, his victory over Goliath strengthened his faith in God's faithfulness and deliverance when Saul wrongly pursued him. **David's strength came from remembering the work of God in his life.** That's what made him a humble person and helped him time and again to strengthen himself in the Lord no matter how terrifying the circumstances looked.

This is a declaration that he repeatedly emphasises in many Psalms. His confidence in God's goodness went through the roof. When he had wronged someone, he humbled himself before God, no matter the cost, and waited on God in repentant brokenness until he was convinced that he had obtained His forgiveness. When people came against him for unjust reasons, he still waited on God to avenge him. Either way, God was his guide.

David never depended on men to rescue him from his woes at any time. We never see David relying on any man's approval. His heart was always after God, to know every instruction directly from Him. This can be seen very clearly when we study his life. That's the reason why God called him a man after His own heart.

7. ARISE, O LORD; SAVE ME O MY GOD! FOR YOU HAVE STRUCK ALL MY ENEMIES ON THE CHEEKBONE; YOU HAVE BROKEN THE TEETH OF THE UNGODLY.

After David fled from Absalom and ascended the mountain with his people, he worshipped God. He understood the fact that praise and thanksgiving to God crippled the enemy. **When we refuse to focus on the problems and instead focus on God, we are able to receive His grace more efficiently to fight whatever comes our way.** Fear and worry, 2 of satan's chosen devices, have never been of help or profit to anyone so far. These are literally dungeons that we lock ourselves into, knowing well that it is a very unpleasant place to be in. God has definitely given us the strength to stay away from these harmful feelings. If we want to, we just have to appropriate His grace, firmly back off, and refuse to enter that place of fear and worry. We need to walk away from the door instead of entering that place and trying to come out. Seek God's help. Do what needs to be done, starting with focusing on God by worshipping and magnifying Him. We have the assurance that He will do what needs to be done because God has put all things under the Lord's feet and has ordained Him to be the head over all things to us (Ephesians 1:22).

David had this revelation because he never forgot all the ways in which God had delivered him from animals and humans. He aptly says that God struck his enemies on the cheekbone. That is embarrassing! Absalom's household was literally shattered, and there is no further mention of his lineage after that. Ahithophel committed suicide! This slap would have taught the enemy never to reconsider fighting David again. It would have been very painful.

Teeth are very important structures in our mouth. We very well know that once the permanent ones are knocked off, they can never grow back. Not only does it disfigure a person, but it also makes them physically weak since they won't be able to eat food satisfactorily without them.

Perhaps the slap on the cheekbone was so hard that it knocked out the teeth too! Well, that's one blow anyone would remember. Let me throw in something interesting here. Injury caused to teeth is a medico-legal case and is punishable under the law. It is considered a grievous injury because of its severe nature. Rectifying it is very expensive and requires expertise. So if the enemy's teeth were knocked off by God, we know for sure that the enemy had been dealt with severely.

It is always wise to leave vengeance in the hands of Almighty God when He clearly says "Vengeance is mine, and I will repay". It would be foolish to take things into our own hands. Let's learn from this story how David left it to God to protect him and bring him back to the holy land and his position as king. David had greatly sinned against God in Uriah's case. But God had dealt with him in this matter. It was not Absalom's place to rake up vengeance against David again. Absalom was destroyed and never had the chance to stand before his father again. David also made it clear that he loved God even if Absalom were to continue as king and David was to continue living as a vagabond.

God spoke a very important blessing over Abraham, saying, 'I will bless those who bless you and curse those who curse you.' The benefit of this blessing rests on everyone who is justified by faith. When a person puts himself against us, he is actually fighting God and is doomed to failure and destruction, provided we haven't wronged anyone! That's exactly the reason why the Lord Jesus asked us to pray for our enemies and bless those who curse us, in the hope that somehow they may have a change of heart, repent, seek forgiveness from God, and be averted from impending destruction.

8. *SALVATION BELONGS TO THE LORD. YOUR BLESSING IS UPON YOUR PEOPLE.*

This is a loud declaration of the truth. It is very important for us to have absolute assurance in this matter. This personal assurance is an indicator of our faith, trust, and hope in God. If we are able to declare this fact beyond the shadow of a doubt, we do well.

Salvation is a word that includes many things. Apart from deliverance from the enemy (as applied here), it also includes healing, wholeness, and forgiveness. In other words, it is the term that describes all that God has done and continues to do for us. When we can boldly and confidently say that God is light and in Him is no darkness, we are declaring that salvation belongs to God. God is not responsible for all the evil happening in the world today.

All evil entered the world because man chose his wisdom above God's in the Garden of Eden. It was mankind who opened the door to all misery, invited it in, and hugged it wholeheartedly. Even today, mankind is bent upon living life and partaking of the tree of the knowledge of good and evil when they decide to do things their way instead of God's way. Nevertheless, God provided a way to Himself through His Son. Satan can never offer mankind salvation; he can never rescue us in any manner; his only objective is to steal, kill, and destroy. He also rewards his followers with the same evil; he can never do any good.

Salvation belongs only to God! His blessings are always upon His people. We, the children of God, are always blessed. That is the truth. Even though we may feel otherwise about the circumstances, the truth that we are blessed still remains. It is up to us to renew our minds to this simple truth, which is of immense help when we embrace and stand on it. For example, the word describes Joseph as a very prosperous man when he was a servant to Potiphar and also when he was unjustly locked up in prison. **'Blessed' is who we are.** It is not defined by what we have. When we know we are blessed, we can flourish like a palm tree in the desert, no matter the circumstances. If we believe that materialistic wealth is what defines or determines our blessed nature, we are absolutely mistaken. Since we are already blessed, these things will be added to us. It's just a by-product of being blessed. It doesn't define it. That's exactly what the word teaches.

Psalm 4

INTRODUCTION:

This Psalm was probably written in succession to the previous one. The betrayal by Absalom was still fresh. David shares his insight and experience of his walk with God through it while all this happened. He describes the futility of man's pride, the peace he experienced even while he was fleeing from Absalom, and advises us on how to tackle our anger at any injustice that we may suffer.

1. HEAR ME WHEN I CALL, O GOD OF MY RIGHTEOUSNESS! YOU HAVE RELIEVED ME IN MY DISTRESS; HAVE MERCY ON ME AND HEAR MY PRAYER.

Here we see the declaration of the covenant of grace ('God of my righteousness') by David, who was an old covenant saint. Today, we who believe can stand before God because He has imparted His righteousness to us. None of us can approach Him otherwise. In truth, God does not owe us anything. But because He loves us, He provided redemption from our sins and imparted to us His Son's righteousness. That qualifies us to stand justified before Him. That's the reason we can boldly enter His presence and place our requests before Him. That's the reason we are heard! David approaches God in this manner, declaring that God is his righteousness.

David often remembers and declares the deliverances God granted him in most of his Psalms. He was ever mindful of the way God brought him through on a daily basis. This is actually a strong source of strength for God's children. He also declares very clearly in other Psalms that God relieved him from 'ALL' his distresses. That is not an overstatement. When we study David's life in the Word of God, we can see how intimate his relationship was with God. He was ever thankful to God for deliverance from all his enemies.

Our lives are established when we realise that God deals with us at all times according to His mercy and grace. There is no other way for man to approach God. Salvation life is flooded with God's grace and mercy. Often, we tend to forget that and revert back to justifying ourselves by our works. Whether we do good or otherwise, always remember that we can approach God only on the basis of His mercy and grace. These 2 attributes of God are inseparable. They always go hand in hand. Because we lack the ability to renew our minds, we receive His mercy and ignore His grace. While His mercy provides forgiveness for all our sins, His grace is what helps us live a holy life going forward.

While growing up, I thought that I was forgiven for my sins up until I confessed them and was water baptised, but after that, I believed that I would be held accountable for any sins I committed. I was ignorant of the baptism of the Holy Spirit. Later, when I studied His word and heard the teachings of God-sent preachers, I realised the obvious flaw of this doctrine. If salvation were to be so (as I had understood before), then there would still be no hope for man. Man would still go to hell, and God's work of redemption would not serve the purpose it was supposed to. Because even after salvation, it is not possible for us to totally keep away from sin, as is the experience of most. Then there is no use for the Lord Jesus having died to just wash away a fraction of our sins (so to speak). Romans 6:10 clearly states that He died once for all our sins (past, present, and future sins put together). He died much before I was born; so all my sins were in the future, and I believe He has forgiven me for all of them. That's His mercy. Now knowing that I am forgiven, I reach out to the open hands of God and receive His grace to help me live the 'New Creation Life' that is ordained for all His children. **God's grace doesn't give us the licence to sin; it keeps us from sinning!** Grace is what empowers us to live right. When we believe right, we live right. Both mercy and grace are gifts of God to mankind and are available to all who receive them with a humble heart.

2. HOW LONG O YOU SONS OF MEN, WILL YOU TURN MY GLORY TO SHAME? HOW LONG WILL YOU LOVE WORTHLESSNESS AND SEEK FALSEHOOD? SELAH.

This verse is a paraphrase of Psalm 2:1–3. From the very beginning, God declared that man's thoughts and intents are wicked continually. The prophets warn us of this time and again in their books. The Lord Jesus spoke along the same lines in His Sermon on the Mount. At the fall that happened in Eden, the focus of man shifted from God to himself. It is the goodness of God—His love, mercy, and grace—that redirect our focus back to God.

God's glory is clearly displayed in creation. Creation directs us to God. It provides undeniable evidence that God exists. But instead of understanding this point, we see people worshipping the sun, moon, stars, trees, animals, birds, snakes, and what not! In other words, man has turned the glory of God (displayed through His creative works) to shame (by worshipping the creation instead of the Creator)! I believe that the sun itself would feel disgusted about the fact that men worship it instead of God.

The world's definition of love, prosperity, success, friendship, humility, etc. is very different from God's definition. We will be led astray by the principles and traditions of the world if we are not aware of the truth in God's word, and this is much to our loss. Ignorance of the truth has wrecked the lives of innumerable people. The word states that people perish because of a lack of knowledge. Knowledge here refers to God-centred knowledge that comes only from the word of God. Another cause of man's destruction is an improper understanding of the Word. The Lord Jesus explained this in detail when He taught about the parable of the sower recorded in Matthew 13, Mark 4, and Luke 8. God makes sure to send out His word to every corner of the world. The deficit in reception is always on our side.

We are taught to have foresight even as we grow up. Most parents teach their children to save money. But how often do we think about eternity? Even most Christians are securing property and inculcating worldly ambitions in their children instead of teaching them to seek God first with all their heart, mind, and soul. If we were to look at everything in the light of eternity (heaven or hell), I am sure that most of us would live differently. All of our worldly ambitions and desires are futile, worthless, and false when they do not have God at the centre of it.

The sun is the centre of the solar system, and all the planets revolve around it. This is the pattern that our lives should follow. No 2 planets are the same. Each is different in size and feature. The sun denotes God's position and power; the planets correlate to the different aspects of our lives—career, marriage, parenting, relationships, etc. Each of these varies in importance and should be centred around God. God's word assures us that God has each of us on this earth for a specific, unique reason, and that's the best place for us to be in. Unfortunately, we make all the plans and try to fit God somewhere in there. It is similar to expecting the sun to revolve around each planet. That doesn't make sense, right? This is the sole reason for the failures most Christians face. If only each of us would seek the will of God for our own lives and strive to fulfil that with His grace, our lives would reflect His glory!

Many ambitious people who have been a great success according to the world's standards have confessed this fact shortly before their death or at the far end of their lives only to realise the futility and vanity of their ambitions. But death is a point where it is too late to turn around. We are blessed when God reveals this to us as we study His word and receive it for ourselves. We are blessed with the ability to portray God and speak into the lives of many through the way we live our lives. It's all about **"PERSPECTIVE".** When we look at everything through the light of God's word, we are using the **'eternity perspective'** (that is wisdom). If we restrict it only to this earthly life, we lose out on the actual worth and purpose for which we were created.

The truth remains the truth, irrespective of who accepts or denies it. This life will come to an end one day. The Day of Judgement is inevitable, and there is a crowd that enters heaven and another into hell. Every man has been given the privilege of making his choice according to his own free will. Choose wisely! We can never be exempted from the consequences of our choices. Our life here on earth is not even a notable fraction of eternity. Eternity never ends!

3. ***BUT KNOW THAT THE LORD HAS SET APART FOR HIMSELF HIM WHO IS GODLY; THE LORD WILL HEAR WHEN I CALL TO HIM.***

It brings me much joy when the Lord shows me certain New Covenant truths declared so boldly and clearly in the Old Testament. This is the truth of 'Election by Grace'. When we study Romans 8:29–30, we learn that God already had a protocol laid out from the foundation of the world for His elect people.

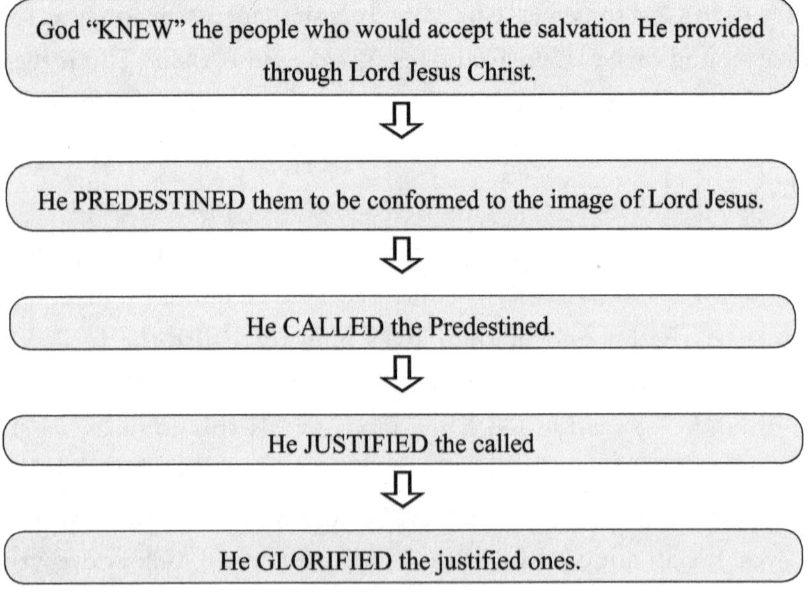

David is speaking this exact same thing. Let alone the unbelievers, even most believers are unaware of this astounding truth. Many people stop at

Salvation and don't go beyond that into the abundant life. If we renew our minds to the ocean of revelation of God's word, it won't be difficult for us to hold onto our calling and accomplish it for the glory of God since He supplies grace in abundance for this very purpose. He has finished His part. We just need to do ours.

If we, the children of God, understood the fact that God has set us apart and hears our every request, we would live very differently. The authority He has handed out to us will not be wasted. We can live such victorious lives that the world would envy us for it. Instead, many waste their time begging God to do what He has already done. They wail, beg, bawl, and say they are not being heard at the end of it all. Revival happens when man opens his heart to receive all that God has already released. He did not withhold His only Son from us. How can He keep anything else from us (Romans 8:32)? It's just common sense!

When we have children, it is easy to understand certain things. As parents, we do our best to see our children lack nothing good. We also do our best to keep them away from harm. Yet when it comes to our relationship with God, we shed tears for everything! How awkward is that? Certain preachers encourage the people to wail and shed rivers of tears for even small things. It is good to come to the level of understanding that God hears us when we CALL, just like the way we respond to our children when they call us.

4. *BE ANGRY, AND DO NOT SIN. MEDITATE WITHIN YOUR HEART ON YOUR BED AND BE STILL. SELAH.*

5. *OFFER THE SACRIFICES OF RIGHTEOUSNESS, AND PUT YOUR TRUST IN THE LORD.*

Do you feel that you are in David's shoes right now? Were you put down or betrayed by one you loved dearly? Does your heart ache more because you know that your loved one is doing something that is destroying them? Take this excellent advice that David has written here!

It's not a surprise if we get angry at injustice done to us (provided we come clean). David was angry here when Absalom killed Amnon and fled. Lord Jesus was angry at injustice (at the money changers and people who did business inside the temple). It is one of many feelings that God has given us. But anger is meant for us to take a step towards justice and not injustice. We need to have control over anger and not vice versa. Only God can help us do that!

When we allow anger to have the upper hand, forcing us to do wrong, we are giving place to sin. It, in turn, grows into wrath, which is cruel. Absalom was angry with Amnon, but he did not cause any physical harm to Amnon. But when this turned to wrath, Absalom killed Amnon. God has given us the grace to channel our anger in the right manner. For David, it was to meditate on God's word, lying upon his bed and being still (i.e. not taking any unwanted action against Absalom). For Lord Jesus, it was a righteous indignation concerning His Father's house, and He made a whip of cords and drove out the money changers from the temple. He did this not once, but twice. God's way for each of us is unique at every instance. The step we need to take is made known to us if we are sensitive to His voice. We should learn to wait on Him and make the right move as He guides us.

The guidance of God will always make us do the right thing. He will never lead us into any evil. He expects us to do right always and wait on Him to avenge us at the right moment. There is none who can avenge like God. None can outsmart Him. During times of temptation, we need to remember Psalm 1:1 – not to walk in the counsel of the ungodly, or stand in the path of sinners, or sit in the seat of the scornful. Wait on Him and just watch Him work the impossible for you.

6. *THERE ARE MANY WHO SAY, "WHO WILL SHOW US ANY GOOD?" LORD, LIFT UP THE LIGHT OF YOUR COUNTENANCE UPON US.*

This is a very dangerous statement a believer can make when they are disappointed or dismayed, and it happens because their faith is weakened. I cringe when I hear someone say that because I know that is a lie from the pit of hell. Most often, because of this, we end up taking things into our own hands and make matters worse. Patience is nowhere around. This is the root cause of further distress in perilous times. The unbelievers have this mindset all the time and operate on this very principle.

Have you heard the saying 'Stand on your own feet'? As believers, we are required to stand on the foundation of Lord Christ; not our feet or legs or hands (self-confidence). Any other foundation other than Lord Jesus doesn't have a chance of withstanding a storm. When we stand confident in Him, He strengthens our legs, feet, hands, and every other part of our body to bring His goodwill to pass in and through our lives. Educating oneself is good. Gaining knowledge is good too. But if we put our confidence in our education and knowledge instead of trusting God to lead and guide us, we will be at a great loss. 'Trusting God' and 'patience' go hand in hand. It is a fruit of the Spirit. We have it deposited in our spirit when we are born again. We need to learn to use it. It's a spiritual muscle that needs constant exercise to get strengthened further in our lives. If we see everything the way God sees, it wouldn't be difficult to have patience because we know that God will come through for us.

What we really need at trying times is the opening of our understanding. We need to know and acknowledge that God is still seated on His throne and that He has never lost a battle, ever! When we open our hearts to this truth, we are able to place everything into the hands of the Living God and allow Him to fight the battle for us. He helps us with patience when we need it most. God is the only One Who can show us good. We need to practice what David recommends here because it obviously worked for him and it will definitely work for us too.

Sometimes we may see our loved ones in this situation. We should pray for them along these lines. God not only hears our prayers but He is also more than willing to disperse their darkness with His light.

Psalms teaches us many short powerful prayers like these. It teaches us what exactly we need to petition God when we face a particular situation.

7. YOU HAVE PUT GLADNESS IN MY HEART, MORE THAN IN THE SEASON THAT THEIR GRAIN AND WINE INCREASED.

This verse describes the outcome of David's trust in God and doing the right thing. What satisfies a worldly person? Is there anything that truly satisfies a carnal person? Probably an ambition fulfilled would ignite some joy. But it is most surely short-lived because they tend to rely on a continuous supply of good circumstances to maintain their joy. In other words, their joy is sourced from the outside and can be tampered with. Lord Jesus described in the Sermon on the Mount how gentiles seek after food and clothing primarily. The reason why worldly joy is temporary is because it depends on an external factor. So if that factor is withdrawn or if we lose interest in it, that joy crumbles.

Agriculture and animal husbandry were the 2 common occupations of people in those days. Harvest was celebration time for those in agriculture. They looked forward to it from the time they sowed the seeds. They thought that a good harvest was the outcome of their sweat and toil, crediting and praising themselves as people do now. But David just did one thing. He trusted in God wholeheartedly and did what God told him to do (no sweat or toil), and yet the gladness he had even while waiting was greater than the joy of harvest which those people had. In other words, David was rejoicing in his place of exile more than Absalom did sitting on the throne in Jerusalem!

Every one of us who trusts God this way is entitled to the same joy every day of our lives, irrespective of the circumstances. The reason for this is, joy is placed in our spirit when we are born again. It is something that originates from the inside and has the power to change our external situations. This joy doesn't end and cannot be destroyed. Joy that flows from within makes us abound in thanksgiving, praise, and worship to God. This is what makes mountains move and keeps our hearts stable in times of distress.

8. *I WILL BOTH LIE DOWN IN PEACE, AND SLEEP; FOR YOU ALONE, O LORD, MAKE ME DWELL IN SAFETY.*

The results that David had because of trusting God are astounding and something that we should covet. We can have it too, provided we follow the same pattern:

- ✡ Believe God 100%.
- ✡ Follow His guidance.
- ✡ Allow the gifts of the Spirit to work in and through us.
- ✡ Refrain from self justification.
- ✡ Let God avenge us.

David lived in peace, slept in peace, and awoke with gladness in his heart all because he believed right. His understanding of God was priceless. He knew Who God is : The Great I Am! Since he focused on this fact alone, he was able to come through and get out of all trouble.

To be able to lie down and sleep in peace after a long day definitely qualifies as one of the greatest blessings a person can have. Ask the world; it would confess that too. The number of people approaching doctors and counsellors for insomnia is on the rise. They want to know if a cup of green tea or soaking their feet in hot water before sleeping would help. **The bottom line is this: if your heart is at peace, you sleep well.** When it is disturbed, no amount of tea or feet soaking is going to help. May we realise this for ourselves and also help others realise this fact too. Our physical body needs rest. Most problems could be avoided if we could just get a normal good night's sleep. God's grace is what enables us to do just that.

Being safe and away from harm is God's blessing. We have seen and heard of bodyguards turning on people they had sworn to protect and assassinating them. We can't trust man to keep us safe. That being said, it is the duty of a husband to protect his wife and children, for parents to protect their children when they are young and vice versa when parents grow old, for shepherds of churches to safeguard their flock, etc. This is the protection standard instituted by God Himself and He is right at the top of the line. The problem arises when God is not in the picture and one man trusts another man to keep him safe. That will never work out. Man always fails without God. God's protection is what we need every single day. This is provided for us in the midst of trials and persecutions too. God's angels are assigned to each of His children to keep them safe (Psalm

91:11). But this protection is only for those who boldly confess before the world that Jesus Christ is Lord (Luke 12:8). Those who take it for granted cannot avail this benefit. Can you perceive the depth of David's confession and the confidence he had in God as his protector? Let's learn to walk in that path too. With so much assurance given to us by these counsellors, what else do we need to convince us?

Psalm 5

INTRODUCTION:

This psalm emphasises an established truth: we can approach God only because of His mercy and grace. No human can justify himself before God by his works. It is God who chose us, called us, and justified us. The starting and ending point is God. He is the author and finisher of our faith. God doesn't owe us anything. Motivated by love, He provided atonement for the whole world. In His humility, He hears us when we approach Him. We don't score points based on our goodness. That's what David is conveying to us through this Psalm. This is a Psalm that teaches us biblical humility.

1. ***GIVE EAR TO MY WORDS, O LORD, CONSIDER MY MEDITATION.***

2. ***GIVE HEED TO THE VOICE OF MY CRY, MY KING AND MY GOD. FOR TO YOU I WILL PRAY.***

3. ***MY VOICE YOU SHALL HEAR IN THE MORNING, O LORD; IN THE MORNING I WILL DIRECT IT TO YOU, AND I WILL LOOK UP.***

I'm sure that most of us think that by rising up early in the morning to worship God, we are doing God a favour. How easy is it to rise up early in the morning every day and worship God consistently? And if we were to do that, how many of us would do it for the reason that we love God or just do it as an obligation to try to score some bonus points?

David approached God for Who He is—The God of the universe. It is an awesome thing indeed that Almighty God, who created and governs the entire universe, would even bother to listen to each and every one of our prayers. If we could just understand the magnificence and glorious splendour of our God, we would realise how great a favour He has shown.

There were many times that I read this Psalm and thought that David was asking God to hear him because of his effort to rise early and seek Him. But no! This is not about that. This is David realising the greatness of God and giving due respect to the King of the universe. Furthermore, he admits that before each day starts, he wants God to give him the necessary instructions for the day, showing David's dependence on God. He is requesting God to guide his words and his thoughts (meditation). That's very important in our daily walk with God.

I once heard a wonderful man of God say there was a reason why God ordained the Book of Proverbs to have 31 chapters. Being the book of wisdom, each of the 31 chapters provides instructions for each day of the month (each month having 30–31 days). This really gripped my heart. Ever since then, I begin my day with the Proverb specific to each date. For example, I read Proverbs 1 on the first day of the month and follow it sequentially until the end of the month. God has instructed me on a daily basis this way for years now, and it has never decreased or lost its efficacy.

Most of us have planners. Tonight we contemplate what needs to be done tomorrow. Some even pen down stuff for an entire year, while others even make post-retirement plans as they begin their career! There is nothing wrong with planning and being organised. But inevitably, most of us go off the deep end while doing that and keep God out of it. This is clear when our planning fails and we start to fret. When we plan things with God at the centre, it is a restful planning accompanied by peace, knowing that He will bring things to pass in a timely manner. The Lord is never late.

Lord Jesus taught us very clearly in the Lord's Prayer, saying, 'Give us this day our daily bread'. This is what David was asking for. A fresh supply of manna was given every morning to the Israelites. Similarly, God releases His favour, mercy, and grace fresh every morning, for the day, in the measure we need them. Only He knows the demand, and only He can supply it. He never gives us the grace to solve tomorrow's issues, today. A supply is dispensed each day. For tomorrow, the supply is kept ready by Him. But this grace to live each day, one at a time, needs to be received by us. Only if we have knowledge of this can we receive it from His loving hands, and this would destroy any level of anxiety a person has.

It is God who puts the desire in us to seek Him early in the morning. His love draws us to Him. People who did so with the right attitude reaped a pleasant reward. For example, Mary Magdalene went to the tomb early on the first day of the week. She was richly rewarded for being the first to see the resurrected Lord! She also had the privilege of telling everyone else that the Lord had risen! God chose a woman to "inform" others about His resurrection! That excites and encourages me to the core! In those days, there was very little value or worth placed on women. Can you see how a person is rewarded when they seek Him early with a true heart?

It is wise to seek God the first thing when we rise up each day and place ourselves and our day into His hands before we get occupied with other things. The God who upholds the universe is more than willing to guide us with His wisdom and give us the abundant life that He has entitled us to have. David had a humble beginning. Yet when he became king, he continued to seek the Lord early. We should not allow our schedule, laziness or excuses to get in the way of seeking God. The moment we realise it, we need to kick away every hindrance and get right back to seeking God.

Often times, during trials, we are tempted to look at other people for help and guidance. After spending restless nights contemplating whom we should approach first the next morning, we forget that God is the One who works through people to help us. We need to seek God, and He will point us in the right direction to the right person, with a witness in our hearts. That does not mean we put our trust in that person. We need to put our trust in God alone and keep it there. People are temporary helpers. God may use Mr. A today and Mr. B tomorrow. Sometimes, we may be that A or B for someone else. On the whole, every single person needs to put their trust in God alone.

4. FOR YOU ARE NOT A GOD WHO TAKES PLEASURE IN WICKEDNESS, NOR SHALL EVIL DWELL WITH YOU.

5. THE BOASTFUL SHALL NOT STAND IN YOUR SIGHT; YOU HATE ALL WORKERS OF INIQUITY.

6. YOU SHALL DESTROY THOSE WHO SPEAK FALSEHOOD; THE LORD ABHORS THE BLOODTHIRSTY AND DECEITFUL MAN.

David had experienced the severity of God's stance towards sin in his own life. Romans 3:10 and 23 says, 'There is none righteous; no, not one' and 'all have sinned and come short of the glory of God'. David knew very well that he was a sinner like any other man. In fact, his sin concerning Bathsheba and Uriah was something that most of us wouldn't commit even in our dreams. But he knew what it was to be in that place and how much of an abomination it was to God. For a period of time after committing that shameful act, he ignored his own conscience and committed the greater sin of murdering Uriah. But he learned that God's mercy was greater and extended to every true repentant sinner. God's mercy drew him out of that place of condemnation when he repented with a broken spirit and a contrite heart.

Sometimes we think that God silently tags along with us when we are continuing in sin and overlooks it. No, that's not the case. David here declares that God is light, and in Him there is no darkness. The minute we have God in our lives, His light dispels every bit of darkness and brings out our hidden sins as well. This is done in order to convict us and not condemn us, so that we can deal with it and forsake it. He is the consuming fire who burns up all the muck in our lives. His word continually sanctifies us when we dwell in it. Though David had numbed himself to sin for a period of time and continued to commit one sin greater than the other, it did not take God long to reveal his pride, wickedness, deceit, and bloodthirsty nature through the prophet Nathan. Even though God had declared long ago that David was a man after His own heart, He disciplined him promptly when he did wrong. David had to pay a huge price for his mistakes in the form of consequences.

God has absolutely no part in evil. As He disciplined David then, He does it for us now. When we do wrong and repent of it, He forgives us. We don't go to hell for the sins we commit. If we have believed in the Lord Christ, then we are not judged by God. But we have to bear the consequences of our mistakes. We need to humble ourselves by never justifying our act in any manner. For example, if a believer breaks traffic rules, the police will detain him. He has to pay the fine or suffer the punishment that the law of the land dictates. That's the consequence. As far as God is concerned, He is not going to send him to hell for that. If he causes a wreck and injures or kills someone because of negligence, he will have to spend time in jail and will be held responsible by many people for that. This discipline cannot be escaped. Still, God doesn't send him to hell for that. This discipline will make sure that we learn our lesson and keep away not only from breaking the rules again, but also from a lot of other wrong things.

There is no way God can indulge with the wicked, boastful people, workers of iniquity, liars, bloodthirsty, and deceitful men. He is watching over all the evil that these people do, constantly warning them (through their conscience), and will make them pay for it at the right time if they don't repent. The word specifies that the wickedness of the wicked will destroy them. That's an established law.

Boasting is a major problem today. It is legalised in the conscience of mankind. Unfortunately, we haven't realised it because we often practice it ourselves. The only way we become aware of the foolishness of boasting is when we are convicted by the Holy Spirit who dwells in us. When we are convicted in that manner, we literally hate boasting in any form. Boasting in ourselves and our accomplishments is absolute foolishness and detrimental to our walk with God. In truth, everything that we are and all that we have is gifted to us by God. If He doesn't give us favour or wisdom, we would be hopeless today. In 1 Corinthians 4:7, Paul says, 'For who makes you different from another? And what do you have that you did not receive? Now if you did indeed receive it, why do you boast as if you had not received it?' The absolute truth is that boasting in the flesh amounts to nothing. In Galatians 6:14, Paul says explicitly, 'But God forbid that I should boast except in the cross of our Lord Jesus Christ.' If at all we are tempted to boast, it should always be centred on the Cross of our Lord Jesus Christ. May we learn by practicing every day to increase Him and decrease us (John 3:30). Proverbs 10:32 says, 'The lips of the righteous know what is acceptable'. When we are made righteous through our Lord Jesus Christ, the Spirit within us bears witness to what words are acceptable from our mouth. This will automatically block perverse (curses and abuses) and boastful words.

David explains here how God deals with wicked people who continue to step up the ladder of wickedness. It starts with God not taking pleasure in wickedness, hating and then abhorring those who indulge in it. God has indeed taken a stance against wickedness. So we, His children, should not have anything to do with wickedness. We need to flee from it.

7. BUT AS FOR ME, I WILL COME INTO YOUR HOUSE IN THE MULTITUDE OF YOUR MERCY; IN FEAR OF YOU, I WILL WORSHIP TOWARD YOUR HOLY TEMPLE.

For any of us who have stumbled and fallen like David did, can take this hint that he gives and approach God with the right attitude. Humbling ourselves and not justifying our sins, is the way to approach Him. The entrance is His gates of mercy. In spite of the horrific sin that he committed, David knew God's mercy was greater. He didn't run from God when Nathan warned him. Being king, he could have justified himself before any man if he wanted to (though that is not true justification). But he humbled himself immediately, fell on his face before God, and truly repented of the evil he had done. Under the old covenant, there was a way of atonement provided for sins through animal sacrifices. David could have taken repentance lightly and just got done with it by offering that sacrifice. But he knew very well that God was not interested in those sacrifices. **God has always looked at man's heart and intentions, requiring**

men to repent with a contrite heart. That's what David chose wisely and also declared boldly in the Psalm that he wrote. As a result, God forgave him, strengthened him to face the consequences of his wrong choices, and kept him going in life to accomplish His will through him.

8. *LEAD ME, O LORD, IN YOUR RIGHTEOUSNESS BECAUSE OF MY ENEMIES; MAKE YOUR WAY STRAIGHT BEFORE MY FACE.*

David's sin was very well known to his enemies too. His own sons used his poor morality against him. They took it upon themselves to punish him, thinking they were in God's place. But none of us can take God's place to punish another man for his sins. That position belongs only to our sovereign God. Even though David was anointed to be king, he never stood against Saul to avenge himself, even when he had the opportunity to kill him. He declared that he would not lift his hand against the Lord's anointed. Saul died in battle. David was raised to the position of kingship in a couple of days following Saul's death because he patiently waited on God instead of avenging himself. He first became king over Judah and ruled for 7 and a half years, while one of Saul's sons, Ishbosheth, ruled over Israel. Ishbosheth was assassinated by his own men, and then David was anointed king of both Israel and Judah.

Contrary to this, Absalom exalted himself to the place of king while David was still king. He took it upon himself to punish his father. Even though David loved him as his son, Absalom counted his father as his enemy. Fearing that harm might come to his subjects because of Absalom's wrath, David fled the country. He could have very well fought against Absalom, but he chose not to. He waited on God to justify him and bring him back to kingship if the Lord willed for it to be so. In other words, he depended on God's righteousness. He knew his was worthless.

David feared faltering in his path, especially before his adversaries, including his own sons. He did not want to return evil for evil when they contended with him. His own sons, Absalom and Adonijah, contended with him even until his death. The distress is greater when a loved one stands against us. He constantly depended on the Lord for His guidance at every point. He had learned his lesson well through the discipline he received from the Lord after his sin with Bathsheba. Hence, he never took a chance of putting himself against God again. Even though his enemies raked up his sin before him time and again, he depended on God to rescue him in His time and His way.

9. FOR THERE IS NO FAITHFULNESS IN THEIR MOUTH; THEIR INWARD PART IS DESTRUCTION; THEIR THROAT IS AN OPEN TOMB; THEY FLATTER WITH THEIR TONGUE.

All the features described here generally apply to the ungodly man. However, the people referred to here are not unbelievers. They are the ones who call themselves God's children but display these characteristics at the heart level. The Lord Jesus warns us of wolves in sheep's clothing, warning us of so-called Christians who behave the same way. The early church was constantly warned to watch out for and keep away from such. The world has plenty of them now. David had to face many of his own people who behaved in this manner. During his last days, Joab (the commander of his own army), Adonijah (his son), and Abiathar (the high priest) turned against him.

The way a person talks about others to us is the same way he or she will talk about us to them. If they are not faithful in keeping secrets that others trusted them with, neither will they be faithful in keeping the secrets we tell them. This is a very good way to discern the character of a person and keep away from them. When they open their mouths, it stinks (not literally, though). But all that they can say is bad about everyone. It is very easy for them to put down another and flatter us. If we don't pay attention, we can get carried away, give into their flattery, and suffer the same consequences that their victims suffered. People can sweet-talk us into destruction. They do that for their own profit. As long as they can get something done through us, they'll flatter us to the skies. The moment we realise their deception and put ourselves on guard, their behaviour makes a U-turn! It is much better for us to stand on guard right from the very beginning with such people. This is possible only when we depend on God for discernment every day. We can save ourselves a lot of trouble that way.

The Book of Proverbs constantly warns us against flattery. Most of us automatically stay away from people who would rebuke or speak evil of us. But unfortunately, the soothing effect of flattery fools us. Wisdom is not to allow flattery to affect us in any way as much as negative things spoken over us. Instead of flattery and negativity, let us pay attention to what God says about us, because that is what matters. When people forcibly wanted to make the Lord Jesus king, He withdrew from them and did not commit Himself to man, knowing what was in man. They proved time and again that as long as He satisfied their physical and emotional needs, they would worship Him. The moment they dint, they wouldn't even hesitate to stone Him. Never base your life on the opinion of men (good or bad). Seriously, it doesn't matter at all. **What matters is what God says about you. That is everything!**

10. PRONOUNCE THEM GUILTY, O GOD! LET THEM FALL BY THEIR OWN COUNSELS; CAST THEM OUT IN THE MULTITUDE OF THEIR TRANSGRESSIONS, FOR THEY HAVE REBELLED AGAINST YOU.

David described his adversaries as those who stood against God. His understanding regarding them was deep. David's sons, his trusted commander Joab and high priest Abiathar, rebelled against him one after another. His trusted counsellor, Ahithophel, stabbed him in the back by supporting the rebels and giving them odious advice. Nevertheless, David knew that God had anointed and crowned him as king. He never strived to obtain that position by deception (like Absalom). Only based on the anointing did he become king over Israel and Judah. This happened much later (approximately 13 years) after the prophet Samuel anointed him to be king. During all this time, David never fought against Saul because he (Saul) was the 'Lord's anointed'. David had that fear. He knew that God is the one who brings down one and raises up another. He waited patiently on God to seat him on the throne of Israel.

David's sons, however, did not do that. While he was alive and still king, Absalom, followed by Adonijah, took it upon them to become king. Both of them were older than Solomon. Yet God had promised David through Nathan, much before his sin with Bathsheba, that his son, who would build the temple, would be the one to succeed him on the throne too. That clearly referred to Solomon. Yet both Absalom and Adonijah tried to take it by force. Neither of them was interested in God and His plans for Israel. They just wanted to usurp power and exalt themselves. David was confident that both sons were wrong in what they were doing. He didn't take it personally, though, because he clearly saw their rebellion directed against God. He knew that God had appointed Solomon to be king. Young Solomon followed his father when he fled from Absalom. He too waited on God to appoint him as king at the right time. He did not exalt himself before his father or brothers.

These rebels had also recruited people who served their father and made them rebel against the authority that God had placed. Joab, Ahithophel, and Abiathar are examples of people who served David faithfully during perilous times and yet defected later on. David's prayer to God regarding his adversaries is very astounding. He prayed that their wicked counsel should turn back on them. In more than one place in the word, we read that the wickedness of the wicked will destroy them. Eventually, that is what happens if one continues to be wicked. That's exactly the reason why God asks us to love our enemies and pray for them. When they willfully wrong us, they are putting themselves against God. By praying for them, we hope that their darkness dispels and that they will allow God to speak into their lives. They may be enlightened about their sin and shown the way to get out of it. Perhaps they may repent and receive God's forgiveness, or else they will be doomed to destruction.

All this being said, we need to make sure that we haven't wronged the person who is fighting us. When the fault is ours, we must be quick to apologise and set things right. We can't ask God to avenge us when we are wrong. We should receive God's grace to help us apologise and set things right with the one whom we have wronged before things get worse (Proverbs 25:8–10, Matthew 5:23–25).

11. BUT LET ALL THOSE REJOICE WHO PUT THEIR TRUST IN YOU; LET THEM EVER SHOUT FOR JOY, BECAUSE YOU DEFEND THEM; LET THOSE ALSO WHO LOVE YOUR NAME BE JOYFUL IN YOU.

12. FOR YOU, O LORD, WILL BLESS THE RIGHTEOUS; WITH FAVOUR YOU WILL SURROUND HIM AS WITH A SHIELD.

Whether David was fleeing from Absalom or being betrayed by Adonijah, he was able to lie down in peace and sleep. This shows the place of favour and peace that God's children inherit. Even though there was much turmoil from his own blood, other people showed him kindness, which was from the Lord. Favour is something that we inherit at salvation. Not many of us are aware of that. The very presence of God in our lives defines us as favoured and prosperous. This in turn brings tangible (visible) good into our lives. Wealth in itself does not define us as prosperous or successful. That is a misconception of the biblical principle of prosperity. God's presence in us makes us blessed and prosperous, and as a result, tangible perks follow. When we seek God, these things are added to us (Matthew 6:33). Even if these visible things are shaken off, it does not disqualify us from the status of being blessed and prosperous. We continue in that status because God is still with us and the physical entities can and will be replaced again. This is well evident in David's and Joseph's lives. After the death of Absalom, Israel and Judah reinstated David as king according to the Lord's will and timing.

For those of us who know God and trust in Him, there is much reason to rejoice in the fact that God will always fight our battles for us and give us victory at all times. When we submit to Him, He stands for us, and all of heaven backs us up. Through trial or persecution, we must strive to rejoice because God defends us! Knowing that deliverance is only in His name, we can expect good things to happen. This is certainly possible because the Lord has instructed us to see the victory in our hearts and confess it, even before our eyes see it. If we can see it with our hearts first, it's just a matter of time before we see the victory with our physical eyes. If we first see it on the inside (imagination of our heart), then we will see it on the outside (physical realm). That is God's way to appropriate His victory in our lives. When we are so filled with assurance of victory, how can we not rejoice?

The Lord's work is straightforward and clear. He blesses the righteous and surrounds them with favour, as with a shield. The reason for that is that we are placed in the Lord Jesus Christ, who is the Beloved of the Father. We are given His righteousness which attracts the blessing and favour of God. The word shield here holds a different meaning. It's much more than the shield of a soldier, which only protects a person from the front. The shield that God speaks about is a 360-degree shield that encloses a person like a sphere. It is protection and favour provided in every area of our lives. Be it academics, career, parenting, marriage, relationships, etc., the Lord is with us, protecting and prospering us.

Psalm 6

A MUSICAL PSALM

INTRODUCTION:

An eight-string harp is a small harp (more like a basic, beginner, or simple version). It was probably more affordable or easy to make than the other types of harp. This particular Psalm was to be played on an 8-string harp, making it more personal. David played the harp as a shepherd boy. This talent was further refined when he was anointed by Samuel and the Holy Spirit came upon him. He was a musician. He also prepared many instruments when he was in kingship, especially for the worship in the temple.

David mentioned precise melodies for certain Psalms. Songs have a great impact on the mind and soul of a person. We teach children to learn certain things better by singing them so that they remain in their long-term memory. Above all, music was created by God, and worship is elevated so much more when we sing to Him. All can talk, but not all can sing. Singing or playing instruments is a God-given talent that is meant to be used to worship and glorify only Him.

The essence of this Psalm is that David approached only God for forgiveness for the sin he had committed. This sin had wrecked his soul and his physical body, causing much grief. In other words, he approached God with a broken heart and a contrite spirit. He also talks about the enemy's accusations that were meant to torment him. But he did not fall into the trap of condemnation that his enemies laid out for him. While seeking God's forgiveness, he did not allow the enemy to feed on his guilt. He knew very well that God is merciful, gracious, and had forgiven him.

1. O LORD, DO NOT REBUKE ME IN YOUR ANGER, NOR CHASTEN ME IN YOUR HOT DISPLEASURE.

We, as believers, tend to sin sometimes due to the weakness of our flesh. When we do, most often we find ourselves condemned and escaping from our fellowship with God. But that is not the right thing to do. When we sin, the first thing we need to do is go to God. He is the only One who can help us! Forgiveness and deliverance both belong to Him. This should be our foundational belief. We can save ourselves much trouble if we first go to Him instead of committing more blunders to cover up the first one. His mercies are greater and more powerful than our blunders.

When we have wronged someone, it is imperative for us to apologise and set things right with them. But if they are not in a position to forgive us, then we need to wait patiently and allow God to work peace between us. We have no right to talk bad about them or blame them for anything if they don't forgive us. At the same time, we need to keep away from the trap of condemnation that they set before us.

There are many examples of the Lord's chastening in the Bible. Basically, it can be classified into 2 types:

- ✡ Chastening because He loves us: this is done by His grace and mercy and leads to our restoration. It is compared to the relationship between a father and son. The father corrects and disciplines his son because he loves him.
- ✡ Chastening because of His anger: the classic example of this is the way He deals with the ungodly and wicked people who willfully reject His goodness, e.g., the Canaanites. This leads to absolute destruction and even the loss of life. It applies to people who are beyond any hope of repentance, despite the long-suffering nature of God.

David was under the Old Covenant. Yet he had a revelation of God's mercy and pleaded with God to deal with him by chastening him in love. For whatever sin he had committed, he knew that he was well deserving of death. That's the reason he asks God to deal with him in mercy and to forgive him for his sin.

2. *HAVE MERCY ON ME, O LORD, FOR I AM WEAK; O LORD, HEAL ME, FOR MY BONES ARE TROUBLED.*

3. *MY SOUL ALSO IS GREATLY TROUBLED; BUT YOU, O LORD-HOW LONG?*

It is absolutely essential to have a good understanding of who we are with and without God. Without God, we are just breathing corpses dragged towards hell in every work we do since we are empowered by carnality (flesh). With God, it's a totally different deal. When God is the centre of our lives, He takes over completely and makes life worth living. The only thing that beats carnality (flesh) is the Spirit of the Living God working in us.

David had the Spirit of the Lord in him since the day he was anointed by Samuel. There is no mention anywhere in the word of this spirit being lifted off from him, like how it happened with King Saul. That's the reason for his conviction and repentance. On the contrary, we never see Saul repenting for any wrong he had done. He steadily declined in life until he finally died. When we falter, it's the Spirit of God in us who convicts us and makes us return to God and be reconciled with Him. God has already reconciled the world to Himself through His Son (2 Corinthians 5:19). This loving Spirit convicts us and doesn't condemn us. There is an element of hope in conviction. Satan is the one who condemns and accuses us. God never condemns His children. It is His goodness that leads us to repentance. God is always known to be merciful to people who ask Him for His mercy. But the stubborn in heart willingly despise His mercy.

Even though God elevated David from shepherd to king, he knew his place. After being enthroned as king, he did many wrong things. But he never justified himself before God. He always returned to God for His mercy and forgiveness. He acknowledged the weakness of his flesh and never blamed others for his sin. God's presence in our lives should set us apart from the worldly people who are more than happy to point their fingers at everyone else. We should know who we are with and without Christ very clearly.

The effects of sin in a believer's life are devastating if not repented for. By submitting to sin, we open the door for satan to come in and wreck us. It may not seem the same for unbelievers because satan doesn't waste his time on someone who is not a challenge to his ministry; they are wrecking their own lives. But the children of God who do His will are a constant threat to him. Since God deals with us and wants us to get out of sin, He puts a holy dissatisfaction in us concerning our disobedience. This discomfort persists in us until we repent of it and receive His forgiveness. There is much physical (bodily) and emotional (soulish) weakness that we go through when we live in sin; that is what sin does. When we repent and turn to God, He works in us to prune away all those unwanted things, gives us grace to face the consequences of our mistakes, and finally restores us. This seems very painful, but nevertheless, He is with us and gives us grace to come through it. Continuing in sin without heeding God only increases stress (troubled soul) in our lives, causing our bones to weaken (osteoporosis). Scientific evidence has proven this today. There is absolutely no peace for a believer who continues in sin. Most importantly, humility is needed. We cannot justify ourselves before man or God for the wrong we do. We must humble ourselves, take responsibility for whatever wrong we have done, wait in patience, and walk in obedience to His leading, even as He sets things right for us.

How long should we pray for forgiveness? Let me ask you something: how much can we eat? We eat until we are filled and the hunger is satisfied. Similarly, we should not step away from fellowship with God until we know for sure and are assured in our hearts that God has forgiven us. It can be 10 seconds or 10 days. The truth is that God is quick to forgive. But we delay in receiving His forgiveness because we often battle the guilt in our conscience. Once we receive His forgiveness, the enemy has no chance to shake us with condemnation.

4. RETURN, O LORD, DELIVER ME! OH, SAVE ME FOR YOUR MERCIES' SAKE!

5. FOR IN DEATH THERE IS NO REMEMBRANCE OF YOU; IN THE GRAVE, WHO WILL GIVE YOU THANKS?

David felt that the Lord's Spirit may have departed from him. I don't believe that's true, though. It could have been the magnitude of his guilt that made him feel that way. If the Lord's Spirit had indeed left him, he would have turned out to be just like his predecessor, Saul. It is told that once the Lord's anointing had departed from Saul, a distressing spirit came upon him. Saul continued to do wrong, yet he never repented. Neither did he feel guilty. We never see him calling upon God the way David relents and repents. He became a total reprobate with no place for repentance. But David kept coming back to God. That is a sign that the Spirit of God was drawing him to God. That is a practical sign for us in our lives too.

An unbeliever makes very light of sin. He wouldn't probably even bother to make restitution for it because there is nothing in him to draw him towards God. At a basic level, a conscience is given to every human to turn us away from wrongdoing. But many people have their conscience seared so bad that it is powerless. Some very legalistic unbelievers would cut a deal with God, trying to pay back for their wrong deeds through certain religious rituals. But we are well aware that it is useless. God expects repentance from the heart. It's not something that is external only.

This particular sin had vexed David's soul and body to the point where he thought he would surely die. He knew he was hopeless without God, and death was certainly imminent. There is so much we can learn from the confessions and emotional turmoil that David writes regarding the after-effects of sin. It's just not a good place to be in.

Death is never an answer to anything. It was not even a part of God's original plan. It crept in because of the fall. But it was conquered by our Lord Jesus Christ when God resurrected Him. Eventually, death will be completely abolished when the Lord Jesus Christ returns and our physical bodies are transformed directly into glorious bodies that suit eternity in heaven, bypassing death. Our physical bodies are of no use after death. Whatever has to be done has to be done when we are alive and breathing. Much can be accomplished when we are alive. David asks for this privilege.

David counts praising and thanking God as a pleasure. The thought of death abhorred him for the fact that he couldn't praise God in the grave. He wanted a consistent and continued relationship with God and probably a peaceful passing on later. He never wanted to die from guilt and condemnation.

6. *I AM WEARY WITH MY GROANING; ALL NIGHT I MAKE MY BED SWIM; I DRENCH MY COUCH WITH MY TEARS.*

7. *MY EYE WASTES AWAY BECAUSE OF GRIEF; IT GROWS OLD BECAUSE OF ALL MY ENEMIES.*

A true sign of repentance is a broken spirit and a contrite heart. It is not a show done before men. It's was a personal affair between David and God. True repentance originates in the heart, followed by a correction of our character and a sincere attempt to keep from falling into the same pit again. It is a 180-degree turn from the wrong path.

The outcome of sin is always distressing. It's really not a place intended for the children of God. All the incidences (life examples) quoted in the Bible are written for our admonition and guidance so that we can see the results of obedience to God or disobedience to His word. They are our counsellors (Proverbs 11:14).

David attributes his eye growing old to all the tears he had shed. So much of our physical problems are rooted in our emotional turmoil and our adamancy to wallow in our wrong beliefs. Once the root is taken care of, then the rest of the tree will also be healthy. There is no lasting help medication can provide when the root of the problem is not addressed.

David was sick and tired of being in that state of depression. He wanted out of it as soon as possible, the way God would give it.

The main reason for all this turmoil was probably because David's enemies brought back his sins to remembrance repeatedly and felt responsible enough to punish him. It wasn't God who reminded him of his sins or held him responsible for them once He had forgiven him. They probably spoke very painful and hurtful words that made David go to God again and again instead of fighting his accusers. For some reason, the accuser (satan) brought it up before him through his enemies. When we don't like someone reminding us of our sin and guilt for which we have already obtained forgiveness from God, we shouldn't do the same to anyone else either. It's never our job to be an accuser like satan or a judge like God.

When we find ourselves in turmoil akin to David's, it would be good to examine our lives and make sure that we are not living in sin or persisting in wrong beliefs. If we are, we need to forsake it, walk away from it, hold onto God's ways, and get delivered. As far as our enemies are concerned, God will handle them!

8. DEPART FROM ME, ALL YOU WORKERS OF INIQUITY; FOR THE LORD HAS HEARD THE VOICE OF MY WEEPING,

9. THE LORD HAS HEARD MY SUPPLICATION; THE LORD WILL RECEIVE MY PRAYER.

10. LET ALL MY ENEMIES BE ASHAMED AND GREATLY TROUBLED; LET THEM TURN BACK AND BE ASHAMED SUDDENLY.

At this point, we can actually understand why David was so depressed. It was his enemies who held him guilty for his sins. Such things really tend to bring a man's spirit down. **Constant condemnation works ruin**. We must realise the depth of sorrow that accusation brings, whether someone does it to us or we do it to others. We must not indulge in this business of accusation. We should also be aware that satan is the master accuser, and he will never stop accusing the children of God. It's his work, and he is good at it. When we practice that, we are being his instruments. With a log in our eyes, we certainly should not attempt to pick out the speck in our brother's eye.

David was confident in the Father's love for him, and since he was firm in his relationship with God, it didn't take him long to get back on track. He never attempted to avenge or even justify himself. He waited on God to shut his enemies' mouths. He boldly declares to his enemies that when God has forgiven him, no one had the legal right to hold his sins against him. No one has the right to do that to us either, nor do we have the right to do it to any of God's children who have repented before God and set their hearts right before Him. This is where Romans 8:33 and 34 come in strongly: 'Who shall bring a charge against God's elect? It is God who justifies. Who is he who condemns? It is Christ who died, and furthermore is also risen, who sits even at the right hand of God, Who also makes intercession for us'. We should never allow the accuser to pin us down. People who indulge in accusing the brethren will definitely end up ashamed and troubled.

Psalm 7

INTRODUCTION:

Before we get into the explanation of this psalm, let us study a bit of history. David was from the tribe of Judah, and Saul was from Benjamin. Saul ruled Israel for many years (at least a minimum of 20 years). But the Lord rejected him and his descendants from kingship in the second year of his reign (1 Sam 13). Following this, God commanded Samuel to anoint David, a young shepherd from Bethlehem. But this was a private affair unknown to Saul (or anyone else for that matter).

The tribes were at peace with each other during those days. But the selection of a king from a particular tribe was indeed a prestigious matter. Saul had many loyalists from his own tribe who stood by him to the end and, even after that, supported his son Ishbosheth as king following Saul's death.

It is very clear in the book of Samuel that there were certain loyalists of Saul who spoke wrongly about David to Saul, accusing the former of wanting to kill him. Saul is known to have heeded these men and persisted in persecuting David wrongly. Prior to Saul developing envy over him, David behaved wisely and fought many battles for Saul with great victory. David was under total subjection to Saul. Even after Saul started to wrongly persecute him, David tried to help him. But Saul did not appreciate the help. The same music that David played to calm him down did not have any effect on him when Saul fell prey to jealousy. Proverbs 27:4 says, "Wrath is cruel and anger a torrent, but who can stand before jealousy?"

Even while David was playing the music, Saul tried to pin him to the wall using his spear. It did not take long for Saul to realise that David was anointed and posed a threat to his throne and lineage. Saul's loyalists also envied David and added fuel to the fire by speaking ill of David to Saul. Cush was probably one such person. People became David's enemies for all the wrong reasons. David had never wronged any of them personally.

This rivalry continued even years later when David fled from Absalom, and a Benjamite named Shimei cursed David loudly in the presence of all the people, deeming this a curse from God for having dethroned Saul. Yet David did not fall prey to this condemnation, nor did he avenge himself when he was restored to kingship following Absalom's death.

In spite of all this persecution, David never lifted his hand against Saul because he was the Lord's anointed. He feared God. But that same fear of God made him fight and kill the gentiles (Canaanites), whom the Lord had commanded him to vanquish.

1. O LORD MY GOD, IN YOU I PUT MY TRUST; SAVE ME FROM ALL THOSE WHO PERSECUTE ME; AND DELIVER ME,

2. LEST THEY TEAR ME LIKE A LION, RENDING ME IN PIECES, WHILE THERE IS NONE TO DELIVER.

David sought God and trusted only in His deliverance. David was a mighty man of war. He wasn't one of the cowards who would hide at the sight of his enemies. He had fought and killed the lion and the bear while shepherding. He confesses very distinctly in 1 Samuel 17:37 that it was the Lord who delivered him from the paws of the lion and the bear. Following that, he slew Goliath. He had fought many wars under the leadership of Saul and was victorious in every single one. Yet when it came to his own people persecuting him, David never fought back or argued with them.

David never gave a second thought to fighting back when it concerned threats from animals or gentiles. But when it concerned his own people, he never even entertained the thought of harming them (except for Uriah the Hittite), irrespective of which jewish tribe they were from.

A significant incident occurred when he was hiding from Saul in a cave. Saul happened to come into the same cave to rest a while from his pursuit of David. While Saul slept, David's men advised him strongly to kill Saul, citing this as a God-given opportunity. Yet David cut off only a piece of his robe, later regretting having done that. From a distance, with the piece of the robe in his hand, David tried to convince Saul not to heed the deceiving voices. He always approached God to justify and avenge him. He never really trusted in his own strength, even though he was a mighty man of war. He always knew that it was God who strengthened him for the battles he had to fight. He gave total credit to God. He repeatedly confessed that his enemies were stronger than him and could easily tear him apart if God didn't stand up for him. David never entertained a plan B just in case God did not come through. He knew that death was certain if God did not help him.

David also acknowledged the fact that God works through people. He had a few loyalists, like Zadok, the high priest, and Prophet Nathan, who encouraged him with words from God. He received their advice but never put his trust in anyone but God alone.

When we acknowledge the truth of God as supreme, it sets us free from ourselves and others. We cannot be caught trotting around with self-confidence. It's either God or no one else. No plan B! That increases the strength of our relationship with God, even as we learn to totally rely on Him alone.

3. O LORD MY GOD, IF I HAVE DONE THIS; IF THERE IS INIQUITY IN MY HANDS,

4. IF I HAVE REPAID EVIL TO HIM WHO WAS AT PEACE WITH ME, OR HAVE PLUNDERED MY ENEMY WITHOUT CAUSE,

5. LET THE ENEMY PURSUE ME AND OVERTAKE ME; YES, LET HIM TRAMPLE MY LIFE TO THE EARTH, AND LAY MY HONOUR IN THE DUST. SELAH.

I love the way David personalises his relationship with God by calling Him repeatedly **'My God'**. During those days, God was not addressed as Father.

In fact, people were so guilt-ridden and condemned that they could never relate to God on a personal level. But today, we have this privilege given to us by the Lord Jesus Christ. Yet, through all the good and bad times, David personalised his relationship with God, calling Him 'My God'.

Our relationships can be classified into 2 categories:

- ✡ Our vertical relationship with God.
- ✡ Our horizontal relationship with other humans.

Justification is a term used between God and us. It is He who justified us. When we believe and accept the Lord Jesus as our Saviour, we are justified by God, and we are given the legal right to approach Him. It is to say that our sins are paid for, and in exchange, the Lord Jesus has given us His righteousness to enable us to stand before God. Only forgiveness of our sins does not qualify us to stand before God; it is only part of the deal. The Lord Jesus stamps us with His righteousness and qualifies us to go into the presence of the Father. That's the only way justification works. It's never done by our works, either before or after salvation.

When it comes to justification between us and other people (in our horizontal relationships), it needs some pondering. Many things can happen in our horizontal relationships. Either we can wrong other people, or they can wrong us. In this particular excerpt, David is discussing with God about this very thing. Let's ponder on this now.

- ✡ When we wrong others, the solution is simple. Since we stand guilty before God and man, no matter what the reason is, we have to apologise to both, ignoring our ego. We need to give time to the person whom we have offended to forgive us. If they do, then it's good. Get on with life and we shouldn't repeat the same mistake again. But if they don't, then we should leave it in God's hands, provided we truly apologise, compensate if necessary, and set our behaviour right.
- ✡ When others wrong us, if they ask for forgiveness, we are commanded to forgive 70 times 7 (unlimited). There should be no place for avenging ourselves when we believe in God. If they

don't apologise and continue in their prideful and wicked ways, we should still hold nothing against them in our hearts. At the same time, we need to move with godly discretion concerning our further relationship and interactions with such people. It is not wise not to waste our time. Anger and resentment only poison our souls; they do not affect the offender. Proverbs 11:17 clearly states that 'The merciful man does good for his own soul, but he who is cruel troubles his own flesh.' Science has proved this fact. Repaying our adversaries by doing to them what they did to us will only be repaying evil for evil—something we are commanded to keep away from. In doing so, we also become wicked. That is not the place for God's children.

Here, David is standing on the basis of his innocence in his horizontal relationship. He is not justifying himself before God but rather pondering the way he had behaved with this person. He had examined himself and was ready to accept and suffer the consequences if he had faltered in any way with Cush. David reasoned with God, not with Cush.

It is important for each of us to examine ourselves this way. When we see that someone is behaving wrongly towards us, we need to make sure that we haven't wronged them in the first place instead of ruthlessly judging them. We need to introspect on a daily basis. We can even go one step ahead and talk it out with them. If they give a valid reason, then we have to do what is necessary to set things right with them instead of discussing this matter with any other person.

6. *ARISE, O LORD, IN YOUR ANGER; LIFT YOURSELF UP BECAUSE OF THE RAGE OF MY ENEMIES; RISE UP FOR ME TO THE JUDGEMENT YOU HAVE COMMANDED!*

The rage of man can never be justified, especially when it arises due to jealousy and ego. The very basis for that type of anger is faulty. David calls upon God to judge his enemies. God is the God of justice. At the same time, He shows mercy and compassion on those who repent and return to Him. If a person stubbornly continues in his evil ways, God's mercy and grace don't find a place to work in his life.

Saul persecuted David for many years. There was a time when his madness resulted in the slaughter and destruction of an entire city of priests who had given David refuge (ignorantly though) while he was fleeing from Saul. Not only that, David's parents and brothers also joined him at the Cave of Adullam probably because Saul persecuted them also. David sought a safe abode for his parents from the king of Moab until things got better. David had to unjustly suffer living in the wilderness and betrayal by many people, including people from his own tribe (Ziphites) and people whom he had helped (people of Keilah), just because he was anointed by God. David hadn't wronged any of these people personally. Things were not handed to him on a silver platter (similar to Joseph, Daniel, and Moses). They all stayed faithful to God in the midst of trial, testing, and persecution.

David had spent much time reading the scriptures available in those days. He must have meditated on the lives of his ancestors- on Abraham, Joseph, and Moses, etc. He knew that God would judge and deal with the unjust. Therefore he waited on God to do exactly that even as the intensity of the enemy's rage increased.

It is certainly good to ask the Lord to help us in times of persecution. Along with granting us patience, He is more than able to stand up for us and do the spectacular. When we pray for our enemies, He will even open their eyes to see their wrong and repent from it.

7. SO THE CONGREGATION OF THE PEOPLE'S SHALL SURROUND YOU; FOR THEIR SAKES, THEREFORE, RETURN ON HIGH.

Just the way David saw the Lord working in the lives of his forefathers, he probably knew that one day millions of people would be reading about him also. People who take time to pen down their testimonies and their walk with God in order to share with others to encourage and edify them need to be appreciated. This is a desire that God puts in their hearts. He is the source of this desire and gives them the grace to do so. Thank God for that!

When we observe the ways of the Lord, not only in the life of David but also in the lives of many of His children in the Word, our spirits are lifted high, and we are effortlessly pushed to lean on God's faithfulness. This is because we know the beginning and the end. David repeatedly declares that the Lord delivered him from 'ALL' his distresses. When we study his life, we see that David is not exaggerating by any measure. Hence, faith arises in our hearts and makes us trust God more and more. It builds us up. We are the congregation that David is referring to here. Their life stories are meant to be our counsellors. The factual stories written in the Word are for our benefit that we may meditate on them and know God, His ways, and the way we should conduct ourselves.

When we experience this deliverance in our lives, akin to the examples written in the Word, our testimonies also become strongholds for us and those who hear them. We look back and remember God's faithfulness. This builds up our muscle of faith and hope in God.

8. THE LORD SHALL JUDGE THE PEOPLES; JUDGE ME, O LORD, ACCORDING TO MY RIGHTEOUSNESS, AND ACCORDING TO MY INTEGRITY WITHIN ME.

God is impartial. Just because we become His children, He doesn't make light of our sins. Due to an unrenewed mind coupled with weak flesh, a believer may continue to sin, in which case we have to bear the consequences of our actions, though God does not condemn us to death and hell. If we know God and transform ourselves by renewing our minds according to God's word, we will not be overcome by the urge to sin. There is this beautiful song that says, 'O my soul, you are not alone; there's a place where fear has to face the God you know'. The more we know God, fear, worry, and sin are driven out because none of these stand a chance before Him.

The eyes of God are in every place, keeping watch over the evil and the good (Proverbs 15:3). God will punish the wicked and will not allow His children to suffer injustice forever. God is all eyes on our horizontal relationships, and He will justify His children before the wicked. The evil will bow before the good and the wicked at the gates of the righteous (Proverbs 14:19).

We should always trust God and do what is right. We should never compromise or let go of our integrity, no matter how much we may be tempted by the enemy. God is the one who justifies the blameless.

9. OH, LET THE WICKEDNESS OF THE WICKED COME TO AN END, BUT ESTABLISH THE JUST; FOR THE RIGHTEOUS GOD TESTS THE HEARTS AND MINDS.

10. MY DEFENCE IS OF GOD, WHO SAVES THE UPRIGHT IN HEART.

Wickedness still persists in this world. But this is the cry of the soul that trusts God. Wickedness vexes the heart of the righteous, just as Lot's heart was vexed by the sin of Sodom and Gomorrah. Lot finally saw the consequences of his choice. All that glitters is indeed not gold. When the Lord returns, this wickedness will completely be abolished, and we will all witness it. Even the whole of creation is waiting for that day (Romans 8:20–22)!

When we are justified by God through the Lord Jesus Christ, our Saviour, we are established in righteousness. Even though we may have to leave this body by means of physical death, we have already passed from death to life in the spiritual realm when we were born again. We, the justified, are established by God once we are saved. No demon can tamper with our born-again spirit, which is sealed by the Holy Spirit of promise (Ephesians 1:13–14). We can know these facts when we spend time with God, studying His word.

The most deceptive life one can live is the one lived to please our carnal senses. This life was chosen by Adam and Eve when they ate the fruit of the forbidden tree. Eve decided to make it look good on the outside by pushing God's truth and command aside. In fact, she added to what God said! Generally, man is not concerned about his heart as long as he looks good on the outside. A big house, an expensive car, an elaborate lifestyle, doing charity with media coverage, etc. may fool other people, but not God. People who don't walk according to the wisdom of God get carried away by these things. When we seek first the kingdom of God, the rest of the necessities are added to us as an additional blessing. When these material blessings come in, they will not wrongly influence the heart of a man who truly and consistently seeks God. The number one desire of his heart will still be God. Luke 5:11 is an excellent example of this.

God told Samuel in 1 Sam 16:7 not to look at the outward appearance of man but instead at his heart. This is the lesson God teaches His children through His word. God looks at the heart and mind always. He wants us to do the same, even when we consider ourselves. We need to keep a constant check on ourselves to make sure our attitude is right before God. Many times we may be tempted to do the right thing with a false motive, or vice versa; either is wrong. God tests our motives and actions. He is merciful to us when we repent. For example, the Lord Jesus multiplied the 5 loaves and 2 fish for the 5000 people who followed Him to hear His word. This miracle definitely involved His disciples because they saw the food multiply right before their eyes. This incident should have impacted them deeply. But shortly after that, they had to come up with food for the 4000, and they had 7 loaves and a few little fish. Comparing the 2 incidences, they had more supply to feed a lesser population. Yet they forgot the miracle that happened while feeding the 5000 and ended up answering carnally to the Lord. This is where we also fail. Our hearts and minds need to constantly remember God's faithfulness in the past and rise up higher. This will happen only if we deliberately take time to fellowship with God daily, study His word with the help of the Holy Spirit, and constantly rehearse His faithful works, giving Him thanks for all things.

For every person who accepts the Lord Jesus' sacrifice and submits his life to Him, personal guidance, robust deliverance, and direction are provided (Proverbs 11:3-6). The righteousness of the Lord Jesus Christ is ours! He is our defence always.

11. GOD IS A JUST JUDGE, AND GOD IS ANGRY WITH THE WICKED EVERY DAY.

12. IF HE DOES NOT TURN BACK, HE WILL SHARPEN HIS SWORD; HE BENDS HIS BOW AND MAKES IT READY.

13. HE ALSO PREPARES FOR HIMSELF INSTRUMENTS OF DEATH; HE MAKES HIS ARROWS INTO FIERY SHAFTS.

Our Lord God is extremely gracious and merciful. At the same time, He is just. The way He accomplished salvation was through the death of His Son, our Lord Jesus Christ. Even though salvation is made available to us freely, it cost God His only Son—His everything. Today, if mankind can approach God, it is only through the blood of the Lord Jesus. He is The Only Way, The Truth, and The Life. There is no other way to the Father apart from Him. He has justified every one of us who has accepted the Lord Jesus as our Saviour.

God hates wickedness and sin, always. He is unchanging. He has provided a way for everyone to be saved. But He is angry with people who adamantly and rebelliously reject His Son and hold onto sin. Those who deliberately do so condemn themselves and invite the judgement of God into their lives. The Ark is right before them. It's their choice to enter in and stay safe **OR** stay out and drown in the flood waters. Those who repent and accept Him inherit His mercy and grace.

The flood during the time of Noah teaches us the way God deals with mankind. The flood waters are a sign of God's judgement, and the Ark that Noah built is the sign of His redemption. Noah built the Ark over a period of 100 years! Yeah, that's a long time. It probably became a popular tourist attraction. I believe that every person who watched him build the Ark was given an opportunity to repent and turn to God. But none repented—not even Noah's own siblings. It was Noah and his wife to start with, and a couple of years later, his sons were born, and they joined him later with their wives. Noah had taught his sons well. But no one else believed him enough to even want to be saved. So when the flood came, all flesh died except the ones inside the Ark. Similarly, the Lord Jesus is our Ark. All of us who believe in Him are safely shielded from all the judgement happening outside. Any person who wants to escape it has the privilege of entering the Ark and staying there, i.e., believing and accepting the Lord Jesus Christ as their Saviour. Thereby, we escape the judgement of God that comes from rejecting His Son. We who believe continue to live in the Lord Jesus into eternity and have escaped the judgement of God.

God is not tempted with evil; neither does He tempt anyone with evil (James 1:13). Anything evil is from satan. We cannot attribute any bad thing to the Lord. God does not use evil to threaten us into salvation. **It's His goodness that leads us to repentance (Romans 2:4).** So it's clearly understood that sickness, disease, disasters, accidents, danger, evil, etc. are not devices of God to get us to receive salvation. That's not His strategy. That is the devil's strategy to reward people who have followed his deception by being ignorant of the word. But God uses these circumstances to bring us to Him by demonstrating His goodness to us at such times (Romans 8:28). The only way satan can touch us is by persecuting us for The Words' sake. This persecution is akin to the persecution that our Lord suffered when He walked on this earth.

The word clearly tells us how the world will end. God has made His instruments ready for the Day of Judgement. As long as man has breath in his nostrils, he is given time to repent and accept the Lord Jesus. Once our breath is taken away, there is no more opportunity to change ourselves. Satan and his followers, both people and fallen angels, will be thrown into hell. Our God is extremely longsuffering and has given everyone enough time to come to Him. Rejecting Him for any reason cannot be justified before Him.

God's eyes are in every place on earth, watching over the good and the bad. It's just a matter of time until we see the wicked being justly paid for their dealings. As much as God deals with those who reject Him, he also deals with those who accept Him, but live wrong. He corrects us in love, just as a father corrects his son, whom he loves. It's not 'judgement and condemnation' but rather based on 'conviction' for us. He helps us come out of the pit, providing us with all the grace and mercy we need. Believers continuing in the path of wickedness are foolish and will reap likewise now and in eternity. We need to stay on guard and flee from doing evil.

The first and foremost thing that God uses to judge this world is His word (the sword). It is a fearful thing to fall into the hands of the Living God. No one in their right mind should dare to stand against God. Yet we know that there are plenty of people who have the audacity to ignore and challenge God! The word says that there will come a day when every knee will bow and every tongue will confess that Jesus Christ is Lord. I believe that day is not far away.

14. BEHOLD, THE WICKED BRINGS FORTH INIQUITY; YES, HE CONCEIVES TROUBLE AND BRINGS FORTH FALSEHOOD.

15. HE MADE A PIT AND DUG IT OUT, AND HAS FALLEN INTO THE DITCH WHICH HE MADE.

16. HIS TROUBLE SHALL RETURN UPON HIS OWN HEAD, AND HIS VIOLENT DEALINGS SHALL COME DOWN ON HIS OWN CROWN.

The way of the wicked and ungodly is very predictable. Every person born into this world (except the Lord Jesus) has a fallen nature. Because of this sinful nature that we are born with, we tend to sin. It is not the other way around, i.e., committing sin does not make us sinners, but our sinful nature makes us sin. No one needs to teach a child to lie, throw a tantrum, or be selfish. It is built-in and automatic. Proverbs 20:11 says that even a child is known by his deeds, whether his work is pure or right.

However, at salvation, this is rectified. Our dead (sinful) spirit is removed, and the life-giving Spirit of God is embedded in us. Our Lord Jesus gives us the position that Adam forfeited and even more than that. That's exactly why we need to be **Born Again**. Then God's Spirit takes hold of us and gently guides us into all truth (Romans 8:11). Since the nature on the inside is totally changed, we can absolutely expect our behaviour on the outside to change as well! Right believing will lead to right living, and not vice versa.

Wickedness is most often conceived in the heart before it is practiced. It's just like a weed that is planted in the soil and grows effortlessly, feeding on the nutrition that needs to go to the good plants. The good plants need more tending and care to grow well, while the weeds grow just like that! Similarly, when we want the seed of God's word to grow and bear fruit in our lives, we need to deliberately spend time with Him and have patience, faith, and hope in God to bring it to fruition. The weeds grow faster. But we need to keep the weeds away by primarily preventing its seeding in the first place. But if, by any chance, we have allowed it, then we should diligently uproot it at the earliest. As one man of God said, we cannot prevent a bird flying over our head, but we can certainly prevent it from building a nest on it. Evil thoughts do tempt us at times. But we should never allow it to germinate in our hearts. The sooner it is uprooted, the better.

God shows us the way to prevent seeding of the weeds in our hearts in **Philippians 4:8. "Finally, brethren, whatever things are true, whatever things are noble, whatever things are just, whatever things are pure, whatever things are lovely, whatever things are of good report; if there is any virtue and if there is anything praiseworthy, think on these things."** Only the **WORD OF GOD** satisfies all this criteria. So the only way to keep the 'evil out' is to get the 'word in'. Only the word does the work in us effortlessly to make sure our hearts are growing the right virtues.

Using our imagination is an important aspect of our Christian life. By default, our imagination tends towards death. We always fear the worst. But when we are born again, we can turn that around and direct it towards life. Imagination is seeing things with our hearts. When we learn to see things with our hearts, it doesn't take long for them to manifest. The word of God is supposed to paint these pictures in our minds, similar to the way we can picture an apple when the word apple is spoken. When we allow that to happen and we couple it with faith, God's word comes to pass in our lives. That's the power of incorporating God's word and faith into our imagination. It keeps us going. It is something powerful that the Lord has blessed us with. Every single one of us should put our "imagination" to good use.

Fear can also paint pictures in our imagination. But we need to avoid that. This can be accomplished only with the help of God. From birth, fear has effortlessly painted a lot of distressing things in our imagination. Today, there is more help from the media with regards to this. Once we are saved, we need to undo this by renewing our minds to the Word Of God and allowing the word to accomplish that.

God repeatedly warns us to guard our hearts. Our heart is the place from which life flows (Proverbs 4:23). It is most important for us not to allow our hearts to harbour the muck of this world. Our eyes and ears need to be trained to refuse worldly lusts, and our tongues need to be tamed. These are the main entry points to our hearts. So we also need to set a guard over these and feed our hearts the right things.

When a person begins to dig a pit, he starts at a point and works his way down. The deeper he goes, the more difficult it is for him to come out. So is the way of the wicked. Wickedness is akin to digging a pit towards hell. The deeper one goes, the nearer they get to hell and farther away from heaven. There is an excellent example of this in the book of Esther. Haman was a very wicked man who, for the sake of his enmity with Mordecai, planned to wipe out the entire Jewish race. He dug a pit so deep that he finally died in it. Shortly afterwards, his entire family was wiped out! Plotting against His people is counted a very serious offence by God Himself. People who do such things never get away. God takes it upon Himself to defend His children against these evil doers.

The children of God should stay away from the temptation to repay the wicked with wickedness. God handles justice for us at all times. There is much warning for us in the book of Psalms and Proverbs to never avenge ourselves. Resorting to payback is never supposed to give a believer peace; rather, it causes conviction and unrest. Leave the vengeance part in the hands of God. He can handle that far better than us.

17. I WILL PRAISE THE LORD ACCORDING TO HIS RIGHTEOUSNESS, AND WILL SING PRAISE TO THE NAME OF THE LORD MOST HIGH.

David began this Psalm being in much distress over the words of Cush the Benjamite. But remembering God's faithfulness and His gloriously proven attributes, he concludes this Psalm praising God. His heart is so lightened remembering Who God is, His supremacy, His sovereignty, and His goodness.

This is the reason why we need to glorify God and praise Him at all times, more so when things are not going well. It not only changes our perspective, it shifts our focus onto God and His might. Our problems shrink exponentially when we magnify God, and we actually allow God to change our situation because faith has its way. Looking directly at the sun makes us blind to everything else around us. Try it! Its light is so powerful that it takes much time for us to regain our vision of other things. So how much more when we focus on the One who created the sun and is infinitely greater than it?

The Lord showed Joshua a unique way to conquer Jericho - a heavily fortified city with thick walls and many giants. The Israelites (men of war and the priests holding the Ark of the Covenant) were supposed to march around the city once every day for 6 days in absolute silence. Only the horns had to be blown as they marched around the city. But on the seventh day, they were commanded to march around the city 7 times. They had to start the march before dawn and cover a distance of approximately 14 km around the city (each march around the walls was about 2 km). They were not allowed to take a break or rest in between. They had to do it at a stretch in silence. It would have taken them at least 5 hours to complete this on the 7th day. Imagine the level of fatigue at the end of it. But at that moment when they had finished the final march, God commanded that the trumpets should be blown, and all people had to shout (praises) with one accord. And we can see what happened. Even without the slightest physical movement, the fortified famous walls of Jericho came down flat, crushing all the giants who stood on them, and Israel had to just go in and fulfil God's command regarding them.

We can have a correct perspective of the situations we face by praising God and thanking Him. In doing so, we can do great exploits and glorify the Name of our God.

Psalm 8

INTRODUCTION:

This is a Psalm written by King David, describing the magnificence of God evident through creation and exalting His love for mankind. It is also a Psalm that the Lord Jesus quoted from. It is rich with revelations of the attributes of God and the importance of praise. This Psalm was supposed to be sung with a special instrument, the Instrument of Gath.

THE INSTRUMENT OF GATH:

David was blessed with a special talent to sing and play various musical instruments. It all began when the Lord's Spirit came upon him when the Prophet Samuel anointed him. The first appreciation of this special ability was before Saul, for whom David played the harp when he was possessed by the distressing spirit. When David played the harp, the distressing spirit would lift, leaving Saul refreshed and well (1 Sam 16:23). I believe strongly that David played songs of praise on the harp. This is undeniable evidence of how praising God causes distress to flee. Furthermore, David went on to develop this powerful talent by using it to worship God in his routine. He also made an array of various musical instruments for the Tabernacle and the Temple of the Lord. Music was always a vital part of David's worship. Music has also been used in the palaces of certain heathen kings, who used it mainly for entertainment and as an aid to sleep well. But David used music to worship God more than anything else.

This special musical instrument needs some introduction and history. So let's look back at David's story written in the Old Testament. All was well for a short while after David was employed as Saul's armour bearer and harpist. David would serve Saul for a period of time and then have a short vacation once in a while to go be with his father and tend his sheep. During one such vacation, Israel was at war with the Philistines, and the famous 9 and a half-foot Philistine giant Goliath appeared. Now this guy was an all-arrogant, blaspheming, self-confident nephilim, spewing out his Philistine pride. He was a native of the city called Gath of the Philistines and one of the 5 famous gigantic sons born to a giant in Gath (1 Samuel 21). Have you ever wondered why David picked up 5 smooth stones from the brook to fight Goliath? He was just prepared to slaughter the other 4 too! This giant had placed a tremendous challenge before the Israelites to settle the war without the loss of many lives by having at least one person fight him. None in the camp of Israel, including Saul (who was the tallest in Israel at that time), were ready to take up the challenge. Goliath came and presented his challenge for 40 days, twice every day, in the morning and evening.

During those days, David's father, Jesse, requested that he visit his brothers, who were in Saul's army, to inquire about their well-being and to give them some food supplies. David immediately obeyed his father, handed over his father's sheep to another responsible man, and started out early the next morning to visit his brothers. Once he got there, he heard the blasphemous giant and took up the challenge. The rest is history. David's simple sling fight with the giant was witnessed by all the trembling Israelites as well as the overconfident philistines as it happened in the Valley of Elah between the 2 camps. The outcome of the challenge was so unexpected by both sides that the status changed rapidly with the Israelites chasing the Philistine army and killing them in a great massacre. David finished the job of destroying the enemy when he beheaded him with his (Goliath's) own sword. It is believed that Goliath's head was buried exactly where Mount Calvary stands, on the outskirts of Jerusalem. His sword was later kept in the Tabernacle at Nob. After this great victory that David wrought for Israel, Saul loved him more and never sent him back home again.

David went out and came in and fought many mighty battles on behalf of Israel for Saul after being appointed head of the men of war. That was indeed a prestigious position. David behaved wisely all this while and was so loyal to Saul that the people of Israel loved him even more and took him to be Saul's right-hand man. After one such great victory, the virgins danced before the returning victorious army, praising David over Saul. This caused Saul to boil over with jealousy and envy. Subsequently, Saul wasted no time in demoting David and trying to kill him time and again, either directly or cunningly, by asking him to fight the philistines. He was so blinded by jealousy that he thought he could weary David by getting him married to his second daughter, Michal. But they loved each other so much that Michal helped David escape from her bloodthirsty father. The same music played by David previously did not have any effect now. Finally, David fled from Saul and, on his way out, found refuge in Nob, the city of the priests. Before leaving this place, David asked for and obtained the sword of Goliath that was kept in the tabernacle, some bread and continued his escape. However, the priests didn't know that David was escaping from Saul. Doeg the Edomite, who was **"detained before the Lord"** at Nob at the time, passed on this information to Saul later (to obtain favour in his eyes), and he ended up massacring all the priests but one, Abiathar (Ahimelech's son), who escaped.

Having acquired the sword of Goliath, David fled to Gath. I am not sure how many civilians would have recognised David by his appearance in this place. But surely, most surely, they would have recognised the sword of their hero, Goliath, who was their own breed. They had probably heard of this great hero of Israel who ruthlessly slaughtered their hero. Immediately, they detained and presented him to their king, Achish. But David feigned madness before Achish, and he drove him away. David was relieved and made his way to the cave of Adullam. Up until this point, David was alone. But once he got to the cave of Adullam, many people who were distressed in Israel and the surrounding regions, including his own parents and brothers, joined him there—about 400 people—and he had his own little flock of humans in the wilderness. The crowd soon grew to 600 in number. This was only the male head count. However, Saul kept continuously seeking to kill him, and David had to keep wandering in the wilderness of Judah. So he entrusted his parents to the king of Moab for safety, and that's the last we hear of them.

During this time of great persecution from Saul, who was foolishly wandering from his nest to fight David instead of Israel's enemies, David relocated to Gath and continued to fight the allies of the philistines who were the enemies of Israel- the Amalekites, Geshurites, and Girzites. A tribe of Israel whom David fought for (the people of Keilah) were ready to betray him back to Saul! It's amazing the way David kept away from all the discouragement caused by betrayal and continued to follow God through it all. To beat all odds, his own tribe people (the Ziphites) betrayed him twice to Saul. God granted him a great escape both times. After the second betrayal by these Ziphites, David headed to Achish, the king of Gath, with his 600 men and their families. This is a decision he made out of a holy dissatisfaction with being unable to do what God had called him to do because Saul was constantly tailing him. But David found great favour before Achish, and he treated him well and gave him land in Ziklag, Philistia, for his entire troop. Saul's contempt and hatred for David was no small secret. Most of Israel and their enemies got wind of it, and Achish intended to cash in on this. "An enemy's enemy can be a good friend" was a well-known proverb among the heathen. When Saul heard that David had gone to the philistines, he stopped pursuing him and finally started to focus on fighting the enemies of Israel. David lived 16 months in this region. During his stay here, David kept fighting off Israel's enemies- the Amalekites, Geshurites, and Girzites. But he did not reveal that to Achish (for obvious reasons), who thought that David was fighting against Israel and had become his ally.

During his stay at Ziklag for 16 months, David learned a wonderful truth: "When a man's ways please the Lord, He makes even his enemies to be at peace with him" (Proverbs 16:7). I bet David taught Solomon that! What more? David learned to play the instrument of Gath! Isn't it actually wonderful to praise God using the instruments invented by the enemy, which were actually designed by them to praise their heathen gods? In fact, David used this instrument to sing one of the best Psalms ever—a Psalm that elaborates God's magnificence displayed in creation and His love for us. There is absolutely no groaning or distress in this Psalm; it's just absolute praise!

Can we use the "instruments" of the enemy to glorify God? Yes! If David did it in the land of his enemies, we can too! It magnifies God greatly. Music was created by God and ordained for His worship. It really surprises me when leaders in the Body of Christ belittle music; and satan has used this to his advantage. Primarily, if man could design instruments, it would certainly be God's wisdom working in them. But satan perverted music and the use of instruments through his tactics. Nevertheless, the patent and copyright for it belong to Almighty God. Ponder what you can use from your adversaries lair—instruments that would glorify God and turn the tables on the enemy.

1. *O LORD, OUR LORD, HOW EXCELLENT IS YOUR NAME IN ALL THE EARTH, WHO HAVE SET YOUR GLORY ABOVE THE HEAVENS!*

David has raised a very important topic here, saying how excellent **'THE NAME OF GOD'** is in all the earth. In the first place, we need to look at the significance of the word "name." Speaking in general, everyone and everything around us has a name, primarily for identification (at least in the present day and age). Most parents waste no time in deciding on a name for their child as soon as the baby is conceived in the womb. Until death, that individual is identified by that very name. Even after death, that name is engraved on the tombstone, and he or she is remembered by it. Many mighty men of God are remembered by their names today since God chose to record them in the word. At the very mention of their names, their stories flash before our eyes, provided we have studied about them before.

When God ordained this entity called 'name', at creation itself, He was very serious about its use. He named everything He created and also gave Adam the privilege to name his wife and the animal kingdom. It was not meant to be taken lightly. The name given to a child is supposed to speak blessings over the child's life every time someone calls them. Sadly, today, many people don't have this revelation. In India, the traditional nominal Christians have defected to following senseless traditions and name their children after their forefathers, **even if the name has an adverse meaning.** To them, family pride is more important than what God says. Their traditions overpower the significance of God's word in their lives. The Lord Jesus said in Mark 7:13 that the traditions and doctrines of men make the Word Of God of no effect. Paul warned the Colossians of the same in Colossians 2:8.

God changed the names of quite a few people in the Bible in order to help them expand their vision and achieve their calling. That's the power God assigns to names when it is coupled with faith. He changed Abram to Abraham, Sarai to Sarah, Simon to Peter, Saul to Paul, etc. On the other hand, He gave specific instructions to many parents on what name should be given to the baby being born, even to Mary and Joseph, the earthly parents of the Lord Jesus Christ. Names are very significant because God has ordained words to be significant. In fact, the word says that He calls us by name!

Now let's talk about the Name of God. God is One but Triune—The Father, The Son, and The Holy Spirit. This is evident from Genesis chapter 1. Man's brain cannot wrap itself around, contain or understand Him completely. It is God's will that we should know Him intimately as much as possible. And to those who seek Him as seeking treasure, He reveals Himself to them. He is absolutely above and beyond anyone or anything we can imagine! Men of God who have had an opportunity to look into His glory could not bear the weight of His glory and almost always fell prostrate before Him. The Cherubim and the Seraphim always cover their faces before God and cannot look upon His exceeding glory. On the Mount of Transfiguration, the moment Lord Jesus temporarily pulled back His veil of the flesh to reveal His true glory, Peter, James, and John fell prostrate before Him. Such and more exceeding is His glory. We cannot describe God in a single word. He can never be described completely by a finite number of words! But God gave us His Name or Names in His word, as much as we could take in, to know Him intimately. Being the Supreme Potentate, it is really not necessary for Him to restrict Himself to 'a Name'. Yet, for the sake of mankind, He ascribed Names to Himself that every person in this world could relate to from the beginning, more to our hearts than our brains. The Names of God mentioned in the Word, including the Old and New Testaments, are a long list. Probably a book can be written just based on this topic after a detailed study. Right now, I hope I can help you understand the basics of this topic according to the revelation God has given me.

While studying the Names of God, or for that matter, the Word of God, I found out that it's very helpful to have knowledge of Biblical languages—Hebrew and Greek. These help understanding it better. God is more than able to teach us, even if we don't have this linguistic knowledge either. But those motivated to know more about the word put in an added effort to seek Him, and they are rewarded accordingly. Personally, I don't know any of the Biblical languages, but I have greatly benefited from listening to pastors and teachers who preach the word knowing these languages, and share their revelations with us. God bless them for sharing such valuable information that we tend to miss out on. In that, God makes sure His children get His word through one way or another, provided we seek. God willing, I wish to learn these languages someday. Both of these Biblical languages are very descriptive, Greek more than Hebrew, and they magnify the true sense in which the word is spoken and the manner in which it needs to be understood.

With all the innumerable Names of God mentioned in the Bible, even the sum of all of them fails to draw a circle around God. But they surely do give us good insight and enough knowledge in order to live and finish our lives on this earth victoriously. He gives us as much as we can take in. If we enlarge our cup, we can receive more (Luke 8:18). All this requires an intimate and close personal relationship with God, our Father, through Our Saviour, Lord Jesus Christ, by the revelation of the Holy Spirit.

Being God over all, our heavenly Father loves to identify Himself as **'Our God' or 'the God of Israel'**. He repeatedly says, 'I will be your God' and 'I am your God'. Who on this earth has a God like our God? So high and exalted, yet humbles Himself by identifying with us and coming forward to adopt us as His own.

The first mention of a person who asked God directly about His Name was Moses. And he said, "I AM" is My Name. At that point in time, there was no written record like what we have today. Everything that was written was done by Moses, much after God delivered the Israelites from Egypt. Hence, everything that people knew was through oral records from previous generations. Among all the Names quoted in the Word, the Lord Jesus came especially to reveal the one that is the most significant: **"ABBA FATHER".** And this is the Name that we, the born-again ones, need to familiarise ourselves with. This Name was revealed for the first time by the Lord Jesus and is the most significant. Our relationship with God becomes stronger when we properly understand the essence of this Name. In this world, many have the privilege of having a good biological father. But still, there is much lack, even from the very best of them, in comparison to God our Father. Many people have suffered immensely at the hands of their biological fathers and loathe the very thought of that word. A personal revelation from God is needed to know and understand the true meaning of what the Lord Jesus meant.

According to Rabbinical customs, there are 7 very important Names of God. These Names are considered so holy that the Jews don't ever utter them. Such was the practice during the time of the Lord Jesus. They used alternate names to refer to God while praying or pronouncing blessings over the people. I believe that this sense of unworthiness to even mention the Name of God peaked because of the increasing consciousness of man's guilt and unworthiness rather than the holiness of God. However, there was no particular law in the Old Testament forbidding them to utter God's Name. The Lord Jesus went to the cross and destroyed this load of guilt and condemnation to reveal the Father's love for us and bring us closer to Him. These 7 names of God are as follows:

- ✡ YHWH/Yahweh: The self-existent One.
- ✡ El: God.
- ✡ Elohai: My God (as in God of Abraham, God of Isaac, etc.)
- ✡ Elohim: God is Creator, powerful, and mighty.
- ✡ Shaddai: Almighty.
- ✡ Eliyeh/Ehyeh: I AM.
- ✡ Tzevaot or Sabaoth: God of Hosts

Along with the Names Yahweh and El, certain suffixes were added to personalise God further. A few of these are as follows:

- ✡ El Elyon: Most High God.
- ✡ El Shaddai: Almighty God.
- ✡ El Olam: Everlasting God.
- ✡ El Hai: Living God.
- ✡ El Roi: The Strong One Who Sees.
- ✡ El Gibbor: God of Strength.
- ✡ El Chuwl: The God Who Gave You Life.
- ✡ El Deah: God of all knowledge.
- ✡ Yahweh Maccaddeshem: The Lord, your sanctifier.
- ✡ Yahweh Rohi/ Raah: The Lord my Shepherd.
- ✡ Yahweh Shammah: The Lord is present.
- ✡ Yahweh Rapha: The Lord our healer.
- ✡ Yahweh Tsidkenu: The Lord our righteousness.
- ✡ Yahweh Jireh: The Lord will provide.
- ✡ Yahweh Nissi: The Lord our Banner.
- ✡ Yahweh Shaloam: The Lord is peace.
- ✡ Yahweh Sabbaoth: The Lord of Hosts.

The list continues further, and I would like to encourage the readers to study this further. The reason why so many aspects are described is that for every challenge a person faces, God is the answer. There is no other answer or way other than God the Father and the Lord Jesus Christ. Everything a man ever needs can be supplied only by God. Even if an answer is available from elsewhere, it will be far inferior and temporary in nature. **God is everything that we need and want.** God is **"All-encompassing"** and suits every role. Only He can do that! Total and complete satisfaction exists only in and through Him. The various Names of God describe this very fact.

A few other names are as follows:

- Adoni: My Lord.
- Elah: The Aramic word for God.
- Shekinah: The presence or manifestation of God, Who descended to dwell among humanity.
- AttiyqYoum: The Ancient of Days, Eternal God

There is one special name that I would like to elaborate on: **EhyehasherEhyeh: I AM THAT I AM**

When God spoke this name to Moses, He meant:

- I will be What I will be.
- I will be Who I will be.
- I shall prove to be Whoever I shall prove to be.
- I will be because I will be.
- I will be that I will be.

In Hebrew (aspectual system), this word denotes any action that is not yet complete. So this also points to the fact that God fits into any role, as described earlier.

David knew the importance of God's Name. When we recollect his encounter with Goliath in the Valley of Elah, he makes a bold declaration in the presence of both armies, saying, "you come to me with a sword, a spear, and a javelin. But I come to you in the Name of the Lord of hosts, the God of the armies of Israel whom you have defied (1 Sam 17:45)". Talk about understanding the authority in the Name of the God we worship! Although David had a sling and 5 smooth stones in his hand, it was no comparison to all the weapons that the giant carried. But David's trust was neither in his skill in using the sling nor in the quality of the stones. But he knew that these were equivalent to the Rod of God in Moses' hand, which was used to part the Red Sea and work the various wonders in the land of Egypt. David did not take Goliath's blasphemy lightly. David's trust was in God's Name, knowing that He had given him all the power and authority he needed to slay the giant. A stone pelted from the sling had so much power when it was flung in the Name of God! So are our words!

When David wrote this Psalm, there were many other contemporary religions. The characteristic of most of these religions was that they had a god or goddess for every need: one for peace, another for prosperity, and still others for war, harvest, good fortune, love, etc. So for each of their needs, they had to worship a specific idol. Comparing this scenario to his God, who was Unique and One, David magnifies the Name of God, having a revelation about it. The best part of it was that every enemy of Israel knew the 'God of Israel'. The Name of God struck fear in the hearts of all His enemies. No one could stand against the God of heaven and earth. Some arrogant ones tried to do so and learned their lesson the hard way. God expects us to worship Him, knowing this truth.

If a man observes nature around him or his own physical body for that matter, he is sure to be awestruck at the level of knowledge, wisdom, and understanding incorporated in creating these things. The entire universe is filled with magnificent objects. A person who doesn't pay attention to all these things loses out on a lot. When we just take a moment and ponder on God's creation, we are overwhelmed by its magnificence and splendour - the mountains, the seas, the animal and plant life, the sun, moon, and stars, etc. Every ounce of useful knowledge that we have in the present-day is primarily sourced from God. It is God who gives mankind that understanding, and hence we have all these inventions today. Though some do not acknowledge the hand of God and credit themselves for their inventions, God's good heart allowed the results to benefit mankind big-time. However, man can never ever parallel God in creating anything.

The various laws of gravity, electricity, energy, etc. were put in place by God when He created the world. It was discovered only later by people who went deep into studying it, but they weren't the ones who created it. Ask a doctor, and he'll tell you how awesome a human body is; ask a physicist, and he'll tell you the splendour of how things work at the atomic level. When you actually study the sun, you will be marvelled by its properties! Every created object has a portion of God's glory in it since He created it. But the glory of God is enormously greater than the glory of all these things put together! It's above the heavens! But the goodness of God has allowed us to see and tap into this glory even as He has promised us saying "Christ in us, the hope of glory". God excels in glory above all!

The earth was created perfect. But the fall made the earth subject to corruption (death and decay). This is the reason why death is seen in every created thing. This will cease at the second coming of Christ. Even then, something which is fading away (creation) gives us a sense of awe. But right now, one thing is absolutely perfect - Heaven. It's perfect, having streets of gold, foundations laid with precious stones, gates of pearls, mansions just waiting to be occupied and is being prepared for a time called 'Eternity' by our Lord Jesus Christ. It is glorious! But God's glory is above the heavens. There can be no competitor for the glory of God. When God works in and through His children, bringing His purposes to pass, His glory is revealed because no matter what, the effort of man could never produce an event like that. That's exactly the reason God says in Colossians 1:27 that "Christ in us (is) the hope of glory". The very presence of our Lord God in our lives gives us the privilege to taste this glory when He has His way in our lives.

2. *OUT OF THE MOUTH OF BABES AND NURSING INFANTS YOU HAVE ORDAINED STRENGTH, BECAUSE OF YOUR ENEMIES, THAT YOU MAY SILENCE THE ENEMY AND THE AVENGER.*

This is a very important verse in this Psalm because Lord Jesus quoted this at a very crucial time when He walked on this earth. The actual reference to 'babes and nursing infants' can be studied in 2 ways. Lord Jesus Himself thanked God the Father for hiding the treasures of the kingdom of God and revealing it to babes (spiritually ignorant people like fishermen, His disciples). God is not against the earthly wise. He is the source of all wisdom and knowledge. Proverbs 9:1 says that wisdom has hewn out her 7 pillars. James 3:17 enumerates what these 7 pillars are. The wisdom that originates from Him is first pure (1), then peaceable (2), gentle (3), willing to yield (4), full of mercy and good fruits (5), without partiality (6), and without hypocrisy (7). It is symbolised as the 'Tree of Life' and personified in our Lord Jesus Christ.

A counterfeit wisdom existed in the tree of knowledge of good and evil; this was the worldly/earthly wisdom that belittled the wisdom of God. Satan has firmly parked near this tree and excels in making good use of it even today when he deceives mankind to go by their wisdom instead of what God says. It is subtle, and unless we guard our hearts and minds, we fall prey to his deception. For some reason, Eve thought this earthly wisdom superseded God's wisdom and chose to partake of it. She judged God's wisdom deficient in some way. This resulted in the fall, and this counterfeit wisdom has been normalised to such an extent today that it actively rejects God even when His intent is to help mankind. Humans under the influence of this counterfeit wisdom are filled with absolute pride (even though they may appear to be humble by the world's standards) that they do not agree with God no matter what! But those who are able to receive His grace to overpower and break away from the chains of that counterfeit wisdom can fulfil what the Lord has called them to do (e.g., Apostle Paul).

Let us look at both the aspects of reference this verse may mean:

- ✡ When it literally refers to small babies and nursing infants.
- ✡ When it represents the ignorant people God chose to further His will and kingdom purposes on this earth.

i. Small Babes and Nursing Infants:

David had a good knowledge of the word that was available during his time. Many incidents in his life point to the fact that he had meditated on God's word and obtained vast treasures of wisdom. Two such incidents happened much before he existed and traced down to him. One was the life of Noah's children, and the other was the life of the Prophet Samuel (who had anointed him and played a very important role in his life).

a. The sons of Noah:

Noah was 500 years old when God called him to build the Ark. At this point, Noah's sons were not born. Noah took 100 years to build the Ark. Two years after Noah commenced building the Ark, his first son Shem was born, followed by Ham and Japheth. You can use Genesis 5:32, 7:11, and 11:10 to work out the math. Despite the rampant ungodliness that prevailed in those days, Noah trained his children in the right way, and they helped him build the Ark rather than defecting to the ungodly ways of the world. Can I ask parents how easy is that!? Noah's own siblings, uncles, and aunts, close blood relatives, kept away from heeding the message Noah preached by building the Ark. He had no church to go to or Bible studies to attend or fellowship with other believers. It was just him and his small family. Hence it can be understood, beyond the shadow of a doubt, that even as little children, these 3 boys magnified God by obeying their father and helping him to do what needed to be done.

b. The Prophet Samuel:

The birth of Samuel was nothing short of a miracle. Samuel's father, Elkanah, a Levite, had 2 wives: Hannah (the mother of Samuel) and Peninnah. Hannah was so distressed over her barrenness being ridiculed by her counterpart that she poured out her heart in bitterness of soul and great anguish before the

Lord at the tabernacle in Shiloh. She pleaded with the Lord for **"a male child"** so that she could return him to the Lord's service all the days of his life. **Hannah was a woman of wisdom! She knew exactly what she had to petition for, and she placed God in the centre of that petition.** Eli the high priest saw her distress and confirmed that God would grant her petition. When she fulfilled her vow and presented him to the Lord after weaning, Samuel served in the tabernacle under Eli as a child. Hannah returned to Ramah with a greater blessing to bear 5 more children. What more? After the Ark was captured by the Philippines and Eli died, young Samuel returned to his hometown, Ramah (leaving Shiloh), and settled there till his death. Hannah had to let go of Samuel for a few years (as hard as that may have been). **Finally, the Lord returned him to her for life!** Do you understand that there is a hidden blessing in placing God at the centre of our petitions? He makes sure it comes back to us exponentially! Hannah was exceedingly blessed when God brought Samuel back home! It is said that Hannah was about 130 years old when she bore Samuel!

The word of God was rare in those days, as wickedness was rampant in Eli's priestly clan and the people detested sacrificing to God. The 2 sons of Eli mocked God's sacrifice by usurping the share that belonged to God. They also raped the women who came to pray at the tabernacle. The people were vexed by the behaviour of Eli's wicked sons. Eli gave them nothing more than a sweet rebuke. Knowing that his sons deliberately took the Lord's share of the sacrifice, he partook of the meat and fattened himself. Eli was repeatedly warned by God of the consequences, but he refused to rectify the situation, which he could have handled efficiently if he wanted to 'as a father' and 'as a high priest'. God spoke to the 'boy Samuel' and revealed His judgement on Eli's family to him also. Eli knew that the Lord had spoken to Samuel, was adamant to know what it was, and believed him when he (Samuel) told him God's word. This in itself shows that out of the mouth of babes, God brought forth the truth and ordained strength.

c. <u>At the time of the Lord Jesus:</u>

At the latter end of His ministry on earth, the Lord Jesus triumphantly entered Jerusalem riding on a donkey. The multitudes laid down their clothes and palm branches on the road before Him, as prophesied by the prophet Zechariah centuries earlier in Zech 9:9. The people who welcomed Him into Jerusalem thought that the Lord Jesus would physically fight against the Roman authority to deliver the Jewish nation. Hence, all the way, they cried out, saying, 'Hosanna to the Son of David! Blessed is He Who comes in the Name of the Lord! Hosanna in the highest!"

On the contrary, and probably much to their surprise, Lord Jesus set His face against the injustice that the 'chosen' of the Lord were indulging themselves in. The Lord Jesus walked straight to the temple, made a whip of chords, and drove out all the men doing business inside the temple (with the acknowledgement of the religious leaders of that time). There was none who could stop Him from doing what He did—not the Pharisees or Sadducees, Roman officials or soldiers, the Herodians, nor the chief priests, scribes, or elders. Can we picture this? Why were their hands tied? It was because no one could touch the Son of God until His time came to be crucified (John 10:18). He walked on this earth as the Son of Man, with so much power and authority! He authoritatively quoted the word of God, openly saying **"It is written."** This is so similar to the way He shut up satan during the wilderness temptation. When He quoted the word of God, it disarmed anyone and everyone who wanted to harm Him. This is a very important key for us to remember and practice in faith when we are tested.

After He had driven them out, the blind and the lame, who regularly sat outside the temple begging, came to Him. He healed them, showing everyone what was actually to be done inside the temple. He reversed the priorities that the religious leaders of those days had set. The destitute who were begging outside were brought into God's house and given hope, while the hypocrites were thrown out and taught a lesson they'd never forget.

Now remember that this was shortly before the Passover, and people from all over Israel came to the temple in Jerusalem to celebrate the feast along with their entire family. At this time, when He healed these blind and lame people, the (literal) children who were in the temple cried out in the temple, saying, "Hosanna to the Son of David!" (Matthew 21:15). This totally put off the 'big ones', and they questioned the Lord Jesus concerning the children's declaration. This is when He quotes this verse and says, "Yes. Have you never read, 'Out of the mouths of babies and nursing infants, you have perfected praise'?" Lord Jesus plainly told them that it's David's prophecy fulfilled! What the wise ones could not see or accept was percieved very clearly by the little ones and accepted readily by them. That's the beauty of this verse.

When David declared this, he said that God '**ordained strength**' from the mouths of babies and nursing infants. But when the Lord Jesus quoted it, He said that God had '**perfected praise**' from the mouths of babies and nursing infants. Equating both, we can say that 'perfected praise' is equivalent to 'ordaining strength'. Therefore, praising God endows us with strength. Do you feel weak in your body and soul? The simple solution is to just praise God more and more!

Why is 'Praise from the mouth of children' so important to God? For once, God loves children, and He is greatly magnified when they worship Him with pure, innocent hearts (unlike the cluttered hearts of adults). The Lord Jesus also told us that unless we change and become like little children, we will never enter the kingdom of heaven. I have observed in my own children the sincerity with which they pray. They don't think twice before asking Him for things that may seem insignificant to us. Sometimes I am taken aback by their level of understanding when I hear them speak to God. During our family prayer one night, when my daughter was 6, she didn't hesitate to randomly strum her little guitar, making absolutely no melody. She just strummed all the strings as loudly as she could while we sang and didn't seem to care that her music didn't make any sense. She just wanted to do her best to praise God. She was so influenced by her older teenaged brother who plays fabulous music! We learned not to shut her up. Both my children have challenged me to come up higher in worshipping God.

During this study, I did some research into the education of Jewish children, which helped me understand a lot of things. I wish to briefly share what I learned with you all. Since this is again a vast topic, I would encourage everyone to research it for themselves.

Our Almighty God explicitly commanded Israel in Deuteronomy 6:6–9 regarding passing on the word of God to their successive generations, saying, "And these words which I command you today shall be in your heart. You shall teach them **diligently** to your children and shall talk of them when you sit in your house, when you walk by the way, when you lie down, and when you rise up. You shall bind them as a sign on your hand, and they shall be as frontlets between your eyes. You shall write them on the doorposts of your house and on your gates."

The Jews sincerely followed this command and, from a very early age, put in much effort to teach their children the word of God. Children were first tutored at home by their parents, and as the days progressed, a system of education was put into place where tutors were hired to come home and teach the children, or the children were sent to schools that were set up either in or near the synagogues. By the age of 5, the children had to study the written Torah. By 10 years of age, they had to study the oral Torah- the Mishnah. This was a study by repetition and consisted of the concise and precise laws dictating how the written Torah's commandments are achieved. By 13 years of age, they had to perfect themselves in the Mitzvoth, which consisted of about 613 commandments that the Pharisees held very strictly. This was written by the so-called Jewish scholars by human interpretation of God's laws. By 15 years of age, they should have studied the Talmud, i.e., comprehension of the oral and written laws and contemplation of the laws. So education in Jewish culture was a serious affair.

Initially, all this education was done informally by the parents at home, followed by the priests in the annexes to the synagogues, and later taken up by the scribes and pharisees. The priests were the ones who performed the duty in the temple, made copies of the book of law, and also taught the children. But during the 70 years of exile, the Jews were scattered all over, and people known as 'scribes' came into being. They were mostly Levites. The most elite among the Levitical priests became involved in politics as there was no king over the nation after they returned from exile. These were the Sadducees. They believed in only the written Torah and paid no attention to the oral Torah, the prophets, or the writings of the doctrine of resurrection from the dead. Biblical scholarship and exposition were passed on to a special class of scribes from the time of Ezra. Now the scribes became the people who made written copies of the Word of God and taught the people the laws and commandments of God.

Yet another group was called the Pharisees. These also came into existence after their return from exile. A person from any tribe could become one. They dedicated their lives to strictly adhering to and following the written and oral Torah, the Mitzvoth, and the Talmud. They did not encourage hellinisation (acceptance of Greek culture), which the Sadducees supported to benefit their politics. They were confident that they had Mosaic authority when interpreting the laws of God. This is how the Mitzvoth came into existence. These Pharisees had come to a purely carnal conclusion about the laws of God and burdened the general population with unnecessary rules and regulations. Such man-made laws were always criticised by the Lord Jesus. To the Pharisees, adultery was only something committed through physical contact. But the Lord Jesus raised the standard to it being a matter of the heart.

The commandments put forth by these scribes and Pharisees were burdensome to people, and the Lord Jesus exposed their hypocrisy time and again. Lord Jesus instructed the people to follow the commandments of God quoted by the Pharisees from the book of the law but not to follow their deeds because they were self-righteous hypocrites who lived holy outwardly for the praise and respect of men. Lord Jesus was against their version of interpretation of God's laws because most of it had to do with benefiting themselves.

During the exile, 3 institutions were set up in foreign lands.

✡ House of Assembly: synagogue

✡ House of prayer: proseuche

✡ House of study: Midrash

These were carried forward when they returned to their homeland. It was at one of these places that even the Lord Jesus was educated. Children entered the temple very early in life. The Bible gives us an account of the Lord Jesus being in the temple at the age of 12. At this age, the Lord Jesus' knowledge and understanding of the Word baffled the religious teachers of those days. The principles followed by the

Pharisees, scribes, and Sadducees were passed down to the children at a very tender age. When the Lord Jesus challenged their doctrine, they counted Him as a major threat to their future. The moment the children in the esteemed temple of Jerusalem cried out praises to the Lord Jesus, they were very upset. These children were their future, the ones to carry forward their legacy of hypocrisy, and the Lord Jesus was undoing it effortlessly. The young minds related the word they were learning to the practical demonstration of godliness that the Lord Jesus showed them, and they were all in awe of Him. Now they had a new "Model" to follow, with the Lord Jesus shifting the focus from the flesh to the heart. This must have given the young ones such great relief compared to the heavy burdens imposed on them by their Rabbis. It is always difficult or nearly impossible for people bathed in self-righteousness to receive the love offered by God.

ii. <u>When It Represents the Ignorant People God Chose to Further His Kingdom Purposes on This Earth:</u>

In 1 Corinthians 1:26-29, the Apostle Paul clearly tells us the standard of God's selection. He excels at choosing the 'foolish', the 'weak', the 'base', the 'despised', and 'things that are not' in order to display His splendour and glory to the world. To this day, this selection still holds good. Even the Lord Jesus used these criteria when He chose His disciples on earth. It is not that God is against the rich, educated, famous, or smart people. If they humble themselves and give God the first place, He partners with them too! The clever and smart ones find it difficult to submit to that criterion.

I'd just like to sidetrack here momentarily and extrapolate this to us today. When I was studying in school, I often saw teachers being favourable towards the brilliant students. The same is happening even today in my children's school. It is not uncommon and is written off as normal most of the time. I wasn't one of the 'brilliant ones' and often went unnoticed by most and targeted by some teachers at times who deliberately flunked me. It did affect my psychology, and my academic performance would go down. It was very rare that a teacher would notice or pay attention to a student like or worse than me. But one kind-hearted teacher did, and she was my third-grade class teacher (Mrs. Medhora). She treated all students equally but gave special attention to the ones obviously left out by the rest as insignificant. And till today, she is the only teacher (among all those in more than a decade of schooling) that I am in touch with. I have the highest regard for her! Her love for me at that tender age of 8 has impacted me till today, and I would certainly wish for all the Christian teachers to be like her. **There is no point in teachers glorifying themselves in the lives of brilliant students. Pick the ones who are dull and work on them. When they excel, the world will applaud your effort. That is humility!** I dare my fellow believers in the teaching profession to try this. The Lord Jesus set the precedent for this perfectly!

The reason why God chose them over the wise, the noble, and the mighty is because they were quick to receive the grace of God and allow Him to work in and through them. On the other hand, the self-sufficient ones depended on their intellect and accomplishments. The measure of grace provided to set aside their insufficiency or self-sufficiency (pride) is the same for both parties. For some reason, humans find it easier to lay aside their insufficiency than their self-sufficiency. That's exactly why the Lord Jesus had a cabinet of fishermen and tax collectors to perform His wonders rather than a bunch of Pharisees and Sadducees. While the former had more insufficiency than self-sufficiency, the latter excelled in a false sense of self-sufficiency!

God is impartial. It is man who has failed to receive His abounding grace in order to follow and fulfil His will. The same grace was received by the pharisee of the pharisees, the Apostle Paul, and he succeeded in turning the world 'right side up'. God used him so effectively to deliver astounding truths, which are a blessing to us even today and will continue to be so.

The main purpose of accomplishing His praise through the mouths of babes and infants was to "silence His enemies". Who and what are the enemies of God? It is satan and all that he does. Also, all things that end in death are the enemies of God. Sickness, poverty, lack, and all the works of the flesh mentioned in Galatians 5:19–21 are the enemies of God. When we come under the influence of any of these, we need to step up and increase the outflow of praise and worship from our lives, along with acknowledgement of God's truth regarding them. This is the way the enemy and the avenger are paralysed and overcome.

So far, we have spoken about "babes and nursing infants praising God" in 2 aspects. There are many instances mentioned in God's word where, when such praise was offered, the enemy and avenger were totally silenced. They could go no further in their evil plots. However, they had to look for a new way to persecute the children of God, and yet they faced the same fate every time.

Some believers preferred martyrdom to deliverance. Lord Jesus said in Matthew 10:28, "Do not be afraid of those who kill the body but cannot kill the soul. Rather, be afraid of the One who can destroy both soul and body in hell." The people who died through martyrdom knew this secret. Hence, they did not accept deliverance and looked forward to a better resurrection (Hebrews 11:35). But the wicked people who slaughter the children of God are not aware of this truth. They think they have attained victory by murdering them. Such murderers will have greater accountability in this life and on the Day of Judgement. For every martyr who lays down his life, there are more number of disciples being made every day. Since the day the Lord Jesus ushered in the Kingdom of God on this earth, it has always grown and flourished. There is no power in the universe that can stop this exponential progress at any point in time.

3. *WHEN I CONSIDER YOUR HEAVENS, THE WORK OF YOUR FINGERS, THE MOON AND THE STARS WHICH YOU HAVE ORDAINED,*

When we study the Psalms, we notice that David observed nature intently - the land, seas, sky, animals, birds, water creatures, etc. I personally believe that David learned more about nature while he was shepherding his father's sheep as a young man. This was the **'Preparation Time'** for David. If we have a personal revelation of this concept, discouragement and negativity can literally be wiped off from one's life. From the time when we come to the knowledge of God to the time of tangible fruition, there is a preparation time. The length of this time totally depends on how we handle it. If we know that it is precious and vital for us to learn and get trained as much as we can, then we do well. God prepares us for all that is up ahead. Joseph underwent this training for 13 years in the house of Potiphar and the prison. He learned everything he could, and it helped him when he stood before Pharaoh. David also had the same training in the wilderness when he was shepherding his flock and also while dodging Saul. But the work that God does during these times is phenomenal and helps in building a strong foundation. This is basically **'foundation building time'**, and stronger the foundation, the stronger the building! Never underestimate or despise the value of your preparation time. Most of the growth in this season is like the root of the plant that goes deep into the ground for good anchorage. The shoot still may be tiny. The growth happening underground is not visible to the outside world. But once the root is established, it takes no time for the strong shoot to grow up, and the world will see the work of God.

However, in today's world, the availability of gadgets driven by the latest technology and the quality of the entertainment streaming on media has made very little time available for people to think straight. For most people, time with God is just 5 minutes in the morning and another 5 minutes at night. This is a typical religious person doing stuff just to satisfy his ragged conscience. It is unprofitable for us and God. If God is not the first and the last and everything in between in our lives, it is basically meaningless. The crowd (Christians included) are drawn to all the ungodly activities and entertainments. While many observe nature, they end up making gods out of creation and don't attribute God as their maker. It's not uncommon to hear the word 'mother nature'. She is a common deity in almost every heathen religion and is one of the greatest insults to Father God.

Social media and other media also have a significant influence on our lives. When used in the right manner by listening to godly content, it contributes to our edification. On the other hand, it can also be a source of maximum filth. Being distracted by all the rubbish piped into our minds through these channels is one reason we neglect to observe God's power and magnificence displayed in nature.

Meditating on God's word and His work should be a vital part of a believer's life. David "considered" the heavens. In other words, he didn't just see the creation of God, but he pondered it. Pondering, meditating and considering God's word is absolutely life-changing because of the revelation given to us by the Holy Spirit through them. Our perception is elevated to the kingdom level. God hid many of His attributes in nature and gave us the privilege to search them out! All it takes is time and willingness from our end. When there is revelation, hope and faith arise, bondages are broken, and the impact of knowing God's truth sets us free.

When God created everything in the beginning, He ordained certain laws that would govern this world as long as it exists. These laws can never be undone unless God suspends them temporarily for His hand to be revealed (through miracles). One such law is given in Gen 8:22. "While the earth remains, seedtime and harvest, cold and heat, winter and summer, day and night shall not cease." These laws hold good even to this day and will continue to do so. Observing nature teaches us all these godly laws and encourages us to put them into practice in our lives. It is very practical for a farmer to take this in a literal sense and follow the law of seed-time-harvest. But we need to extrapolate this principle into our personal lives and sow the word of God in our hearts, patiently wait on it, and see the outcome (harvest). We reap what we sow!

During the time of David, there were not many scientific types of equipment available to observe celestial bodies. They had to mostly rely on their eyes only. Neither did they have the knowledge that science has imparted to us today (evidence-based). Yet David knew by revelation the magnificence of the celestial bodies. The lunar cycle was the basis on which they counted their days, weeks, months, and years. The position of the sun and the moon in the sky has been used to set a time-system in place from time immemorial. The position of the stars established directions, especially while travelling by land and sea. With the resources available to them, they gathered much information and gave God glory for it. David never doubted 'The Creator'.

Modern-day education has succeeded in making highly educated fools who have brought in the theory of evolution to completely omit the role of God. This is a good example of a satanic perversion of the truth. But there is no way one can get anywhere trying to propagate these useless and baseless theories, which they themselves cannot prove no matter what. God never interferes with or forces these 'geniuses' to change their minds when they adamantly stick to their propaganda. But on the contrary, God has used educated people who have laid down their earthly pride and want to prove creation through archaeological evidence and scientific experiments. These people have done exceptional work in proving God's awesome creation.

At creation, God spoke in Genesis 1:14, saying, "Let there be light in the firmament of the heavens to divide the day from the night; and let them be for signs and seasons and for days and years." Mankind has seen the fulfilment of this for ages. Not only did David read this truth in God's word, he also considered the magnificence and beauty of the work of God's fingers. God has spoken many great and awesome truths in His word. Anyone who takes the time to consider all this will surely be rewarded with revelations that will impact their lives forever. Sometimes, the repeated reading of a particular verse imparts a new revelation every time. For example, when I was writing this, it occurred to me that God placed the sun, moon, and stars in such a way that the earth should benefit the most. In other words, the earth was first designed, and then the sun, moon, and stars were created in order to serve the earth! People worship creation today rather than the Creator and don't realise that it is Almighty God who created the sun to serve the earth and its inhabitants. So who exactly should we be worshipping?

Due to the fall of humanity, creation took precedence over the Creator. Even today, many Christians consistently regard zodiac signs and believe that stars control their destiny. How naive can people be? Hey, God is the one who placed the stars there and has depicted the story of the Messiah's work in the skies. Starting with Virgo (the virgin, September) to Leo (the lion, August), the truth of God- the Gospel- is displayed for the whole world to see. I recommend that you look it up and study it further. The misinterpretation of the zodiac signs occurred because those who interpreted them left the Creator out of the equation. Astronomy is God's work, but satan perverted it into astrology. God would have been more than happy to reveal the truth behind it if only they had asked Him for it. The Magi from the East were able to come and worship the King of the Jews because they paid attention to astronomy, and God used it to instruct them!

Today, almost every religion on Earth worships the sun as a deity, calling it by different names. Festivals commemorating the magnificence of the sun god, nephilim-like fictitious creatures and half human-half animal beings are prominent in India. How much would that grieve the loving heart of God? Even many Christians don't realise their folly when they compromise by wishing their friends and colleagues on the occasion of these festivals, dressing up likewise and participating in these events. They would rather hurt God's heart than offend humans, glorifying their so-called tolerance. That is absolute hypocrisy!

Here me out on this please. Always remember that when you wish people on the occasion of their (heathen) festivals, saying 'happy so and so' etc., you are essentially saying, 'Have a good time worshipping your idols and continue being lost!' What more? I have heard Indian preachers and pastors voicing wishes from the pulpit to showcase their 'tolerance'! Would you do the same if God Almighty was visibly present on the scene? I dare you! How are you witnessing the gospel to a lost world when you yourself are indulging in idolatry, sir? How are we any different from the Israelites who compromised with the Canaanites during their festivals in which they worshipped demons and other creation? We cannot deceive

Almighty God! Since the day the Lord revealed this to me, I have never wished anyone for their heathen festivals. I don't mind even if it costs me that friendship. The Lord's approval is more precious to me. Stand by your convictions no matter the cost!

If you are feeling discouraged or dismayed for any reason today, just spend time observing God's creation and allow God to speak His truth to your heart. That will undoubtedly lift the burden within no time.

4. WHAT IS MAN THAT YOU ARE MINDFUL OF HIM, AND THE SON OF MAN THAT YOU VISIT HIM?

God created mankind after He had created everything else in the world. Everything was kept ready for man and his wife. There was not a need left unattended for them; they lacked nothing. It was a beautiful and perfect life in the Garden of Eden. To make it more worthwhile, God gave man a job to take care of His creation (even before giving him a wife), along with the authority that he needed to accomplish this task. God loves His creation, and all His creation adores Him. The basis on which God established His relationship with us is "**LOVE**." It's not sympathy, empathy, pity, benevolence, or even obligation for having created us. He started with love, and it continues into eternity. There is no end to His love for us. God intends us to have a good life (Jeremiah 29:11), and life can be good only when it is God-centred. There is hope and a future for every man who is wholly dependent on God.

Despite the perfect environment that Adam and Eve lived in, they chose to rely on their own knowledge by partaking of the forbidden tree. Right there we see God giving us the best example of what happens when man chooses himself over God. Most often we think that satan is destroying lives. While that is certainly true, the greater truth is evident from the Garden of Eden.

Every day and every moment, we are constantly choosing between the 'Tree of Life' (God's Wisdom) and the 'Tree of knowledge of good and evil' (our wisdom). Satan does not have access to the Tree of Life; he cannot come anywhere near it. But he has his little hut built right under the Tree of knowledge of good and evil, and is more than willing to help everyone (through deception, fear, worry, etc.) who chooses to eat the fruit of that tree. How often are we tempted to eat that fruit!? When we do so, it is akin to giving a thief our house keys and allowing him to come in and go out as he pleases. This is the subtle way in which he usurps our God-given authority.

Eve and Adam did the same and lost their position. Yet, God did not abandon them at this crucial guilt-ridden point. While showing them that their attempt to cover their nakedness with fig leaves (self-righteousness/ work of the flesh) was useless, He clothed them with the skin of the first animal sacrificed in the Garden of Eden, which pointed to the future sacrifice of His beloved Son, displaying His plan of redemption for mankind. He also taught them and the succeeding generations, the significance of observing these animal sacrifices. He continuously upheld man, wanting to redeem him from the life of curse he had chosen and deal with him in mercy. He did all this motivated by **AGAPE LOVE.**

The arrogance and self-confidence of man demanded the laws of God in order to justify himself before Him. So He gave them what they wanted - The Ten Commandments. It was definitely impossible to keep all these commandments. But the reason He gave them these was to show that there was no good their flesh was capable of to justify themselves before God; they all needed a Saviour! Knowing very well that they would fail the law, He showed them the way to atone for their sins through animal sacrifices that pointed to the Messiah. **They were declaring the future redemption by faith in offering these sacrifices.** God kept His part of the deal, but man failed every time.

Still motivated by love, He ordained the New Covenant through Lord Jesus Christ for us. This covenant absolutely magnifies His love for us. Knowing our weaknesses, He brought into effect a covenant so great through our Lord Jesus Christ that it is absolutely foolish for man not to accept it. Through this covenant, God always lives in and through us.

At every point in time, God has always been 'MIND-FULL' of us. For many years, I overlooked the significance of this word. It is not just mindful (as in he remembers us every once in a while); it is MIND-FULL! We fill His mind 24x7! God etched this on my heart when I heard Don Moen sing 'My Creator King.' He perfectly split the word 'mindful' in the chorus, dragging the 'mind' and adding the 'full,' emphasising it beautifully. What has man done for God that he deserves this place? Absolutely nothing! At every instance, the thoughts of mankind were continually evil and rebellious. Motivated by love and love only, and not by anything else, He continues to lead us.

'VISIT':

God is omnipresent. He is in every place at every time. But man failed to appreciate His presence because of his sins and his sin conscience. The good news is that Lord Jesus did away with sin, and the baptism instituted by Him nullifies the sin conscience (1 Peter 3:21). The purpose of water baptism and the need for it is very clearly explained by the Apostle Peter in this verse. At times when man felt that God was far away from him, God made sure to assure man that He was very much present and willing to deliver. This is what David terms here as "VISIT." From the beginning, God always promised to be with us. God is unchanging. We need to have the correct perspective on this. When we do that, we will always be aware that God is with us. He has stayed His ground always. It is we who move away. Note that it was the prodigal who left home, and the father was still rooted in his house (Luke 15) and was watchful always for his son to return.

I believe David could have also meant that 'God answers us.' God is our good God who listens to our prayers and answers them according to His will (because, lacking discretion, we are capable of asking for things destructive to us also). All over the Bible, He repeatedly encourages all of us to approach Him, and He will answer us. He answers us because He is good and obliging, not because of our merits or good works. No matter what situation we may be in, He is always ready to hear and answer us. His mercy, portrayed through the sacrifice of His Son, is so great that it overpowered the sum of all the sins of the human race. His grace is so rich and abundant that each of His children can live according to His will, provided they receive it.

David said in Psalms 139:8, 'If I ascend into heaven, You are there; If I make my bed in hell, behold You are there,' and in verse 2 of the same chapter he says, 'You know my sitting down and my rising up; You understand my thoughts afar off.' Man cannot hide from God, and He never neglects His creation. No matter how far we may have gone from Him, the only One who can draw us out and get us to a broad place is our Almighty God. He is our only hope, and deliverance belongs only to Him.

5. ***FOR YOU HAVE MADE HIM A LITTLE LOWER THAN THE ANGELS, AND YOU HAVE CROWNED HIM WITH GLORY AND HONOUR.***

6. ***YOU HAVE MADE HIM TO HAVE DOMINION OVER THE WORKS OF YOUR HANDS; YOU HAVE PUT ALL THINGS UNDER HIS FEET,***

7. ***ALL SHEEP AND OXEN- EVEN THE BEASTS OF THE FIELD,***

8. ***THE BIRDS OF THE AIR, AND THE FISH OF THE SEA THAT PASS THROUGH THE PATHS OF THE SEAS.***

This passage is astounding. When I studied this in depth, the revelation blew my hat off! I hope you enjoy reading this as well and studying this for yourselves.

Genesis 1:1 says, 'In the beginning, God created the Heavens and the earth.' So God created the heavens first and then the earth. The angelic beings were created before mankind. They belong to the host of heaven, and we belong to the host of earth. God is God of all the hosts together.

God's word provides a good insight into the subject of angels. While the names of a few prominent ones are mentioned (Archangel Michael and the Messenger Gabriel), it also gives us information on the types of angels like Cherubim and Seraphim. Angels were created perfect and for a reason. Their primary purpose was and is to worship God (akin to the purpose given to mankind). Also, God has told us that angels have been given the responsibility to protect (Psalm 91:11) and minister (Hebrews 1:14) to us (mankind). They are messengers from God to man as well as mostly invisible beings who carry out the spoken word of God (Psalm 103:20).

The angels live before God - in His very presence, ministering to Him. They see the face of God (Matthew 18:10). They walk back and forth to the earth, carrying out the tasks that the Lord assigns to them. Jacob's dream establishes this fact for us. However, 'Angelic service' is not for everyone. It is for the children of God who have accepted or are going to accept salvation in this life. The ladder that the angels climbed up and down is our Lord Jesus Christ, indicating that believing in Him is essential to receive angelic service. One more criterion was further added by Lord Jesus in Luke 12:8, 9: 'Also, I say to you, whoever confesses me before men, Him the Son of Man will confess before the angels of God. But he who denies me before men will be denied before the angels of God.' Therefore, angelic protection and ministering cannot be taken for granted by anyone and everyone who do not stand as an open witness for God. We need to be very clear on the doctrine that we believe and follow and make sure that God's word is our source/foundation.

Psalm 103:20 says that the angels of God who excel in strength, do His word, heeding the voice of His word. Angels have been put into the service of mankind from the very beginning, even from the Garden of Eden. Before I start giving further insight into this subject, which is very interesting, I request you to study Ezekiel 28, Isaiah 14, and Revelation 12. These 3 passages put together reveal the history of Lucifer (satan/ devil).

Angels are vested with supernatural powers. They walk between heaven and earth, having access to God's presence, go from one end of the earth to the other in no time, and can be visible to a person while being invisible to others. In this respect, angels are superior beings to us. This is what David meant in verse 5.

Ezekiel 28 clearly tells us that Lucifer (satan) was the anointed cherub who was placed in the Garden of Eden to cover and protect Adam and

Eve (verse 13, 14). Besides being the seal of perfection and full of wisdom, he was covered with every precious stone - sardius, topaz, diamond, beryl, onyx, jasper, sapphire, turquoise, and emerald with gold. He had an inbuilt system of timbrels and pipes. In other words, he was the perfect specimen of beauty and wisdom. He walked across the fiery stones between heaven and earth. Unfortunately, these 2 attributes - beauty and wisdom, corrupted him, causing his heart to swell with pride (Ezekiel 28:17). Lucifer never verbalised this pride orally, but he did so in his heart. He said in his heart that he could exalt himself to God's position (Isaiah 14:13-14). In order to retain his splendour, he corrupted his wisdom. He traded God's wisdom for futile personal gain of wanting to take the place of God and usurping all the worship and adoration that belongs to Him.

I believe one of the things that irked Lucifer was the relationship that God had with mankind. He witnessed that in the Garden of Eden. Man, who was created a little lower than the angels, had direct access to God and not through any mediator like him. Lucifer was jealous of this fact, and at some point during this time, succeeded in acquiring 1/3rd of the angelic host to himself. The ultimate point of his downfall occurred when he said in his heart that he will be like God. Following this, Almighty God banished him from heaven along with his crew. He was stripped of all his beauty and wisdom. Revelation calls him the fiery red dragon having 7 heads and 10 horns. Ever since then, he lives on earth, targeting the children of God, as said in Revelation 12.

This made satan really mad at God. He continues to be so until today. He works evil in rebellion to the plans and purposes of God. He always produces a counterfeit to God's standards and has succeeded in deceiving the world. When people succumb to his deception, he overpowers them. It always starts in the mind and heart of man. Nevertheless, his deception is only for a period of time and will soon come to an end.

It could be possible that Adam and Eve knew Lucifer by appearance since he was in the Garden. After his fall, he did not approach them directly but rather through a serpent; the serpent was an animal. This needs some thought: he succeeded in bringing the serpent (animal kingdom) under his control before he could touch the humans. Hence, I believe that the animal kingdom fell first. Animals were given a blessing but not authority; man was given blessing and authority. That certainly makes a difference, and man could have fought back with just his words. Once satan had the serpent under his control, **satan's next target was Eve; not Adam**. Through Eve, he got to Adam. He always starts at the weaker one and works his way up cunningly. We need to be aware of that. For this reason, **God forbade women to have authority over men, especially in the church** (1 Corinthians 14:34-35, 1 Timothy 2:11-14). I don't see why this straight-forward command is overlooked so easily today. God commanded us ladies to keep away from this one forbidden tree; but some daughters of Eve want to adamantly partake of it! There are thousands of other good trees in the garden for us. We should delight ourselves in those, isn't it?

When God made man and put him in the Garden of Eden, He gave Adam the responsibility of taking care of the garden and a specific command to not eat from the tree of knowledge of good and evil. Later, God made Eve from Adam's rib. Hence, when God gave this command to abstain from the forbidden tree, Eve was not yet created. The duty to inform Eve belonged to Adam. Now we cannot be sure of whether or not Adam informed his wife word-for-word regarding God's command. Because when the serpent approached her, questioning God's command, she added to what God had primarily said (Gen 2:3). In exaggerating, she lied; **or** Adam had added to what God said when he informed Eve about the forbidden tree, in which case he lied.

The word tells us very clearly that there were 2 trees in the midst of the garden: The Tree Of Life and The Tree Of Knowledge Of Good And Evil (Gen 1:9). Until the serpent brought her attention to it, I don't think they were tempted to eat its fruit. It is possible that Eve could have been ignorant of the facts or could have thought herself to be wiser than God. This cost her and the rest of mankind greatly. Adam's role in all this cannot be belittled. The word says that he was with her when Eve ate the fruit. At this juncture, I would like to extrapolate this into our lives. The word of God is the storehouse of knowledge, and God is the One who gives wisdom and understanding. Unless we spend quality and quantity time in His word, under the guidance of the Holy Spirit, we will likewise fall prey to satan's deception, like Eve. Wrong teaching/ preaching also does much harm. God clearly said that His people perish for lack of knowledge.

Satan basically questioned God's word before Eve, indicating that God had hidden something very vital from them. Everything in the garden was good all along. "Evil/ death" wasn't in their dictionary. Satan presented the concept of 'evil' in a very interesting manner and 'initiated' her to use her wisdom and reasoning. To her, 'evil' would have been something that God had hidden from them. The least she could have done was just approach God and ask Him about it before she decided anything for herself; after all, God fellowshipped with them every day in the Garden of Eden. Instead, she fell in the exact same manner that Lucifer fell. She opted to govern her own life and give more importance to her 5 senses. She never argued verbally or spoke blasphemy directly to God. All the disobedience originated in her heart, and she simply gave into it. Ultimately, the lust of the flesh (fruit was good for food), the lust of the eyes (fruit was pleasant to the eyes), and the pride of life (tree desirable to make one wise) came into full-blown effect, as quoted in Genesis 3:6. **Notice that all this revelation did not come to her after she had eaten the fruit to test it, but rather before she ate it.** This shows us very clearly that if we think about something and meditate on it, we will end up doing it. So we can well avoid sinning if we stop thinking and meditating on negative and ungodly things. Adam was with her all along, and we don't see any resistance from him in this entire matter! Men, watch out! Eve succeeded in pulling him down with her.

When God created man and woman, He clothed them with glory and honour. Even though the English Bible says 'crowned', the Hebrew word literally means 'surrounded'. It was this attribute that made even the dinosaur obey the words that man spoke. Even the mightiest of all the beasts and other animals had to bow to the word of man. Such was the authority given to mankind when God spoke the blessing over them. Even though they were totally naked from the time of creation, this clothing of glory and honour covered them. Hence they were never aware of their nakedness. But once they ate the fruit, poof! This glory and honour were lifted immediately, and the first thing they realised was their nakedness. This was the first sign of death starting to work in mankind. From this point, the countdown to the end began, and the clock has been ticking ever since.

For all of us who would waste no time in blaming and deriding Adam and Eve, let's consider this: Even though the prevailing circumstances were different for them and us, the bottom line remains the same. From time immemorial, God established living life by choosing one of 2 options: either we choose to live life partaking of the Tree of Life i.e. living life God's way **OR** we can live life partaking of the Tree of Knowledge of Good and Evil, where we decide what is best for us and set God aside or tuck Him in somewhere. Satan has nothing to do with the trees. He has no ownership of the forbidden tree either. Note that God planted both the trees in the Garden among many other trees. God has given us all a choice. Both trees exist even to this day in our world. You can choose God's way **OR** your way. When we have simplified this truth to this basic level, it is possible that we ourselves may be found guilty, similar to Adam and Eve. It won't be surprising to find a good number among the Christian population who are living partaking from the forbidden tree today, the main reason being ignorance, a hardened heart, or frank disobedience by falling prey to their culture and traditions. I have personally witnessed the deception caused by traditions and the major role it has played in the Christian population in my country.

So then, what role does satan have in all of this? The answer is very simple. When man chooses to live by his own standards, he moves away from God. When we move away, satan is more than happy to help us ruin our lives through further deception. The more we trust in ourselves, deeper is the pit we dig for ourselves, and the more difficult it is to come out. Meanwhile, satan has a feast, rejoicing to see God's creation rebelling at Him. That is basically his goal.

However, as long as we are alive, there is always hope. If you find yourself in such a sinking situation, God is closer than you think. Reach out to Him instead of running away from Him. Once you repent and return, take a stand to obey Him no matter what, and allow God to work

His will in your life. **Destroying ungodly and unbiblical traditions is the need of the hour**. God is a gentleman. He never forces anything on us. But when we submit to Him, He puts all of heaven's forces to work on our behalf. I am a testimony to that fact! Do yourself a favour and kick the serpent out the minute you see him. Do not entertain anything or anyone who contradicts God's word. All Eve had to do was ask the serpent to shut up by voicing God's command. The word had the power and ability to kick the tempter out, as the Lord Jesus demonstrated this for us in the wilderness temptation for 40 days. There was no place for any more talk when He said **"IT IS WRITTEN"**. Satan had no option but to flee and leave Him alone. So start equipping yourselves with the word of God!

The events that happened in the Garden of Eden were very disappointing. Yet God salvaged the whole thing, which cost Him the life of His only Son. He never abandoned His choice creation. Right at the point of pronouncing the curse on the serpent, Adam, and Eve in the garden, He gave the promise of "The Messiah" who would redeem the whole world, and fulfilled His promise through our Lord Jesus Christ.

With the coming of the Messiah and His finished work on the cross, His robe of righteousness has been given to us. When we believe this absolute truth with all our hearts, we can utilise that same magnificent glory and honour for the furtherance of God's kingdom on earth. David speaks of this authority in the present tense, confirming this fact.

9. O LORD, OUR LORD, HOW EXCELLENT IS YOUR NAME IN ALL THE EARTH!

Now, along with David, we can also praise God and His attributes after having realised His work for us and in our lives.

Psalm 9

INTRODUCTION:

Most of David's Psalms were accompanied by music chosen by him. It is indeed wonderful to see him using the wisdom that God had given him in choosing the right instrument or music style for his Psalms. There is an anointing that comes through such wisdom that is well able to minister to the hearts of people more effectively. He had discernment regarding which particular style would go best with each Psalm.

David was first introduced to us in the book of 1 Samuel as a shepherd boy who sincerely took care of his father's sheep. After the prophet Samuel anointed him, the Spirit of the Lord came upon him, and he was blessed and strengthened with more talents (1 Samuel 16:18), one of which was music. David probably developed this further while tending the sheep. This pattern of God imparting skills is also seen in the life of Daniel. This provides exceptional practical study material if one is willing to study and utilise it to glorify God.

The tune for this Psalm as given by David is called 'MuthLabben' in Hebrew, meaning "Death of the Son". It could be that David composed this Psalm following the death of any of his sons. David loved all his sons. But a few did not reciprocate his love. I have previously elaborated on the story of Absalom's rebellion.

1. ***I WILL PRAISE YOU, O LORD, WITH MY WHOLE HEART; I WILL TELL OF YOUR MARVELLOUS WORKS.***

In the Psalms, one particular attribute of David's character stands out: the **'remembrance of God's faithfulness'**. He constantly remembered the fact that God heard and answered his prayers. Most of us prayerfully place lot of requests before God. But how many of us return to give Him thanks for answering our prayers? How many of us would go one step ahead and testify about His faithfulness to others, declaring His goodness? Furthermore, how many of us will remember His previous deliverance when we come up against a fresh challenge? Let me elaborate this with a beautiful incident in the life of the Lord Jesus that shows that there is a special 'acknowledgement' from God for every 'Thank You' we offer back to Him. Our 'thank you, Lord' is never the end!

In Luke 17:11–19, we read the story of the 10 lepers. This happened in a village in the region between Samaria and Galilee. This group of 10 was a mixed population of Jews and Samaritans. Most of us are aware of this devastating and debilitating disease known as leprosy. It was considered a curse for sinning, and all the lepers were to be housed outside the camp of Israel and labelled as unclean or untouchable. They could not enter or roam inside the city as it was a contagious disease, living a lonely life and almost always died early. They were a despised lot. As the Lord Jesus was passing by this village, these 10 men cried out to Him for mercy.

The basic thing here is that they were well aware that they were sinners and that sin was the root cause of their sickness. So when they approached Him, they asked for mercy so that they might be set free from the curse of sin. Our ever-merciful Lord Jesus simply asked them to go show themselves to the priests, even without touching or waving at them. It is admirable to observe the faith of these 10 men, who immediately obeyed Him without question or doubt. As they went, they were cleansed. Surely this must have been a visible miracle for all 10 as the raw areas of flesh disappeared on the way! But this miracle of our Lord overwhelmed only one person, a Samaritan, who immediately turned around and went back to the Lord Jesus, fell facedown at His feet, glorified God with a loud voice, and gave Him thanks. Lord Jesus acknowledged his 'Thank You' in a special way—this healed Samaritan leper was made 'Whole'! (Luke 17:19, KJV).

The Leprae bacilli chew away the digits and disfigure the affected ones severely, in addition to causing skin sores. When he returned to thank the Lord, not only were his skin sores healed, but his digits (fingers and toes) and face were restored to normalcy. How wonderful is that!? In essence, this is exactly what happened to David too. Not only did God punish his enemies, He restored the throne and the kingdom to him. God is indeed blessed when we thank Him, but He outdoes us by loading us with greater benefits each time.

As important as thanksgiving is, being witnesses to His goodness and awesome works should be the hallmark of every soul that is touched by God's loving hand. It should be a virtue of His children. All of the Lord's apostles, including the one who replaced the son of perdition, Judas Iscariot, were excellent witnesses of the Lord. It's their witness that helped spread the gospel to the whole world. Their witness turned the world right side up and surely helped many souls to a relationship with the Father through salvation in the Lord Jesus Christ.

When we receive salvation, God lives in and through us. He works in our lives, making all things beautiful, and through us, he spreads the fragrance of His goodness into a world drowning in sin and hopelessness. Witnessing should be a day-to-day activity for every believer. Witness, encourage, and edify! Never underestimate the power of witnessing to a lost world. You never know how many lives will be changed by a single witness that comes from a believer's mouth.

The great commission is given to us based on this very principle after the Lord finished His work of redemption on earth and ascended to the Father.

2. *I WILL BE GLAD AND REJOICE IN YOU; I WILL SING PRAISES TO YOUR NAME, O MOST HIGH.*

This portrays the 'attitude' of a believer. No matter what the circumstances are, good or bad, we have to retain an attitude or character of thanksgiving and joy. Knowing that it is just a matter of time and that victory is already ours, helps us to maintain this attitude.

David has written quite a few Psalms describing the ordeal he suffered because of his sons. The outstanding attribute he displayed in them was his strong trust and faith in God. Despite being in such a desperate situation, he not only kept his thoughts clear, but he also stayed calm and slept in peace, knowing that God would give him justice.

It is indeed easy to rejoice when all is well. But David shows us that we need to maintain thanksgiving and praise even during the storm. It begins when we exalt God above everything else. When we constantly look at the sun for a couple of minutes and then turn away, our vision is blurred and takes quite some time to adapt to the surroundings. So it is when we choose to focus on God and magnify Him. Then praising and thanking Him at all times is effortless, and we train ourselves and help that muscle to develop. Any problem would look minuscule compared to the might and splendour of our Almighty God. We are assured beyond the shadow of a doubt that God fights for us, and we need to look at every battle from a victory standpoint since God has never lost a battle. We need to wait on God with patience, seeking His justification while God works on our behalf. At the same time, we should make sure that we are not justifying ourselves when we are wrong.

When we continue with this attitude, it puts us on the road to deliverance, and it is just a matter of time before we see the magnificent work of God unfold in our lives. Praise, thanksgiving, and worship disarm satan and his army, as well as every human who follows him, and this, in turn, causes us to abound more in thanksgiving and praise to God. It is a never-ending cycle. Praising God is indeed one of the weapons He has provided us for spiritual warfare. It should originate sincerely from our heart. Use it well! It accomplishes a lot.

3. *WHEN MY ENEMIES TURN BACK, THEY SHALL FALL AND PERISH AT YOUR PRESENCE.*

4. *FOR YOU HAVE MAINTAINED MY RIGHT AND MY CAUSE; YOU SAT ON THE THRONE JUDGING IN RIGHTEOUSNESS.*

5. YOU HAVE REBUKED THE NATIONS, YOU HAVE DESTROYED THE WICKED; YOU HAVE BLOTTED OUT THEIR NAMES FOREVER AND EVER.

David was a man of war. He entered the battlefield very early in life. First, he was employed as Saul's armour-bearer cum musician. While serving Saul, he learned the tactics of warfare. Preparation time is never wasted time. He went on to fight Goliath and was catapulted to a higher position in Saul's army. When Saul's jealousy was aroused by David's success, he was forced to flee from him and live in hiding. He dwelt in the wilderness and enemy territories, which added to his knowledge of warfare. All these events in David's life served a good purpose, as God worked all these things to benefit him and made him fight well against all of Israel's enemies—the Philistines, Moabites, Ammonites, Amalekites, etc. David gave 100% credit to God for all his victories. He knew very well that his enemies fell because God routed them. He constantly acknowledged God's merciful hand in all of it.

When we encounter difficulties and trials in our lives, we often assume that God is also taken by surprise. It is true that God is very much with us at all times, including the trying ones. But we have to 'know' and acknowledge that He is seated on His throne. Our difficulties don't push Him off the throne. He continues to be the 'Sovereign God' and 'Supreme Potentate'. That in itself should boost us up to hold our heads high! David said that 'He sits on His throne, judging righteously'. No one can threaten God!

One more striking feature, very evident through his Psalms, is that David never tried to justify himself before God or man. He did speak of his innocence at times, but he always asked God to deal with him based on His mercy and grace. This is the sign of true humility. Many times we take matters into our own hands due to a lack of patience and try to work things out. David had learned a very costly lesson when he erred with Bathsheba and murdered her husband. This event had so many distressing repercussions for his family shortly after. But through all of it, David held onto God for dear life and came through every consequence by His grace.

What Absalom did to him was very wrong. Even while his father lived, he usurped the throne and kingdom wrongly. Absalom totally ignored God! Adonijah followed suit. David had enough reasons to justify himself and take it back. But he kept his integrity. He preferred to let go and let God justify him if it was His will. David was always ready to accept God's decision as final. He was also ok if things did not go in his favour and turned the other way around (2 Samuel 15:25–26). He recognised and respected God's decision.

Before long, as he expected, the Lord brought justice to David and defeated his enemies. This not only concerned Absalom and Adonijah but also the enemies of Israel. God went to war every single time and routed his enemies. By the end of David's reign, every enemy of Israel was subdued, and his son Solomon had a peaceful, war-free reign. When God executes justice and judgement, no one can stop it. God always stands up for His children and safeguards their justice. When we have the Great God of the universe holding our lives in His hand, why would we even want to justify ourselves or take matters into our own hands?

Anyone who takes it up to tamper with the children of Almighty God condemns himself (as long as we are not at fault). They literally put themselves against God. From ages past, we know that God has never lost a battle and that none of God's adversaries has ever succeeded against Him. They were all subdued every single time. Knowing this truth will drastically change our approach to the people who put themselves against us wrongly. We can just pray for them so that they turn away from their wickedness.

In the word, we see God subdue giants like Goliath as well as kings, nations, and kingdoms that stood against His children. Egypt was wiped out when they hardened their hearts. Babylon is in heaps today. Every nation against which a prophecy was spoken has come to that expected end. God is God! No one can stand against Him.

The wicked person's name will be blotted out forever. This is declared by God in more than one place in the word. The wicked here refers to the unsaved. Even the kindest, unsaved person is wicked. Due to their charm, they may look good to many; but it's just a matter of time before they are all forgotten. The moment an unsaved person breathes last on earth, his desires, hopes, ambitions, etc. all perish. That is literally the end of him. He has no heritage on earth or remembrance in heaven. Rather, only a place called hell waits as an eternal residence. No one in their right mind should ever desire to be in that place. On the other hand, every believer enters eternity with God. Also, their hopes and dreams continue on this earth even long after they are gone because it is all God-centred.

6. ***O ENEMY, DESTRUCTIONS ARE FINISHED FOREVER! AND YOU HAVE DESTROYED CITIES; EVEN THEIR MEMORY HAS PERISHED.***

7. ***BUT THE LORD SHALL ENDURE FOREVER; HE HAS PREPARED HIS THRONE FOR JUDGEMENT.***

8. ***HE SHALL JUDGE THE WORLD IN RIGHTEOUSNESS AND HE SHALL ADMINISTER JUDGEMENT FOR THE PEOPLES IN UPRIGHTNESS.***

One day, the entire world will cease to exist. Life is not a fairy tale. God has set a particular time for the Day of Judgement. Most of the ambitious exploits of men are soon forgotten once they breathe their last. They may be written in history books and taught to succeeding generations, but they are short-lived. Personally, I found these historical accounts very boring in school. Today, most of this knowledge is unused in my life. It rather points to the very same point these verses project: 'the futility of men who had no regard for God'. Almost every nation has changed over the ages, and nations that once existed in all glory (ex. Babylon) are now in ruins. Academic curricula in schools and colleges have been teaching these so-called 'great conquests of man' only to open people's eyes to see the hand of God bring His divine purposes to pass. What did the great conquerors gain? Nothing! But these men spent an entire lifetime amassing wealth and fame for themselves at the cost of precious human lives.

God is longsuffering. He is patiently waiting and giving every man a chance to know the truth and accept it. There will never be a person who dies without hearing the 'Truth'. It's just a matter of acceptance (to life) or non-acceptance (to destruction). While all the myopics on earth are wiling away their time and energy, running behind name, fame, and fortune, God is patiently waiting and accepting all those who repent and turn to Him. On the set day and time, once the gospel has been preached to the whole world, He will roll up the heavens, and the earth will melt away. All the futile efforts of mankind will just vanish into thin air, never to be seen or heard of again. The unbelief of this world will not deter the established plans of God. All our earthly trophies, medals, and certificates are useless. Paul called them dung! That's the perspective we need to possess. While God causes His children to prosper and succeed in earthly competitions, these accolades should never be the ground on which we stand and build our lives. Praise God for it, enjoy it, and move on in His calling.

The end of the world and the Day of Judgement are inevitable. There is coming a day when satan and his entire demonic army, including all the souls that rejected the Lord Christ, will be shut up in eternal damnation in hell. Therefore, as long as we have breath in our nostrils, we have time to make a wise decision and choose to live according to the truth of God's word, having received His salvation.

When we talk about judgement, there are many aspects to it. As far as believers are concerned, we have passed from death to life, and we are not condemned along with the world. God judged the Lord Jesus on the cross on behalf of all mankind. He carried our sins. This is God administering judgement for the people in uprightness. **But salvation is appropriated in the lives of only those who have accepted it; it is not accounted to anyone and everyone by default.** Man's good works (self-righteousness) or the blood of animals (as in the Old Testament sacrifices) cannot wash out the iniquities of mankind. God knew the perfect solution to this hopelessness right from the very beginning, when He foretold the coming of the Messiah. Almighty God accounted all our sins in the flesh of the Lord Jesus and judged Him on the cross. God never made light of sin. In fact, He made a way to abolish the effects of sin that oppressed mankind all along. But this can be appropriated only to those who believe in and accept His sacrifice. For those who ignore and deliberately reject His salvation, there is absolutely no hope whatsoever. **There is only one sin for which people will be judged by Him: the sin of rejecting His Son (John 16:9).**

The Lord Jesus gave us a very good insight into the ministry of the Holy Spirit. In John 16:8–11, He tells us the work of the Holy Spirit when He comes. The Holy Spirit was poured out on the Day of Pentecost. Starting from that day, He has been doing what the Lord said He would do: convicting the world of sin, righteousness, and judgement.

- Of sin: This is the sin of rejecting the precious sacrifice of our Lord Jesus Christ. This is the only sin that matters before God now.
- Of righteousness: He reminds every believer that the Lord Jesus has imparted His righteousness to us. This is an everlasting righteousness that indwells our spirits. Satan tries hard to corrupt this understanding. Nevertheless, the Holy Spirit overpowers his condemnation and convicts us furthermore of the truth. We are the righteousness of God in Christ Jesus, our Lord!
- Of judgement: He constantly reminds us that when the Lord Jesus died on the cross, God not only judged our sins but also sealed satan's fate forever. His devastating end and eternal damnation are strongly declared. The work that God accomplished through the cross is brought to our attention repeatedly. All the prophecies concerning the death and resurrection of the Messiah came to pass. All the while, satan tried his best to kill the seed but never succeeded. Finally, at the cross, as declared by God, satan's head was crushed and his treasury was ransacked. There is nothing left for satan to accuse the believers before God (Romans 8:32–34). When we understand this, it empowers us to overcome his deceptions and tactics, especially his relentless condemnation.

Always remember, the Holy Spirit convicts. He never condemns. He convicts so that we can be redirected into the kingdom of heaven. Every single day, the Lord is administering His righteous judgement on our behalf. Lord Jesus is our High Priest and Advocate before the Father for all those who believe in Him. He also guards the paths of justice as far as we are concerned. No one can wrong God's children and get away with it. That account will be settled by Him. When a child of God errs, God chastens us, the Holy Spirit convicts us, and we are redirected.

David saw the judgement of God being passed on to all his enemies, including his own son Absalom. So he never doubted the righteous judgement and recompense of God.

9. THE LORD ALSO WILL BE A REFUGE FOR THE OPPRESSED, A REFUGE IN TIMES OF TROUBLE.

10. AND THOSE WHO KNOW YOUR NAME WILL PUT THEIR TRUST IN YOU; FOR YOU LORD, HAVE NOT FORSAKEN THOSE WHO SEEK YOU.

Oppression is the virtue of satan and his followers. When a person gets into the habit of oppressing others, he is working as satan's right hand. This behaviour can be observed in humans as early as childhood, when certain kids resort to being bullies. Being representatives of Almighty God, we should make sure that we never get into that vice. No one has the right to oppress anyone. Unfortunately, the world seems to have plenty of it today. Starting from relationships to politics, oppression plays a major role.

The good news for believers is that God is a refuge for the oppressed. Are you oppressed in body or soul? Come to the Lord Jesus; listen to and obey Him. He will surely set you above oppression by revealing His truth to you. Oppression is not a godly virtue. It is, in fact, 100% satanic, and God has given us every right to resist and fight against it. He has promised this in Isaiah 54:14, and the way He works it out in us is by "ridding us off fear"—the fear of man! A person can oppress another only if the latter fears the former. The truth of His word will not only set us free but will also help us resist oppression. Let me explain this with a powerful example from the Book of Esther.

The story of Esther is well known to most Christians. Those who are not aware can read through the book once before reading any further. After Haman's plot to annihilate the entire Jewish race all over the kingdom of Persia was exposed by Queen Esther, the king ordered his execution on the gallows he had built for Mordecai. However, the decree signed by the king (under the deceptive influence of Haman) could not be undone according to the law of the Medes and Persians. But the Lord elevated Mordecai, and the king gave him his signet ring after Haman's death. Mordecai was God-fearing, wise, and fearless of men. Being advised to formulate a law to save his people from the ruthless decree of Haman, Mordecai decreed a law permitting and encouraging every Jew to **"defend"** themselves by "destroying, killing, and annihilating" all the forces of any people or province that would assault them (Jews), irrespective of their age and sex (Esther 8:10–11). On the day that Haman had previously ordained (the 13th day of the month of Adar) for the destruction of the Jews, the enemies of the Jews had hoped to overpower them. But the opposite occurred, in that the Jews themselves overpowered those who attacked them. The Jews never charged on them first. They merely defended themselves when they were attacked. Close to 76,000 of the enemies of the Jews were killed (Esther 9) over 2 days. Fearing the law that Mordecai passed, a good number of gentiles in the region converted to Judaism! Do you now understand that we can overcome oppression by being fearless and rightfully using the authority God has given us? If you are oppressed by someone or something for any reason today, go to the Word! The solution to your problem is right there! The Lord will help you fight and overcome it with His wisdom.

Something very important needs to be said here for the benefit of the daughters of God in India and other countries where this type of oppression in marriage is prevalent. The Indian marriage culture is oppressive and biased. Unfortunately, most Indian Christians (the groom's side) support it wholeheartedly and almost always ignore God's command regarding marriage. I have heard only 1 or 2 pastors preach on this because the rest probably indulge in the same or fear losing their crowd. But oh, what a difference it would make in the lives of couples who have broken marriages!

Genesis 2:24 clearly states that 'Therefore shall a man leave his father and his mother, and shall cleave unto his wife; and they shall become one flesh". It is God's established statute concerning marriage. Knowing that people today would ignore it as an Old Testament statute, the Lord Jesus sealed it in Matthew 19:4-6 for the New Covenant people. However, it has been conveniently reversed here in the name of 'culture and tradition', and the women in India have suffered much oppression because of this. This certainly does not mean that the groom has to abandon his parents and not care for them. It simply means that he needs to mentally detach from his parents and make a family with his wife, putting her first and involving her in every decision concerning the new family. In other words, it is a complete reversal of every injustice the majority of Indian grooms and their families indulge in today. Lacking the fear of God, they revert this command to the bride's family instead. They are more than happy to ignore and reverse God's command in order to satisfy their flesh by embracing the heathen culture, which in turn places heavy, senseless burdens on the bride and her family with reckless rules and regulations. May I ask the Christian men, who permitted them to change God's statute? Most marriages breakdown because of disobedience to this simple command the Lord has given. And there are many who wonder why! Even if you tell them, many are unwilling to correct it.

Our children (girls or boys) are loaned to us by God. We are not their owners; God is! He expects us to bring them up to know Him and responsibly walk in His path. Every parent (especially Indians) should understand this very clearly. When the time comes for our children to start their own families, it would be best for us and them to **'let them go'**. When God's command is obeyed, He will make sure that both sides stay happy and blessed! I can challenge anyone on that! God can take care of us much better in our old age than our children can. Many times, He may use our children to do so as well. But they are not the only ones He uses. God has promised us in Isaiah 46:4, saying, **"Even to your old age, I am He, and even to grey hairs, I will carry you! I have made, and I will bear; even I will carry, and I will deliver you"**. We throw ourselves and our children into a lot of heartbreak when we place our security in our children more than God. The Mordecai in us needs to wake up. God loves His daughters and does not authorise **anyone** to oppress them. Daughters! Have you realised that you are His child and the authority He has given you? His word regarding the norms for marriage is clear! Will you stand on it fearlessly and defend yourself? I assure you that all of heaven will back you up, provided you don't misuse that authority to mean something contrary to what God says! **God's foreknowledge of the prevalence of this type of oppression warranted this statute to be engraved in the first book of the Holy Bible and its affirmation by the Son of God when He walked on earth.** Parents! Do not take it for granted. God is watching!

The master of oppression was defeated when the Lord Jesus died on the cross and lost his legal right to oppress the children of God. If we were to value the word of God 100%, this promise would bring a lot of relief and a great deal of hope and confidence. When we know that God has secured us under Himself, we can dare to do great exploits for the kingdom. Since we are fearless, nothing or no one can deter us.

God knows every single person who will accept Him. These are the 'called' or the 'elect'. Even before the elect actually accept Him, God is close to us, knowing that one day we will accept Him. His beauty is exemplified by the fact that His presence is always with us. He never leaves us or forsakes us. A broken, contrite, oppressed, depressed, and wasted heart always attracts His grace. He is ever so close to these souls, wanting to deliver them speedily. But this truth is sometimes overshadowed by our feelings, which arise from our 5 senses, and by satan harping away his deceptive songs of woe in our ears.

The battle is always in our minds. The Lord has exalted His word above His Name! That's how serious He is about everything He has said in the word of God. Exercising godliness is important, and we need to work daily at trusting His word more than anything else. Fasting helps a lot in this. Fasting helps us to deny the sensory input from our 5 senses and trust God more. We can practice fasting from a lot of things today: food, Netflix, Hotstar, gossip, foolish talk, parties with friends, watching sports, shopping, and on and on. **The reason we fast is to take the time we**

spend doing all these other things and use it to study God's word more deeply without any interruption. Fasting is not a means to twist God's arm to accept our demands but rather a mode of subjecting our flesh to His Spirit in us. When we fast from food, our flesh cries out for food and water; but when we persist, we are bringing our flesh under control and helping it to deny the facts (hunger and thirst) in order to accept the truth of the word (man shall not live by bread alone, but by every word of God). Facts and truth do not match all the time. For example, if a person is sick today, the fact is he is sick. But the truth is, "By His stripes, he was/ is healed!" This is what fasting helps us achieve. **It helps us to appropriate and receive the finished work of God.** There is no reason for a child of God to live an oppressed life. **When we accept oppression, we forfeit the blessings of God.** Never in the history of mankind has God forsaken those who put their trust in Him.

Life with God is very practical. We cannot separate God from our routine lives. We were created for life with God. The believer is expected to live every moment with God. He is with us in our waking and sleeping, in our eating and working, in our going out and coming in, etc. When we spend quantity and quality time knowing Him and building our relationship with Him, it becomes effortless to put our trust in Him always. No matter what life throws at us, we know where we stand and Who we need to look up to. By experience, we are assured of the Lord's faithfulness and the manner in which He sustains us. This comes through a consistent and devoted study of His word and walking with Him.

David was very confident in God's faithfulness and sought Him at every stage of life. When we are practical about our relationship with God and include Him and depend on Him, akin to how a child holds on to his parents, we learn His ways. But this is not possible if all the knowledge we have is only theory. Knowledge certainly helps. But wisdom (putting knowledge into practice) is ultimate!

11. SING PRAISES TO THE LORD, WHO DWELLS IN ZION! DECLARE HIS DEEDS AMONG THE PEOPLE.

The primary purpose of all creation is to proclaim the praises of our Almighty God. But because of the fall, this took a hit. Nevertheless, our God salvaged it and brought back this privilege. We are the modern-day dwellers of Zion. It's our privilege and honour to praise God and declare His deeds among all people. This becomes natural and effortless when we are in sync with Him. When we bless God and praise and thank Him, it builds our inner man and exalts the work of God in our lives. Real strength comes from this. **This is how we encourage ourselves in the Lord.** When we make this a regular part of our lives, we can experience joy and strength that comes from within and cannot be nullified by anyone. After all, we are called to be kings and priests unto Him.

It is absolutely essential to bear witness to God's work in our lives and declare His deeds among the peoples and the nations. When Lord Jesus ascended to the Father, He gave us the great commission - To go into the world and preach the Gospel to the nations. This is an absolute command to all His disciples, and we need to do it without any alibi. Along with declaring His word, we can also share the way He worked/works in our lives as a testimony. We are all living witnesses of His goodness and grace, being able to live life only because He lives in and through us. It is not left to us to select the crowd to which we need to preach. Our target should be the world around us, and we need to wait on God to streamline it and work in the hearts of all those who hear us.

Revelation 12:11 says, "And they (witnesses) overcame him (satan) by the blood of the Lamb, the word of their testimony, and they did not love their lives to the death." The word of our testimony is one of the ways we disarm satan and overcome him. This shows how important it is for us to witness to the world. Don't ever let anyone discourage you from using this privilege.

12. WHEN HE AVENGES BLOOD, HE REMEMBERS THEM; HE DOES NOT FORGET THE CRY OF THE HUMBLE.

Romans 12:19 clearly states that God is our avenger. Paul quotes this from Deuteronomy 32:35, which says, "Vengeance is Mine, and recompense".

Pause and think. Not only vengeance, but recompense too! How many times have we required recompense from the hands of people who have wronged us? The recompense of men is far inferior to the recompense of God. Next time you want it, go to God. He will make the thief (satan) pay you back 7 times for all he robbed you of. Every word of God is a word of integrity. But when it is repeated twice, it indicates how serious God is about His word and promises to us. It should settle any and every doubt in our hearts. Beginning with the blood of righteous Abel, God has avenged the blood of all His children. Forgiveness is always available to everyone who repents and turns to God. His mercies never fail. And God is certainly with them when they have to face the consequences of their deeds.

David knew the Lord to be his avenger. He was so sure that God looked on his sorrow and the injustice he had to face that he wrote in Psalm 56:8, "You number my wanderings; put my tears into Your bottle; are they not in Your book?" This is the extent to which he saw God standing up for him. The Lord not only keeps a record of our tears, but He also numbers the hair on our heads (Luke 12:7)! Collecting tears and numbering our hair! What more does God have to say to convince us of His love for us? Not even our parents would do that!

Our Lord is so **MINDFUL** of us and everything that concerns us. When we are established in this truth and have the right perspective, we can see how beautiful life is. Almost every human is concerned about their hair. After all, it affects our external appearance. Every time I comb my hair, there is a certain amount of hair that gets off on the hairbrush. I have often heard family members grumbling about this. But that has never been my complaint because when I see my hair on the brush, the word spoken by the Lord Jesus just resounds in my heart and comes out of my mouth—He numbers the hairs on my head! It has never depressed me, deterred me, or given me sleepless nights. I believe that for every strand that is shed, He restores my scalp with 2 new strands! Some people say, "I wish I had more hair on my scalp." I ask you, "What stops you from placing that request before God and believing Him for it to be answered?" Your words contain power; use it! Instead of confessing the hair fall, confess, "He restores my scalp!"

God's children are very precious to Him. He never discounts their sorrow, whether small or great. Every small detail is recorded by Him because He loves us. When we study the lives of the Lord Jesus, the prophets, and the disciples of the Lord (Apostles as well as others like Stephen), we can see how serious God is about accomplishing what He says. Especially people who chose martyrdom show and teach us a great level of faith and confidence in God. Their perspective on life and death is something we need to have. People who trusted God to that extent were greatly rewarded.

When the Lord Jesus ascended to the Father after His resurrection, God **'seated'** Him at His right hand. When Stephen was being martyred, he saw the heavens open and the Lord Jesus **STANDING** at God's right hand! Do you know what it means when people stand when you enter a room? It's honour and respect! That's what the Lord did for Stephen. The Lord Jesus stood up to receive His child, who was shortly going to enter eternity. Do you know what happened to the one man who arrogantly stood guarding the robes of those who stoned Stephen? God turned his world upside down, gave him an awesome revelation of the New Covenant, which is the main source of knowledge for us today, ordained him as **'THE APOSTLE' to the gentiles,** and got him to write more than half of the New Testament. Yes, that's Paul!

Most often, revenge and avenging need not be the death or destruction of all who wrong us. Even though that has happened many times, the word shows us another facet of this avenging. It can also be a change of heart that causes the ultimate exaltation of God's purposes, as it was with Paul. It's never God's will for even one soul to perish. Those who perish have brought it upon themselves by rejecting the salvation given through the Lord Jesus Christ. The Lord has instructed us to feed our enemies when they are hungry and give them a drink when they are thirsty, to pray for and bless those who curse us. Do you know why? It all starts with the blessing that we have inherited as Abraham's seed (children of promise): "I will bless those who bless you and curse those who curse you". Anyone who curses us (without a cause) is cursed by default because of this blessing. But such people have hope when we pray for them and bless them. They can be turned away from their wicked ways. Proverbs 16:7 says, 'When a man's ways please the Lord, He makes even His enemies to be at peace with Him.' It is very important that we study and know the way the Lord works. His plans and purposes are always great. He knows how to deal with our adversaries. We need to ask Him for wisdom and discretion to live every single day fruitfully.

Acts 3:26 says that God sent the Lord Jesus to bless us by turning us away from our iniquities. Knowing that one facet of "God's blessing" is to turn us away from our sins should encourage and make it easier for us to bless our enemies. The word of God helps us to renew our minds. We would have never thought of this concept of blessing, right? Now that you know, bless your enemies! You are, in fact, opening up a door for God to work and set things right in their lives. Leave the rest to Him. He is awesome in His work.

13. *HAVE MERCY ON ME, O LORD! CONSIDER MY TROUBLE FROM THOSE WHO HATE ME, YOU WHO LIFT ME UP FROM THE GATES OF DEATH.*

14. *THAT I MAY TELL OF ALL YOUR PRAISE IN THE GATES OF THE DAUGHTER OF ZION. I WILL REJOICE IN YOUR SALVATION.*

2 Timothy 3:12 says, "All those who desire to live godly in Christ Jesus will suffer persecution." This applies to all the saints from the beginning. It is true that trouble will come from those who hate us. Trials and persecutions were a part of the Lord's life when He walked on the earth. He also said that His followers will have the same challenges testing their faith. However, the death on the cross could be handled only by Him. We are not called to die for the sins of mankind. But we are commanded to carry our cross and follow Him.

What is this cross we need to carry? Let's have a little insight into this topic. Today, most believers are confused on this matter, as much as I was once. Sickness, lack, poverty, need, loss, etc., are all included under the list of trials and persecutions today by most if not all. Furthermore, I have even heard people call troubled relationships (especially spouses) as the cross we need to bear! If we do not get our understanding clear on this, we are bound to incur much loss in life. To clear the doubt, we should allow the word to enlighten us.

The primary thing is to look at 'The Cross' and find out what Lord Jesus paid for and has provided for us. Also, Lord Jesus told us very clearly about the things which proceed from God and what proceeds from the devil in John 10:10 - The devil comes only to steal, to kill, and to destroy; but Lord Jesus came to give us life and give it more abundantly. If we filter the things that we are faced with using John 10:10 as the perfect sieve, the difference becomes very clear. Endurance is needed for some, while active resistance for the others. The cross was God's ultimate will for Lord Jesus. We need to discern what our cross is.

THE TRUTH REGARDING SICKNESS AND DISEASE:

Sickness and diseases entered the world as a result of the fall. It is a counterpart of death and is not in the perfect will of God. Lord Jesus established this when He made it His mission to enlighten mankind (through preaching the gospel) and **healing 'every type' of sickness and disease.** The reason He indulged in healing was to prove that health and wholeness is God's will for mankind. Isaiah 53:4, 5 says, "Surely He has borne our GRIEFS (SICKNESSES) and carried our SORROWS (DISEASES)." Matthew quoted this verse in Matthew 8:17, from where we can understand what exactly grief and sorrows meant. Isaiah goes on to say, **"But He was wounded for our TRANSGRESSIONS and crushed for OUR INIQUITIES; the chastisement for our peace was upon Him and BY HIS STRIPES WE ARE HEALED."** Peter reaffirms this in His letter, 1 Peter 2:24, saying, **"Who Himself bore our sins in His own body on the tree, that we, having died to sins, might live for righteousness, by Whose stripes you were healed."**

So with these 2 passages quoted, we can most surely come to a conclusion that sin, sickness, disease, sorrows are all paid for. Therefore, we cannot and should not include them in the trial and persecution list. Ignorance of this truth makes us carry unnecessary burdens that we should actually be resisting. These do not qualify for the criteria of the cross we have to bear either. Holding onto wrong principles and doctrines can virtually destroy our lives and credit that destruction to the hand of God. I have heard enough of that baseless accusation!

THE TRUTH REGARDING LACK, POVERTY, NEED:

Let us consider the following verses:

- ✡ Psalm 37:25: 'I have been young, and now I am old, yet I have not seen the righteous forsaken nor his descendants begging bread'.
- ✡ 2 Corinthians 8:9: 'For you know the grace of our Lord Jesus Christ, that though He was rich, yet for your sakes He became poor, that you through His poverty might become rich.'
- ✡ The salutation in 3 John verse 2 reads, 'Beloved, I pray that you may prosper in all things and be in health, just as your soul prospers.'
- ✡ Deuteronomy 8:18: You shall remember the Lord your God, for it is He who gives you the power to get wealth.

From the 4 verses that have been mentioned here (2 from the OT and 2 from the NT), it is very clear that God doesn't assign poverty to His children. God cannot be double-minded. He does not want one person to lack and another to prosper. This attribute does not define His character. He has provided a way out of poverty, lack, and need. He is delighted in prospering His children, and He is the One who strengthens us to get wealth. His commandments and statutes are designed in a manner to guarantee us this.

Deuteronomy 4:6 says "The commandments, statutes, and judgements of God is your wisdom and understanding in the sight of the people who will hear all this and say, 'Surely this great nation is a wise and understanding people'". The onus to obtain God's best is on us through our simple acceptance of the truth. But this simple, plain truth is utterly complicated by people who do not understand. People pull this into extremes and nullify the gift and grace of God in their lives.

God wants to bless us so that we can be a blessing to many other people. This is God's idea of prosperity in plain terms. It's not for us to hoard, boast about, or have a closed fist. The moment a child of God does that with the blessing of God, he becomes like the Dead Sea. God wants the hearts of His children to be like the waters of a river that is always flowing and supplying goodness to all in its path (Proverbs 21:1). If we restrict prosperity only to money and material things, we are very narrow-minded. We need to study the Biblical definition of prosperity to know what it truly is. True prosperity is "God's presence and favour" on our lives.

Now that our doubts regarding these things are cleared, we can narrow down the list of trials and persecutions. These arise mainly when we stand as witnesses for the Lord Jesus Christ. This is what Paul is speaking about in 1 Corinthians 4:11–12 and 2 Corinthians 11:24–27. But it is very obvious that the Lord delivered him from all these perils. In fact, at the end of the book of Romans, it is mentioned that Paul stayed in his own rented house, receiving people and teaching them for 2 years. Unless the Lord had prospered him, how could he pay rent for his house? He called 'trials and persecutions' as "filling up in his flesh what is lacking in the afflictions of Christ, for the sake of His body, which is the Church" (Colossians 1:24). **The only trial and persecution we need to face is the one that arises for the Name of the Lord Jesus Christ.** The rest of the things need to be fought against, like fighting the plague.

If things further confuse you, simply look to the life of the Lord Jesus, so beautifully displayed in the gospels. Study what he allowed and what he did not allow. The Bible is a very candid book. It portrays everything plainly. The weaknesses of people are also clearly mentioned. We never see the Lord Jesus resting because of a head ache or a cold. He never let disease and sickness anywhere near Him. His anointing blessed others to receive healing from all types of diseases, small or big, congenital or acquired. When He was a child, God sent wise men from the east to provide for Him with gold, frankincense, and myrrh to assist Mary and Joseph for their livelihood and up-bringing of the young Messiah in a foreign land. A fish had a coin in its mouth to pay for the temple tax for the Lord Jesus and Peter (Matthew 17:24–27). Yet persecutions came against Him big time. But our Lord beautifully handled all of it in perfect wisdom. When we study this, the Holy Spirit gives us clarity and confidence.

Luke chapter 4 elaborates on the synagogue incident in Nazareth. The Lord Jesus boldly proclaimed the gospel on the Sabbath. Initially, the people agreed with Him. But within minutes, they related Him to being just the carpenter's son and turned on Him. Being filled with wrath at His sayings, they arose and thrust Him out of the city, leading Him to the brow of the hill on which their city was built, wanting to throw Him down the cliff. Verse 30 plainly says that He passed through the midst of them and went His way. How did he do that!? Can you picture a mob so violent, dragging Him down to the edge of a cliff? How did he get loose from their hands? Could it be that He resisted them? And when He did that, could it be that the 12 legions of angels (who were put to His service) pushed the mob back? Think about it! It was still not His time to go.

When such persecutions arise against us from any direction, we have to look to God to carry us through. His mercy and grace are all sufficient, and they never fail. He has allowed us to come to His throne of grace with all boldness that we may obtain mercy and find grace to help 'in time of need' (Hebrews 4:16). It is possible to overcome this hand-in-hand with the Lord. Persecution is a constant instrument of satan. But in truth, every time he uses it, the kingdom of God and the children of God flourish (Exodus 1:12; Acts 8:1). In other words, Romans 8:28 is fulfilled.

Every time we are persecuted for the Lord's sake, it may seem like impending death. But the Lord, who has overcome the world, delivers us every time and sets our feet on a broad place. We need to understand the reason for this deliverance. The main reason is that God loves us and, secondly, that we may declare His deliverance to the nations, especially to the body of Christ. The power of such a testimony is great. I can't be grateful enough to God for the testimonies He has used to encourage me.

These testimonies (in the word as well as in recent times) have constantly uplifted me, reminded me of His faithfulness, and directed me in the path I need to walk in. The Lord has made us salt and light in this world. We need to get out of the salt shaker and stay put on the lamp stand so that we may serve our calling and purpose.

How do we rejoice in His salvation? One way is to give Him glory and continual thanksgiving from the depth of our hearts. Another way is to proclaim His goodness and deliverance to this world and win many souls for Lord Jesus. Yet another way is to remember the way He has delivered us in the past and use that experience to strengthen us when we face new challenges. This helps us face other trials with courage and confidence.

When we do something obviously wrong and are suffering because of those consequences, we cannot classify them as the cross of Christ either. That would be stupidity. It is obvious that we need to repent and set our hearts right with God and make it right with the people whom we have wronged.

Proverbs 11:31 says, "If the righteous shall be rewarded on this earth, how much more the ungodly and the sinner?" We can be absolutely sure that God will handle all our adversaries in the right manner because **HE HAS SPOKEN AND IT IS WRITTEN!**

15. *THE NATIONS HAVE SUNK DOWN IN THE PIT THEY HAVE MADE; IN THE NET WHICH THEY HID, THEIR OWN FOOT IS CAUGHT.*

16. *THE LORD IS KNOWN BY THE JUDGEMENT HE EXECUTES; THE WICKED IS SNARED IN THE WORK OF HIS OWN HANDS. MEDITATION. SELAH.*

17. *THE WICKED SHALL BE TURNED INTO HELL, AND ALL THE NATIONS THAT FORGET GOD.*

Once the word has proceeded from the mouth of God, it is established. God is unchanging, and so is His word. His word is final! This statement made here by David has been repeated time and again in various places in the Bible and is a perfectly established truth. The man who digs a pit will fall into it, and the man who spreads a net for others will have his own foot stuck in it. The evil man is not immune to his wicked plans. He who digs forgets at some point how deep he has dug and makes his exit impossible. The deeper he digs, the closer he is to death. A very good example of this is the story of Haman in the book of Esther. He finally hung on the gallows he had prepared to kill Mordecai. It is good to study this book because of the treasure in it.

The one who spreads a net forgets that God can just about catapult him into the same, making his escape impossible. This is also seen very clearly in the life of Daniel. The wicked people had trapped him by enticing the king to decree an ungodly command. Daniel never had a second thought regarding his stance. He broke it, got thrown into the lion's den, and came out alive! This is such an awesome and encouraging testimony for believers, inspiring us not to compromise on our godly standards. The climax of this story is the horrific end of the wicked conspirators, who were immediately thrown into the lion's den along with their wives and children, only to be shredded in seconds. The word says the lions overpowered them even before they touched the ground!

Psalm 19:9 says, 'The judgements of the Lord are true and righteous altogether'. No one can point a finger at God and say His judgements are faulty or that He could have done it differently. People who do that have no idea of justice and righteousness. Before any person is judged, he has had the plenteous grace available to turn away from his wicked ways because the Lord is longsuffering. When they are foolish enough to forsake the love of God, they invite trouble.

The problem for an unbeliever is basically spiritual blindness. They indulge their flesh so much that they don't realise what they are doing is going to boomerang back at them. Romans 1:20 says there is intuitive knowledge about God in every person. There is not one person in this world who can stand before God and say that He didn't give them a chance. Before the world ends, God has made sure that everyone has heard the gospel. It is just that they choose not to believe in Him for one reason or the other. However, some willfully resort to wicked ways because it excites them. They cannot sleep until they have done evil (Proverbs 4:16). Above all this, they have justified themselves in their hearts to such a great extent that they are totally hard-hearted towards God. They are influenced by the ways of the world and get carried away by them. They compare themselves among themselves, setting standards that are a waste of time. This is a subtle war raging day in and day out in their minds. This is often seen very early in life. Be it an appreciation, an award, a promotion, a position or status, etc., people are always ready to trample on each other to get to the top, no matter the cost. Such will definitely be subject to the words spoken in this verse.

This principle works big time for all the gossipers too. Gossiping speaks more about the person who gossips than the person being gossiped about. No one can climb higher by putting another person down. That is the truth. The end is defined by what the Lord has said.

For a believer, God has set the perfect standard; He is our Lord Jesus Christ. He walked on earth for 33 and a half years and has clearly shown us how we need to live life "God-centred.". We are not called to look in the horizontal direction to set our standards. We need to always look vertically up to Him. He is always ready to give us all the grace we need to keep away from all the foolishness and clamour of this world.

This law has a widespread effect and is applicable to all manner of wickedness performed by individuals and nations. If a nation has to change, the starting point is a citizen—just one person. As the hearts of the citizens change, the nation changes as a whole. Every person is accountable. When nations and their citizens resort to wickedness, they come to a destructive end, and we can understand the judgement of God. Their own wickedness dooms them and brings them to that place. If they learn from their mistakes and repent, God is always ready to help them take the path to the Tree of Life.

The Lord is patient and long-suffering. He expects people to turn from their wickedness and walk in the path of righteousness. But if they stubbornly refuse and die, then they have to spend eternity in hell. When these people were alive, their so-called hopes and desires were corrupted. When they die, it all ends there. There is no fulfilment of their hopes and desires.

Verse 16 ends with the word 'meditation'. This particular concept is worth meditating upon.

18. FOR THE NEEDY SHALL NOT ALWAYS BE FORGOTTEN; THE EXPECTATION OF THE POOR SHALL NOT PERISH FOREVER.

The ungodly and wicked people living in the world put their confidence in their flesh and riches and stand against the children of God. Let us study and understand this verse effectively from the word.

The Israelites were a peaceful but ignorant lot. The only thing that the pharaoh of Egypt had against them was that they flourished massively. They were put up in the land of Goshen, northern Egypt, and basically they were shepherds. They never retaliated, rebelled, or fought for their own separate land in Egypt. Because of God's blessing stamped on Abraham, his descendents grew exceedingly in number and wealth. About 70 people from the household of Jacob shifted to Egypt during the time of the great famine. But by the end of 4 centuries, their number was in the millions. These people were more than happy to stay in the land of Goshen and reside peacefully alongside the Egyptians. For some reason, the pharaoh saw their fruitfulness, prosperity, and increase as a threat and put himself against them, forcing them into hard bondage and labour and slaughtering all their male children mercilessly. **He forgot that he was fighting God!**

The Israelites had somehow forgotten the promise given by God to Abraham. They cried out for deliverance from the oppression so that they could live peacefully in Egypt. Their idea of deliverance was not a walk through the Red Sea and the wilderness to the Promised Land. Goshen was a fertile land, one of the best available areas in Egypt, which the pharaoh had allotted to Joseph's family when they relocated to Egypt during the great famine. They thought this was their everlasting destination. But what God had in mind was mind-blowing. God was mindful of His promise to Abraham.

When Moses was 40 years old, knowing that he was an Israelite, he tried his own plan of deliverance a little too early, which certainly did not go well with both the Israelites and Egyptians. This did not coincide with God's plan. His plan was big! He had already gone ahead and prepared the Promised Land and the compensation that Egypt had to pay Israel for all the injustice they did to them. So Moses had to undergo training in the same wilderness, through which he had to lead the people, and was sent to deliver Israel 40 years later. He led the people out, along with the spoils of Egypt. None of the plagues that God sent on Egypt affected His children who stayed in the same nation. In the end, the strength and glory of Egypt were utterly destroyed, and the Israelites saw this with their own eyes as the Red Sea closed in on the best of the warriors, horses, and chariots of Egypt, and probably the pharaoh too!

Deliverance belongs to God, and all His children are partakers of this inheritance. God is good, and we, His children, will most surely enjoy the benefits of His goodness and grace. There is not a chance that God will ever forget His promises to us. God never forgot the Israelites, who relocated to Egypt along with Jacob. The famine lasted only 5 years after they came to Goshen. They were well taken care of during the famine as well as after it. At any point after that, they could have returned to Canaan and settled back in the land God had given them as a possession and inheritance. Nobody would have stopped them from doing that; especially not the Egyptians. Jacob extended his stay in Goshen by 17 years and breathed his last there. The small flock of Israel had settled off very well in Egypt for 400 years. It was certainly not God's will for them to stay there for 400 years. His will for them was to possess Canaan, the Promised Land. When they were ready, they called out, and He heard and delivered them.

19. ARISE, O LORD, DO NOT LET MAN PREVAIL; LET THE NATIONS BE JUDGED IN YOUR SIGHT.

20. PUT THEM IN FEAR, O LORD, THAT THE NATIONS MAY KNOW THEMSELVES TO BE BUT MEN. SELAH.

Our Lord Jesus paraphrased this and taught it to His disciples in the 'Lord's prayer'. He asked us all to pray 'Thy kingdom come and Thy will be done on earth as it is in heaven'.

When God and His kingdom are revealed, the wicked man and his nation cannot prevail. Every word of God stands firm with an expected end to every action. God's children have been given the responsibility to invite God's kingdom into their surroundings each day. God answers the prayers of His children and rids the darkness by shining forth His light.

Most humans in the world have a tendency to exalt themselves in pride although they know they drastically fall short in every way. Those who do so are certainly led by the evil one, whose intentions have been the same from the beginning. Every generation has seen this perversion. Nations fight in vain to establish themselves by principles that are exactly opposite to God's will. But that has always led to the downfall of nations all through history and still the lesson is unlearned. With events that have happened from 2019-2021, one can see how a minute virus can paralyse the whole world, bring men down to their knees and fall flat on their face before God. God did not send the virus. He is the one who holds back all impending evil on this world. Man invites these things on himself by doing things that God has prohibited for a good reason. The COVID pandemic has been an eye opener and a very humbling experience for millions of people. But I can boldly testify that this pandemic has been a major stepping stone for me into God's calling on my life; this book was birthed in the quarantine during the pandemic.

It is good for man to learn humility through life's experiences and subject his life to God. But those who refuse this offer will certainly be taught to be but men. Another good example to learn this is in the life of Nebuchadnezzar, king of Babylon as elaborated in Daniel 4. This heathen king declared clearly in the end saying "Now I, Nebuchadnezzar, praise and exalt and glorify the King of heaven, because everything He does is right and all His ways are just. **And those who walk in pride HE IS ABLE TO HUMBLE" (Daniel 4:37).**

Psalm 10

INTRODUCTION:

When we study Psalms, one must remember that it is not a sequence of events in order. The entire book has passages authored by more than one person. Nevertheless, the Holy Spirit is the only spiritual author who worked in all these people. Later on, these writings were compiled as one book called 'Psalms' or 'The Book of Praises.' David wrote most of it though.

This particular Psalm is one that has a question and answer format. Due to the anxiety and dismay in his heart, David begins with questioning God but concludes by answering his own questions with a very strong note of confidence in God's justice and power. It seems as though David has penned down his thoughts exactly in the order it would have run through his mind.

The reason for David's dismal question at the onset is very evident as we continue reading the Psalm: he paid undue importance to studying the ways of the wicked, ungodly, or unbeliever. It is good to use this Psalm to note all the virtues a believer should avoid. When we antagonise the wicked characteristics elaborated here by David, we can define the virtues a believer should possess. This Psalm provides us that information.

1. *WHY DO YOU STAND AFAR OFF, O LORD? WHY DO YOU HIDE IN TIMES OF TROUBLE?*

David certainly knew God better than to question Him this way. The reason he had such an untrue thought cross his mind is that he moved away from the place of confidence in God. He shifted his focus from God to studying the lifestyle of the wicked in detail. Most often, that's the major cause for all our dismay too. Our vision of God gets distorted only because we have focused on the wrong things rather than the goodness of God. A believer should be absolutely convinced in his heart, beyond the shadow of any doubt, that God will never leave him nor forsake him. God does not move 10 steps back every time we face a challenge. **The Lord is with us 24x7 and even closer when we are in trouble.**

How do we overcome the voice of our feelings that says God has abandoned us? In order to do so, Paul provides the perfect solution in Philippians 4:8 - to meditate on the true, noble, just, pure, and lovely things. Where do we find all these? Only in God's word! Not in the newspaper, magazines, or social media. The battle is always in the mind before it spills into the physical realm. When we keep our mind in control, we do well. If we take Paul's suggestions seriously, we will not be tossed about by a dilemma every time. We need to practice this.

We can, therefore, conclude that this statement is made because of his anxiety and not one that describes God's stance with His children because David concludes the same Psalm by affirming that God is indeed near to us during trouble, and He brings justice and deliverance for His children.

2. ***THE WICKED IN HIS PRIDE PERSECUTES THE POOR; LET THEM BE CAUGHT IN THE PLOTS WHICH THEY HAVE DEVISED.***

3. ***FOR THE WICKED BOASTS OF HIS HEART'S DESIRE; HE BLESSES THE GREEDY AND RENOUNCES THE LORD.***

4. ***THE WICKED IN HIS PROUD COUNTENANCE DOES NOT SEEK GOD. GOD IS IN NONE OF HIS THOUGHTS.***

5. ***HIS WAYS ARE ALWAYS PROSPERING; YOUR JUDGEMENTS ARE FAR ABOVE, OUT OF HIS SIGHT; AS FOR ALL HIS ENEMIES, HE SNEERS AT THEM.***

6. ***HE HAS SAID IN HIS HEART, 'I SHALL NOT BE MOVED; I SHALL NEVER BE IN ADVERSITY'.***

7. ***HIS MOUTH IS FULL OF CURSING AND DECEIT AND OPPRESSION; UNDER HIS TONGUE IS TROUBLE AND INIQUITY.***

8. ***HE SITS IN THE LURKING PLACES OF THE VILLAGES; IN THE SECRET PLACES HE MURDERS THE INNOCENT; HIS EYES ARE SECRETLY FIXED ON THE HELPLESS.***

9. ***HE LIES IN WAIT SECRETLY, AS A LION IN HIS DEN; HE LIES IN WAIT TO CATCH THE POOR; HE CATCHES THE POOR WHEN HE DRAWS HIM INTO HIS NET.***

10. ***SO HE CROUCHES, HE LIES LOW, THAT THE HELPLESS MAY FALL BY HIS STRENGTH.***

11. ***HE HAS SAID IN HIS HEART, "GOD HAS FORGOTTEN; HE HIDES HIS FACE; HE WILL NEVER SEE".***

12. ***ARISE, O LORD! O GOD, LIFT UP YOUR HAND! DO NOT FORGET THE HUMBLE.***

13. ***WHY DO THE WICKED RENOUNCE GOD? HE HAS SAID IN HIS HEART, "YOU WILL NOT REQUIRE AN ACCOUNT".***

As we read this section of Psalms, it's not difficult to understand David's feelings expressed at the onset. For some reason, he focused more on the wickedness of the wicked than the handiwork of God. The depth of details he has brought out in this passage regarding the character and work of the wicked shows that he literally observed the wicked carefully and meditated on them. He in fact thought that the wicked were prosperous! David was one of those who remembered God and recounted His works constantly. But it seems as though he got distracted by the wicked (negativity). If we are not careful, this can also happen to us. The principle is very simple: **whatever we focus on becomes bigger.** Satan works hard to shift our focus from God to everything else. It may be worry, fear, care, money, pleasure, food, etc. As long as he has shifted our attention from God to 'other things', he has succeeded.

Keeping ourselves focused on God and His word saves us a lot of unnecessary trouble. Studying the wickedness of ungodly people has never benefited anyone so far. It only causes more distress, disgust, and disappointment. When we look at the sun directly, we cannot see anything else for a period of time until our eyes recuperate. So it is with focusing on God. All other things just fade away, especially the works of the wicked, knowing that they never threaten God. David has taken great pain in elaborating on the character and works of the wicked. But this passage defines the virtues a believer should not possess.

Almost everything David lists here about the wicked is known to us. A believer is one who has been set free from the bondage of sin and is exactly opposite to the wicked in character. That's the lesson here. If we just antagonise (oppose) all the virtues mentioned here, we can outline the character of the child of God. Let us list the characteristics of a wicked man and then reciprocate them.

- ✡ The wicked man is filled with pride.
- ✡ He persecutes the poor.
- ✡ He continuously devises evil plots.
- ✡ Boasts of his heart's desire (which is not God-centred).
- ✡ Blesses the greedy.
- ✡ Renounces the Lord.
- ✡ Has a proud countenance.

- Does not seek God.
- God is in none of his thoughts.
- Seems to prosper in his wicked ways.
- He is strong and confident in his evil work.
- He doesn't care about God's judgements.
- He sneers at his enemies.
- He is steadfast in his heart concerning evil.
- He is confident that he will not face adversity.
- His mouth is filled with curses, deceit, and oppression.
- Trouble and iniquity are always under his tongue.
- He lurks in secret places, setting up an ambush.
- He murders the innocent.
- He targets the helpless.
- He preys on the poor and catches them in his net.
- He waits low to trap the helpless, knowing that they will fall under his strength; he is sly and unpredictable to the naïve.
- He is confident that God will not interfere or care about his dealings.
- He attributes forgetfulness, fear, and blindness to God.

David's study of the wicked is definitely exhausting. It is no wonder that he felt God was far away. When we pay so much unnecessary attention to negativity, we are bound to get pulled down by its weight. I have personally experienced and have also seen others being bound by these same chains. But when the Lord showed me that this was very harmful, I sought His grace to get out of that practice. When we concentrate on God, this anxiety just vaporises. I no longer wanted to look in the wrong direction or enter any of the doors that would cause worry or fear. Some may think I am going overboard if I say that it has been a long time since I read the newspaper or tuned in to any news channel. But it has helped me immensely to stay away from a lot of unnecessary negativity and fear of the future.

Every believer should realise that God is head over him and all things are under His feet (Ephesians 1:22). We are seated at God's right hand in the heavenly places in Christ Jesus, our Lord, even while we are alive on this earth. Satan has absolutely no claim to us whatsoever. Previously, I had pointed out, through the word, that his access to heaven is totally shut. We should never, ever exalt the deeds of the wicked and disarm the word of God in our lives, knowing that faith is essential for His word to work in us. God has already pronounced His judgement over the wicked very clearly in His word. Our physical eyes are restricted at times from seeing this judgement happening in the wicked man's life. But that does not change the truth. If God has spoken, it will most surely come to pass.

No matter how evil a person may be, his wickedness is absolutely no match for God. A believer should believe this strongly and act on it. A person who believes in God more than man is never influenced by the circumstances. The wicked may portray themselves as valiant, but underneath they are just as pathetic as satan is; their foundation is falsehood, and hence they can never stand. Looking at the counterfeit prosperity of the wicked, we should not underestimate the truth in God's word. It can never go well with the wicked! I have seen many examples of this, both small and great.

Now let us define the characteristics that we should avoid.

- ✡ **Pride:** God forbids pride in any form in His children. It was the primary sin of Lucifer. The same pride cut off mankind from God in the Garden of Eden. This is the sin that says, 'I know better than God'. It stops His power from manifesting in our lives. Pride is basically exalting oneself above God. A believer lives life, constantly depending on God every moment, knowing that it is impossible to do it right without Him. Pride can be self-exaltation or self-abasement. When we count ourselves above or below what God defines us, we are prideful. Hence, to keep off pride, we have to agree with God about what He says about us and live it out.

- **Devising plots, persecution, and oppression:** This character undoubtedly originates from satan. He is the master of plotting, persecution, and oppression. Any person indulging in the same is definitely influenced by satan, as I have explained earlier. A believer needs to stay out of this always, whether by thoughts, actions, or words. Indulging in these things is highly stressful for the person and his victim.

- **High (worldly) ambitions:** Man is created in the Image of God. The primary purpose of mankind has always been to glorify God by carrying out His will. Man is absolutely incapable of guiding his own footsteps, even though he constantly attempts to do so. A car is designed to work based on the manufacturer's instructions and needs a human to drive it. Similarly, a man has to live his life following the leading of the Holy Spirit, based on the will of God for his life. Then only can he be truly happy and content. Greedy ambitions have always separated man from God, inviting unnecessary distress and disappointment. However good our intentions may be, if God is not at the centre of our ambitions, they are worthless.

- **Blessing the greedy (wicked) and renouncing God:** This is like the 2 sides of the same coin. We cannot do one without the other. When we bless the wicked, we renounce God . Most often, Christians are tempted to say that the wicked continue in their wickedness, and God just doesn't care. By saying so, we are plainly elevating the wicked over God. Our relationship with God is very poor when we exalt the short-lived factual status of wicked men and underestimate the power of God. That's exactly why He says, 'The just should walk by faith and not by sight'. Our circumstances will soon catch up with spiritual reality. A believer should always value the word of God above all circumstances. Another facet of this verse is that when we support man's ordinance above God's, we automatically renounce God. It can apply to any area of our lives. God has given us everything pertaining to life and godliness through the Knowledge of Him (2 Peter 1:3). Man's will and ambitions are almost always based on greed. When we live to satisfy that greed, we cannot fulfil the will of God. A choice must be made.

- ✡ **The wicked does not seek God; God is in none of his thoughts.** This point puts a clear-cut mark between godly and ungodly men. After salvation, it is a believer's duty to seek God at all times for all things, and God should be supreme in his life. Most Christians just take Him for granted and very religiously restrict Him to a Sunday morning box. After that, most go about their lives absolutely devoid of the purposes of God. The next time they remember Him is on the following Sunday morning. But that's not the way it should be. For a believer, God should be in charge 24x7. Every breath, every thought, and every action should be subject to Him in order to have the abundant life that the Lord Jesus died to give us. A person who knows God, will gladly submit to Him in every way, knowing that He makes life splendid and worth living. His plans and purposes are always higher and outstanding compared to anything we may think of. One has to involve God in everything to experience how awesome He truly is!
- ✡ **The wicked have no insight into the judgement of God and are self-confident.** A believer should always seek to know more about God. This can be achieved by consistently studying His word and meditating on it by spending quantity and quality time in it. The revelation imparted to us by the Holy Spirit during these sessions is phenomenal and rejuvenates and refreshes us. We are the benefactors. By studying His word, the Holy Spirit will reveal the way God works. This is Eternal Life (John 17:3). To know Him in an intimate way (akin to how a husband and wife know each other) is to have eternal life. While studying His word, His will for each of our lives is revealed. The Lord Jesus is the express Image of God, and studying His life in the Gospels is an absolute treasure. The truth that we know will set us free, especially from religious legalism and satanic oppression. God's word will always come to pass, and a believer is confident in this. It is not difficult to understand the judgements of God if we are in sync with His word. God's judgement on sin is portrayed clearly in the Cross of the Lord Jesus Christ for every believer. For the unbelievers, plenty of examples like Noah's flood and the judgement on Egypt and Canaan are well elaborated. Proverbs 28:5 says, 'Evil men do not

understand justice; but those who seek the Lord understand all'. God is indeed justified in and by His works.

- **Sneering at our enemies:** It is not for a believer to feel happy when his adversaries fall. Sneering involves carnal contempt and mocking. These virtues do not define God's chosen. Proverbs 24:17–18 says, 'Do not rejoice when your enemy falls, and do not let your heart be glad when he stumbles; lest the Lord see it and it displease Him, and He turn away His wrath from him.' Hence, it is not for a believer to mock, despise, or pass rude remarks over his adversaries. We need to always remember that God is our vindicator, and He will avenge us better than we can avenge ourselves.
- **Self-confidence:** The world has undoubtedly overrated self-confidence. The way it is portrayed seems harmless, though. This training to be self-confident starts very early in life when the little ones are taught to 'believe in themselves'. Have you heard that slogan? But we as believers should always be sure to train our children, even from a tender age, to depend on God for everything. Confidence in God needs to be taught, rather than self-confidence. One day or another, self-confidence is bound to crash. But when we teach them confidence in God, He equips them with grace, and they are enabled to stand against anything that comes their way. Proverbs 28:26 says, 'He who trusts in his own heart is a fool, but whoever walks wisely will be delivered'. When we put our confidence in God, we enjoy His peace, joy, guidance, and deliverance.
- **Mouth full of cursing, deceit, and oppression; a tongue indulging in trouble and iniquity:** Proverbs 18:21 emphasises the power of words we speak. God created man in His own image and put His virtue into us, i.e., He has given our words the power to direct our lives. 1 Corinthians 6:19–20 says, "Or do you not know that your body is the temple of the Holy Spirit who is in you, whom you have from God, and you are not your own? For you were bought at a price; therefore glorify God in your body and in your spirit, which are God's". The demand on us is made clear in this passage. We are required to glorify God in our body (every organ) and spirit.

God tells us repeatedly to 'speak good' and 'choose life'. God's word is good. We need to constantly speak the promises of God over ourselves and our loved ones. Our words should impart grace to the hearers. Ephesians 4:29–32 says, "Let no corrupt word proceed out of your mouth, but what is good for necessary edification, that it may impart grace to the hearers. And do not grieve the Holy Spirit of God, by whom you were sealed for the day of redemption. Let all bitterness, wrath, anger, clamour, and evil speaking be put away from you, with all malice. And be kind to one another, tender-hearted, forgiving one another, even as God in Christ forgave you". As much as we may feel tempted to do otherwise, we must never speak against the good word that God has spoken over us. It is certainly challenging. Others' behaviour also should not influence us to do otherwise. God's grace is always available to us to accomplish this.

✡ **Cunning, crafty, always laying a net for the weak, targeting the helpless and the poor:** This character is very openly displayed by most ungodly men. It is effortless for them to be mean. But there are some wolves in sheep's clothing among the brethren who excel at this. It is not for a believer to display any of these characteristics either openly or in secret in any area of our lives. Our lives ought to be an open book, and we are definitely accountable to God. We represent Him here on earth. Lord Jesus came down to the earth to reveal the Father to us all. Today He still lives in and through us for the same motive. His heart is for the poor, needy, and the weak. These might seem weak to us, but when they are wronged, God stands supporting them strongly because His grace is perfected in their weakness. Hence our hearts have to be filled with the compassion of the Lord towards such people and help them come out of those situations that keep pulling them down. This is very effectively done by sharing the Gospel with them and teaching them the ways of God. When such people accept the salvation offered by God and make Him supreme in their lives, definitely their life takes a turn for the good so that they in turn can help others like them. The Lord has equipped every one of His children for such a ministry so that we can challenge the injustice which these people suffer.

- ✡ **The wicked underestimates God big-time:** How many Christians and believers are guilty of this clause today? Even though they call themselves the children of God, they do not bestow absolute importance on what God says in His word. Their credentials are largely namesake and even show up in the defeated lives they live. Some people just don't allow God's word to interfere with what they believe. One major reason for this is the useless traditions and philosophies (most often unbiblical) they hold on to. For a believer, God's word should be everything. We should live, breathe, and do everything based on God's guidance. The objective is to always glorify God as Supreme and Sovereign. No matter how long the ungodly puts up a show saying God doesn't care, he has to face the truth one day, and there is a day of reckoning!

Now, having discussed at length about the characteristics a believer should not possess, it is equally important to keep away from the company of those believers who stubbornly hold onto these qualities (1 Corinthians 5:11-13). Bad company will corrupt good manners, and a little leaven will leaven the whole lump!

14. BUT YOU HAVE SEEN, FOR YOU OBSERVE TROUBLE AND GRIEF, TO REPAY IT BY YOUR HAND. THE HELPLESS COMMITS HIMSELF TO YOU; YOU ARE THE HELPER OF THE FATHERLESS.

15. BREAK THE ARM OF THE WICKED AND THE EVIL MAN; SEEK OUT HIS WICKEDNESS UNTIL YOU FIND NONE.

David speaks an established truth here. Our God is always watching the whole world and knows every detail. No injustice at any point in time goes unseen or unnoticed by Him. He is omnipotent, omnipresent, and omniscient. He sees all the good and the bad happening in the world today (Proverbs 15:3). He certainly sees all the evil (trouble and grief), knowing very well the author of it all (John 10:10). He is waiting eagerly for the victims to look up to Him for justice because He is the only One who can settle things justly and righteously.

God has already defeated satan and repaid him for all his wickedness. God can move on our behalf only if we allow Him to, i.e., when we submit to Him and request Him to take over with an attitude of submission and obedience. The person who has hit rock bottom and come to the end of himself should have no problem submitting to God. But the one who thinks he can handle life, even from that pit, will truly be at a loss. Proverbs 21:12 says, 'The righteous God wisely considers the house of the wicked, overthrowing the wicked for their wickedness'. The Lord knows very well how to break the arm (strength) of the wicked. One should not take this in a literal sense and say that God breaks the arms and legs of the wicked. David is merely asking God to cut off their source of strength. The deeds of the wicked may land them in physical harm; it is a consequence of their wrong choices. True and lasting justice comes only from Him.

There is a system that God has put into place. All evil will be punished undoubtedly, either in this life or surely in eternity. There is a 'seeking out the wickedness of the wicked' happening right now. God's mercy and forgiveness are ready at the disposal of the repentant sinner who forsakes his wickedness and submits to God. The foreknowledge of God has made place for His longsuffering nature to be appropriated to those who will repent of their sins in the future as well. But to those who scorn and mock God, judgement is already happening, and the man will reap what he sows. The wicked will fall into his own pit, and his leg will get stuck in the net he spreads to trap others. God will not allow the wicked to get away at any point.

What about the wrong things a believer does? There is a searching out here too. The Lord chastens us as a father does his son, because He loves us. This involves conviction and not condemnation. But we need to deal with the consequences of our foolish behaviour. It would be wise to immediately repent and receive His forgiveness. The sooner we do that, we can get right back on track with a good conscience.

16. THE LORD IS KING FOREVER AND EVER; THE NATIONS HAVE PERISHED OUT OF HIS LAND.

17. LORD, YOU HAVE HEARD THE DESIRE OF THE HUMBLE; YOU WILL PREPARE THEIR HEART; YOU WILL CAUSE YOUR EAR TO HEAR,

18. TO DO JUSTICE TO THE FATHERLESS AND THE OPPRESSED THAT THE MAN OF THE EARTH MAY OPPRESS NO MORE.

From the beginning of creation, there has never been a time that God has failed. He is always victoriously seated on the highest throne. Though the ignorant ones may look at the cross as a place of defeat, it (The cross) is the greatest victory accomplished in the history of the universe. Not only was salvation accomplished there, but satan was judged and sentenced to eternal damnation. Having this perspective, we need to look at all things happening today. Which nation or man can stand against God and win? Nations that rebelled against God are lying in ruins today! Nations that ignore God's truth are swelling with lawlessness, grief, and despair. Demonic influence has blinded many to God's truth and is causing them to confirm their admission in hell. How more insignificant is the wicked man compared to all this? When we realise this, we will be overwhelmed by His power and goodness and magnify Him even more.

The major benefactors amidst all these are the humble people - the ones who have yielded their hearts to God. The reason why orphans, widows, and the oppressed are mentioned when humility is spoken about is because their self-confidence is dead and they are more than happy to depend on God. It is also possible for people otherwise (not orphans, widows, or oppressed) to depend on God when we realise that our carnal strength amounts to nothing eventually. When we humble ourselves, God prepares our heart and puts His desires into us - desires that yearn for true freedom and deliverance available through Him - and then He hears and answers. The execution of this justice definitely silences the wicked man who will dare not thwart anymore with God's children. On the other hand, the ignorant and prideful person, who stubbornly continues in the path of rebellion, will surely suffer.

www.ingramcontent.com/pod-product-compliance
Lightning Source LLC
LaVergne TN
LVHW091250150826
845673LV00006B/1384

* 9 7 9 8 8 9 1 8 6 5 2 1 1 *